Me and My Big Mouth!

Me and My Big Mouth!

Your Answer Is
Right under Your Nose

Joyce Meyer

NEW YORK   NASHVILLE

FaithWords
Hachette Book Group
1290 Avenue of the Americas, New York, NY 10104
faithwords.com
twitter.com/faithwords

First published in October 2016
This edition: May 2017

FaithWords is a division of Hachette Book Group, Inc. The FaithWords name and logo are trademarks of Hachette Book Group, Inc.

The publisher is not responsible for websites (or their content) that are not owned by the publisher.

The Hachette Speakers Bureau provides a wide range of authors for speaking events. To find out more, go to www.hachettespeakersbureau.com or call (866) 376-6591.

ISBN: 978-1-4555-4251-2

Printed in the United States of America

LSC-C

Printing 8, 2021

Me and My Big Mouth!

Contents

...But we have the mind of Christ (the Messiah) and do hold the thoughts (feelings and purposes) of His heart.
— 1 Corinthians 2:16

Introduction

As believers, we need to understand the soul and be trained in discerning the activities of it. As defined in this study, the soul consists of the mind or intellect, the will, and the emotions. Since the soul is full of "self," it can and should be purified and rendered a vessel fit for the Master's use. (2 Tim. 2:21.)

Our mouth gives expression to what we think, feel, and want. Our mind tells us what we think, not necessarily what God thinks. Our will tells us what we want, not what God wants. And our emotions tell us what we feel, not what God feels. As our soul is purified, it is trained to carry God's thoughts, desires, and feelings; then we become a mouthpiece for the Lord!

The Word of God teaches us in 1 Corinthians 2:16 that we have been given the mind of Christ and that we hold the thoughts, feelings, and purposes of His heart. We hold them in us, but the uncrucified soul "blocks" them from coming forth. There is a continual struggle between the flesh and the spirit.

The body and soul corporately make up what the Bible refers to as "the flesh." Therefore we will use the terms "the soul" and "the flesh" interchangeably.

Man wants to think his own thoughts, but God desires to use the mind of man to think His thoughts through. Man wants what he desires, but eventually his desires are changed into God's, if he submits himself to the Holy Spirit. Man lives a great deal by his feelings, which seem to be the believer's number one enemy. Feelings can be trained to come under the leadership of the Spirit, but this is a process that requires time and diligence.

This book is about the mouth, and as I have indicated, the mouth gives expression either to the flesh or to the spirit. It can be used to verbalize God's Word or it can be a vehicle to express the enemy's work. I don't believe that any child of God wants to be used as a mouthpiece for the devil, but many are.

Proverbs 18:21 states, **Death and life are in the power of the tongue, and they who indulge in it shall eat the fruit of it [for death or life].** There is no subject in the Bible that we should take any more seriously than the mouth. It can be used to bring blessings or destruction not only to our own lives, but also to the lives of many others.

Countless excellent books have been written on the mouth. When God began placing a desire in my heart to write a book on the subject, I must admit that I thought, "What for? What can I say that has not already been said?" But I do believe God wants such a book written, and I believe it will be timely in the lives of all those who read it.

I pray that the anointing of the Holy Spirit will be on this book in a powerful way to bring revelation, conviction, and repentance. I pray that as you read the words in it, they will burn into your soul a new desire to be a mouthpiece for God.

chapter 1

Learning To Speak God's Language

And Jesus, replying, said to them, Have faith in God [constantly].

Truly I tell you, whoever says to this mountain, Be lifted up and thrown into the sea! and does not doubt at all in his heart but believes that what he says will take place, it will be done for him. — Mark 11:22,23

Do you have problems? Your answer is right under your nose.

At least a major part of it is.

I do not believe that anyone can live in victory without being well informed concerning the power of words.

Usually when we have mountains in our lives we talk *about* them, but God's Word instructs us to talk *to* them, as we see in Jesus' words in this passage.

Are You Talking *About* Your Mountains — Or *to* Your Mountains?

When Jesus said that we are to speak to our mountain in faith, commanding it to be lifted up and thrown into the sea, this is a radical statement and one that deserves some study.

First of all, what do we say to the mountains in our lives? It is obvious that we are not to hurl our will at them, but the will of God, and His will is His Word.

In Luke 4 when Jesus was being tempted by Satan in the wilderness, He answered every trial with the Word of God. He repeatedly said, "It is written," and quoted Scriptures that met the lies and deceptions of the devil head on.

We have a tendency to "try" this for a while, and then when we do not see quick results we stop speaking the Word to our problems and begin once again speaking our feelings, which is probably what got us into trouble to begin with.

A stonecutter may strike a rock ninety-nine times with a hammer, and there may be no evidence at all that the rock is cracking. Then on the one hundredth time, it may split in half. Each blow was weakening the stone even though there were no signs to indicate it.

Persistence is a vital link to victory. We must know what we believe and be determined to stick with it until we see results.

Obedience and Forgiveness Are as Important as Faith and Persistence

> For this reason I am telling you, whatever you ask for in prayer, believe (trust and be confident) that it is granted to you, and you will [get it].
>
> And whenever you stand praying, if you have anything against anyone, forgive him and let it drop (leave it, let it go), in order that your Father Who is in heaven may also forgive you your [own] failings and shortcomings and let them drop.
>
> But if you do not forgive, neither will your Father in heaven forgive your failings and shortcomings.
>
> Mark 11:24-26

To make sure we maintain balance in this teaching, let me say that speaking the Word of God is powerful and absolutely necessary in overcoming. However, it is not the only doctrine in the Word of God.

For example, obedience is equally important. If a person thinks he can live in disobedience, but speak God's Word to his mountains and get results, he will be sadly disappointed, as Jesus clearly stated in this passage.

Mark 11:22-26 must be considered as a whole. In verse 22 Jesus said to constantly have faith in God. In verse 23 He talked about releasing faith by speaking to mountains. In verse 24 He spoke of prayer and the importance of praying believing prayers.

In verse 25 He gave a command to forgive. And in verse 26 He stated plainly that if we do not forgive, neither will our Father in heaven forgive us our failings and shortcomings.

There is no power in speaking to a mountain if the heart is full of unforgiveness, yet this problem is rampant among God's children.

Multitudes of people who have accepted Christ as their personal Savior fall into the deception of trying to operate one of God's principles while completely ignoring another.

Obedience is the central theme of the Bible. For many of us, our life is in a mess due to disobedience. The disobedience may have been the result of ignorance or rebellion, but the only way out of the mess is repentance and a return to submission and obedience.

Don't Ignore the "Ifs" and "Buts"

If you will listen diligently to the voice of the Lord your God, being watchful to do all His commandments which I command you this day, the Lord your God will set you high above all the nations of the earth.

And all these blessings shall come upon you and overtake you *if* you heed the voice of the Lord your God.

Deuteronomy 28:1,2

Please notice the "ifs" in this passage. So often we choose to ignore the "ifs" and "buts" in the Bible.

Consider, for example, 1 Corinthians 1:9,10:

> **God is faithful (reliable, trustworthy, and therefore ever true to His promise, and He can be depended on); by Him you were called into companionship and participation with His Son, Jesus Christ our Lord.**
> *But* **I urge and entreat you, brethren, by the name of our Lord Jesus Christ, that all of you be in perfect harmony and full agreement in what you say, and that there be no dissensions or factions or divisions among you, *but* that you be perfectly united in your common understanding and in your opinions and judgments.**

We see that God is faithful, and we also see that we draw upon that faithfulness by honoring Him with obedience in relationships. Our disobedience does not change God. He is still faithful, but obedience opens the door for the blessing that is already there due to God's goodness to flow to us.

This book would be a tragedy in my estimation if I tried to teach that you and I can have what we say without clarifying that what we say *must* line up with the Word of God and His will. "Speaking to our mountains" is not a magic charm or incantation that we pull out and use when we are in trouble or when we want something for ourselves, and then continue on in carnality and a disobedient lifestyle.

Mere Infants

However, brethren, I could not talk to you as to spiritual [men], but as to nonspiritual [men of the flesh, in whom the carnal nature predominates], as to mere infants [in the new life] in Christ [unable to talk yet!]

1 Corinthians 3:1

As long as you and I are carnal, we should hope and pray that God shows us mercy and that we do *not* get what we say. We will be saying a lot of things that are our will and not God's will, simply because we cannot tell the difference yet. As "babies in Christ," we simply do not know how to talk yet, as Paul tells us here in this passage.

Just as natural babies must learn to speak the language of their elders, so Christians must learn how to talk God's way.

Learning To Speak God's Language

For everyone who continues to feed on milk is obviously inexperienced and unskilled in the doctrine of righteousness (of conformity to the divine will in purpose, thought, and action), for he is a mere infant [not able to talk yet]!

But solid food is for full-grown men, for those whose senses and mental faculties are trained by practice to discriminate and distinguish between what is morally good and noble and what is evil and contrary either to divine or human law.

Hebrews 5:13,14

We need time to learn the Word of God and to know His heart. Although many things are clearly defined in the Word, and it is obvious what God's will is, there are other things that we need to make decisions about that are not spelled out in black and white. We need to know His heart and be led by His Spirit.

The Bible does not tell us what kind of automobile to buy, or when to sell our house and purchase a new one, or what company to work for. If we do work at a company and want a promotion, that desire could be God's will for us, but it could also be covetousness. How can we know the difference?

Time is the answer.

It takes time to know God, to know our own hearts, and to be able to be totally honest with ourselves and with God. It takes time to learn about motives and how to determine whether ours are pure.

"If It Be Thy Will"

...You do not have, because you do not ask.

[Or] you do ask [God for them] and yet fail to receive, because you ask with wrong purpose and evil, selfish motives. Your intention is [when you get what you desire] to spend it in sensual pleasures.

James 4:2,3

I once heard it said that a person operating in faith will never pray, "if it be Thy will." There was no other explanation given; therefore as a young Christian I took the statement to an extreme.

In the same way, I heard that I could have what I said, but nobody told me that I needed to grow up. Perhaps someone did say it and I was so full of myself that I did not hear, but I was definitely out of balance. I wanted what I wanted, and I thought I had found a new way to get it.

There are some things in the Word of God that are so clear that we never have to pray, "if it be Thy will."

Salvation is a good example.

In 1 Timothy 2:3,4 the Bible states that it is God's desire that all should be saved and come to a knowledge of Him. I would never pray, "Dear Father in heaven, I ask in Jesus' name that You save _____, if it be Thy will." I already know it is His will to save that person.

James 4:2 says we have not because we do not ask. Verse 3 says that sometimes we ask and yet fail to receive because we ask with wrong purpose and evil, selfish motives. I realize that sometimes it is hard to believe that of ourselves, but, nonetheless, it is true. It is especially true of the believer who has not allowed the purification process of God to take place in his life. In that state, a person has God in him, but he also has an abundance of "self" in him.

I believe that in those instances when what we are asking for is not clearly spelled out in the Word, and we are not positive that we have heard from God about the issue, it is wise and an act of true submission to pray, "if it be Thy will."

I recall an instance many years ago when my husband Dave and I were vacationing in a lovely spot in Georgia. We were exceptionally tired, and God had made a way for us to take some time off and rebuild our energies. We were enjoying the place so much that we began planning to bring our children back there the following year and take an extended vacation. We were full of our plans and excitedly talking about them. I began to "declare" (make a verbal confession), "We are coming back here next year, and our entire family will be blessed with a vacation at this place."

Suddenly the Holy Spirit spoke James 4:15 to me: **You ought instead to say, If the Lord is willing, we shall live and we shall do this or that [thing].** As I began later to study this Scripture I also noticed verse 16: **But as it is, you boast [falsely] in your presumption and your self-conceit. All such boasting is wrong.**

There is a difference between faith and confidence, and foolishness and presumption. Unless that difference is discerned, the spiritual life becomes a tragedy instead of a triumph.

I do not personally feel that I am weak in faith if I pray, "Lord, I want this thing — *if* it is Your will, *if* it fits in with Your plan, *if* it is Your best for me, and *if* it is Your timing."

Proverbs 3:7 says, **Be not wise in your own eyes....** I have taken this verse to heart and believe it has saved me a great deal of agony.

There was a time in my life when I thought I knew everything and if everyone would listen to me, we would all get along just fine. I have now discovered that I do not know anything at all, at least not compared to what God knows.

We must resist the temptation to play "Holy Ghost, Jr." Instead, we must let God be God.

Balance, Wisdom, Prudence, Common Sense, and Good Judgment

> **Every prudent man deals with knowledge, but a [self-confident] fool exposes and flaunts his folly.**
>
> **Proverbs 13:16**

It seems to me from my twenty years of observation in the Kingdom of God, that people and teachers have a difficult time with balance. The doctrine concerning the power of words, the mouth, confession, calling those things that be not as though they are, and speaking things into existence, is one example where I have seen people get off into extremes. It seems that the flesh wants to live in the ditch on one side of the road or the other, but it has a difficult time staying in the middle of the highway between the lines of safety.

> Be well balanced (temperate, sober of mind), be vigilant and cautious at all times; for that enemy of yours, the devil, roams around like a lion roaring [in fierce hunger], seeking someone to seize upon and devour.
>
> 1 Peter 5:8

Extremes are actually the devil's playground. If he cannot get a believer to totally ignore a truth and live in deception, his next tactic will be to get him so one-sided and out of balance with that truth that he is no better off than he was before. Sometimes he is even worse off than he was.

Wisdom is a central theme of God's Word. As a matter of fact, there is no real victory without it.

In *Webster's II New College Dictionary,*[1] *wisdom* is defined as "1. Understanding what is true, right, or lasting. 2. Good judgment: common sense." I have dealt with many people over the years, both lay people and those in full-time ministry, who simply do not use any common sense.

Wisdom does not operate in extremes. Proverbs 1:1-4 says that wisdom is full of prudence, and prudence is good management.

In this same dictionary, *prudence* is defined as "careful management: ECONOMY."[2] The adjective form, *prudent,* is defined as "using good judgment or common sense in handling practical matters."[3] I believe we might say that wisdom is a combination of balance, common sense, and good judgment.

A teacher of God's Word has to be responsible to explain himself enough to be reasonably sure that believers in all stages of spiritual growth understand him. To make one blanket statement that "you can have what you say," without any explanation, is dangerous to the immature Christian. I believe that as teachers called to train up the children of God, it is our responsibility to realize that not everyone listening to us understands that statement to mean that he can have what he says, *if* what he is saying is in line with God's Word and will for him at that particular time in his life.

People who are carnal listen to every message they hear with a "carnal ear." As they grow spiritually, they can listen to the same message and hear something totally different from what they heard the first time. The message probably was not in error to begin with, but a little more explanation could have prevented the "baby" Christian from living in the ditch for a few years before he learned how to stay in the middle of the road.

Most teachers have a particular "bent" to their teaching — and rightfully so. It has to do with the call of God on their lives. Some are called to exhort and keep the children of God cheered up, to keep them zealous and pressing forward. Others may be called to teach faith, and still others prosperity. There are those who are called to teach almost exclusively on finances. Many have been called to teach and demonstrate healing.

I find that when people are called to do something, they are so full of what God has put in them, if they are not careful they can become lopsided. They can begin to act as if what they are teaching is the only important thing in the Bible. It may not be intentional, but once again I feel that it is our responsibility to make sure that we are presenting our material in a balanced way, remembering the "babes in Christ" who only know what we tell them and nothing more.

I believe very strongly in the power of confession, I believe we should speak to our mountains, and I believe that in many, if not most, instances the answer to our problems is definitely right under our nose (in our mouth). But I also believe very strongly in the maturity of the believer, the crucifixion of the fleshly nature, dying to selfishness, the necessity for obedience and submission to the Holy Spirit.

In other words, I am not trying to teach you something to just help you get out of trouble or to get everything you want. I am hopeful of helping you learn how to cooperate with the Holy Spirit, to see the will of God accomplished in your life.

chapter 2

The Effect of Words in the Natural Realm

...if you acknowledge and confess with your lips that Jesus is Lord and in your heart believe (adhere to, trust in, and rely on the truth) that God raised Him from the dead, you will be saved.

For with the heart a person believes (adheres to, trusts in, and relies on Christ) and so is justified (declared righteous, acceptable to God), and with the mouth he confesses (declares openly and speaks out freely his faith) and confirms [his] salvation. — Romans 10:9,10

In this passage, the Apostle Paul sets forth a spiritual truth applied to salvation, but I believe it is a truth that may be applied to other issues as well.

The confession of a person's belief confirms his salvation before men, but not before God. God already knows what is in his heart.

Confession confirms the believer's position before the enemy of his soul. It declares a change in allegiance. Previously he has served the devil, but notice is now being given that he is changing masters.

The late biblical scholar W. E. Vine defined two of the Greek words translated *confirm* in the *King James Version* as "to make firm, establish, make secure"[1] and "to make valid, ratify, impart authority or influence."[2] The Greek word translated *confirmation* he defined as "of authoritative validity."[3]

So, based on these definitions, we might say that verbal confession makes firm, establishes, secures, ratifies, and gives authoritative validity to salvation.

In other words, confession "nails salvation in place."

Declaring the Decree

> **I will declare the decree of the Lord: He said to Me, You are My Son; this day [I declare] I have begotten You.**
> **Psalm 2:7**

I once saw a movie in which a king issued a royal decree. He wrote down a command or law and then sent forth riders on horseback throughout the county to "declare the decree" to the citizens of that kingdom.

In the Scriptures we see the issuing of such royal decrees in Esther 8:8-14 of the Old Testament, and in Luke 2:1-3 of the New Testament.

In Psalm 2:7, the psalmist wrote that he would "declare the decree of the Lord." What decree? The decree in which the Lord declares that He (speaking of Jesus) is His only begotten Son. (Heb. 1:1-5.)

The written Word of God is His formal decree. When a believer declares that Word out of his own mouth, with a heart full of faith, his faith-filled words go forth to establish God's order in his life.

When the Royal Decree is pronounced, things begin to change!

God's Plan — Our Choice

For You did form my inward parts; You did knit me together in my mother's womb.

I will confess and praise You for You are fearful and wonderful and for the awful wonder of my birth! Wonderful are Your works, and that my inner self knows right well.

My frame was not hidden from You when I was being formed in secret [and] intricately and curiously wrought [as if embroidered with various colors] in the depths of the earth [a region of darkness and mystery].

Your eyes saw my unformed substance, and in Your book all the days [of my life] were written before ever they took shape, when as yet there was none of them.

Psalm 139:13-16

God's plan for our lives has been established in the spiritual realm since before the foundation of the earth, and it is a good plan as we see in Jeremiah 29:11: **For I know the thoughts and plans that I have for you, says the Lord, thoughts and plans for welfare and peace and not for evil, to give you hope in your final outcome.**

Satan has worked hard to destroy the Lord's plan in most of our lives and has had a very high rate of success.

God sent His own Son Jesus to redeem us and to restore all things to proper order. He has written down His will for our lives, and as we believe it and speak it out, it literally begins to become reality.

Some people believe for a great deal of things, but see very little manifestation of them. Perhaps the reason is because they are believing but not speaking. They may see some results of their faith, but not the radical results they would experience if they would bring their mouths as well as their hearts into God's service. (Rom. 10:9,10.)

Some people are trying to live in the blessings of the Lord while still talking like the devil.

We must not make that mistake.

We will not see positive results in our daily lives if we speak negative things. We should remember that what we are speaking, we are calling for. We are reaching into the realm of the spirit and drawing out according to our words. We can reach into Satan's realm, the realm of curses, and draw out evil, negative things, or we can reach into God's realm, the realm of blessings, and draw out good, positive things.

The choice is up to us.

Created and Sustained By God's Word

> **By faith we understand that the worlds [during the successive ages] were framed (fashioned, put in order, and equipped for their intended purpose) by the word of God, so that what we see was not made out of things which are visible.**
>
> **Hebrews 11:3**

The earth that God created was made from no materials that could be seen. As we read in Genesis 1, God spoke, and things began to appear: light, the sky, earth, vegetation, plants that yielded seed, and trees bearing fruit; the sun, moon, and stars; fish and birds; every kind of living creature: livestock, creeping things, wild beasts, and domestic animals. The earth and everything in it were all created out of nothing that could be seen and are today upheld by nothing that can be seen.

In Hebrews 1:3 we read that God is **...upholding and maintaining and guiding and propelling the universe by His**

mighty word of power.... The universe that was created by His mighty words is still being upheld today by the same thing.

You might say, "Well, sure, Joyce, but that is God."

But we must remember that we are created in God's image (Gen. 1:26,27), and we are supposed to act like Him.

Do What God Does...

Therefore be imitators of God [copy Him and follow His example], as well-beloved children [imitate their father].

Ephesians 5:1

Here in this passage, Paul stated that we are to imitate God, to follow His example. In Romans 4:17 we read that God **...gives life to the dead and speaks of the non-existent things that [He has foretold and promised] as if they [already] existed.**

God's Word is His promise to us, and we should speak of those things that He has promised us as if they already existed.

We don't want to forget balance; therefore, let me give an example.

Let's say that a person is obviously sick. He is coughing. His voice is very raspy and about three octaves lower than normal. His nose and eyes are red and watery, and he looks and feels very tired and worn out. A friend says to him, "Are you sick?" What is a proper response he can give that will be filled with faith but that will also be honest as well as courteous to the friend? I believe part of the answer lies in where the friend is spiritually.

...But Do It Wisely

> For although I am free in every way from anyone's control, I have made myself a bond servant to everyone, so that I might gain the more [for Christ].
>
> To the Jews I became as a Jew, that I might win Jews; to men under the Law, [I became] as one under the Law, though not myself being under the Law, that I might win those under the Law.
>
> To those without (outside) law I became as one without law, not that I am without the law of God and lawless toward Him, but that I am [especially keeping] within and committed to the law of Christ, that I might win those who are without law.
>
> To the weak (wanting in discernment) I have become weak (wanting in discernment) that I might win the weak and overscrupulous. I have [in short] become all things to all men, that I might by all means (at all costs and in any and every way) save some [by winning them to faith in Jesus Christ].
>
> 1 Corinthians 9:19-22

The Apostle Paul said that he met people where they were in order to win them to Christ. Besides telling us to imitate God, he also told us to imitate him: **Pattern yourselves after me [follow my example], as I imitate and follow Christ (the Messiah)** (1 Cor. 11:1). That is especially important when dealing with "those without" spiritual knowledge and understanding.

If the friend who inquires about the individual's health is not a Christian, the response should be different from that given to a Christian.

For example, if I were the sick person and I were asked about my health, I might just say, "I don't feel very good, but I am believing for better things." Or I might say, "My body is under attack, but I am asking God to heal me."

So often well-meaning but over-zealous Christians who do not use any common sense have alienated people by acting like creatures from outer space.

We must remember that we believers speak a language that the world does not understand. It would be improper, for example, for us to say to a non-believer, "Well, bless God, the devil may think he has put some disease off on me, but I am not receiving it; I am healed by the stripes of Jesus!" That kind of talk does not show love for the person asking, especially if we know he is not going to have any idea what we are talking about.

People have used that kind of language with me, and although I *do* know what they are talking about, it always feels like a slap in the face. These people are usually very harsh in their attitude and mannerisms. They are so caught up in getting their healing that they are not sensitive to the Holy Spirit. They give no thought to how their words may affect the person who is trying to show them love by expressing concern about them.

Even among believers who do understand each other we can still operate on a level in which we are not verbally "getting in agreement with sickness," but we are not being rude either.

Many people who think they walk in high levels of faith, oddly enough don't show any fruit of the Spirit (Gal. 5:22,23) — especially the fruit of love, the "more excellent way," which the Apostle Paul tells us is not rude or unmannerly. (1 Cor. 13:5.)

Since faith works by love, according to Galatians 5:6, I doubt that my faith would work and I would receive my healing if I were being rude to others.

People don't intend to be rude, they are just out of balance. They think that if they admit that they are sick, they will be making a negative confession. If they are sick, and that fact is obvious to everyone, why deny it?

The truth is that Jesus is our Healer, and truth is more powerful than fact.

The fact was that I was a horrible mess as a result of being abused most of my life. Now the fact is that I have been healed by the power of God's Word and by the Holy Spirit. I did not have to deny where I was to get to where I am. I did have to find a more positive way of talking about my circumstances and allow my conversation to be filled with hope instead of hopelessness, with faith instead of doubt.

As imitators of God we need to do what He does — **calleth those things which be not as though they were** (Rom. 4:17 KJV). Yet we can do that and not be offensive to people who may not understand. We can "declare the decree" in private; then when someone asks, we can surely find a way to remain positive and yet not leave the other person thinking that Christians are aliens from outer space and that everything they believe is weird.

Non-spiritual people have to be taught — and so do we.

The Apostle Paul understood this fact. That's what he meant when he wrote the church in Corinth: **But the natural, nonspiritual man does not accept or welcome or admit into his heart the gifts and teachings and revelations of the Spirit of God, for they are folly (meaningless nonsense) to him; and he is incapable of knowing them (of progressively recognizing, understanding, and becoming better acquainted with them) because they are spiritually discerned and estimated and appreciated** (1 Cor. 2:14).

In a later passage, Paul went on to write to the Colossians: **Behave yourselves wisely [living prudently and with discretion] in your relations with those of the outside world (the non-Christians)....Let your speech at all times be gracious (pleasant and winsome), seasoned [as it were] with salt, [so that you may never be at a loss] to know how you ought to answer anyone [who puts a question to you]** (Col. 4:5,6).

In other words, Paul was saying to the believers of his day, and to us, "Be careful how you talk to those who are not on your level spiritually. Use wisdom and common sense. Be led by the Holy Spirit."

chapter 3

Calling Those Things That Are Not As Though They Are

...God...calleth those things which be not as though they were.

— Romans 4:17 KJV

To me one of the greatest privileges we have as God's children is that of reaching into the realm where God is and calling "those things which be not as if they were."

We should also establish that this practice can work against us if we are calling for things that are not God's will but the enemy's. As a matter of fact, the world seems to be addicted to calling for disaster.

For example, a person sneezes and says, "I'm probably getting that flu that's going around." Or an individual hears some rumor that the company he works for is going to lay off some employees, so he says, "I'll probably lose my job. That's the story of my life, every time things start to go well, something always happens."

These people are also reaching into the realm of the spirit (the unseen realm) and calling those things that are not yet, as if they already were. They are fearing what has not yet taken place, and by their negative faith they are speaking forth the words that will shape their future.

Keep a Confession List

I believed (trusted in, relied on, and clung to my God), and therefore have I spoken....

Psalm 116:10

I recommend having a list of confessions — things that can be backed up by the Word of God — which you speak out loud over your life, your family, and your future.

When I first began learning these principles I am sharing with you in this book, I was terribly negative. I was a Christian and active in church work. My husband and I tithed and attended church regularly, but we did not know that we could do anything about any of our circumstances.

God began teaching me that I should not think and say negative things. I felt He told me He could not work in my life until I stopped being so negative. I obeyed, and one result was I became happier, because a negative person cannot be happy.

After a period of time had elapsed, I felt that my circumstances really were not any different. I asked the Lord about it, and He said, "You have stopped talking negative, but you are not saying anything positive." That was my first lesson in "calling those things which be not as if they were." I had not been taught it by anyone else; God was teaching me Himself, and it proved to be one of the major breakthroughs in my life.

I made a list of the things that I had been learning were rightfully mine according to the Word of God. I had Scriptures to back them up. Twice a day for approximately six months I confessed those truths out loud. I did it in my house, by myself. I was not talking to any human person; I was declaring the Word of God.

I was "declaring the decree!"

I would like to share some of my list with you, but you should do your homework and make up your own list, one tailor made for your situation:

"I am a new creature in Christ: old things have passed away; behold, all things are become new." (2 Cor. 5:17 KJV.)

"I have died and been raised with Christ and am now seated in heavenly places." (Eph. 2:5,6 KJV.)

"I am dead to sin and alive unto righteousness." (Rom. 6:11 KJV.)

"I have been set free. I am free to love, to worship, to trust with no fear of rejection or of being hurt." (John 8:36; Rom. 8:1.)

"I am a believer — not a doubter!" (Mark 5:36 KJV.)

"I know God's voice, and I always obey what He tells me." (John 10:3-5, 14-16, 27; 14:15.)

"I love to pray, I love to praise and worship God." (1 Thess. 5:17; Ps. 34:1.)

"The love of God has been shed abroad in my heart by the Holy Ghost." (Rom. 5:5 KJV.)

"I humble myself, and God exalts me." (1 Pet. 5:6 KJV.)

"I am creative because the Holy Spirit lives in me." (John 14:26; 1 Cor. 6:19.)

"I love all people, and I am loved by all people." (1 John 3:14.)

"I operate in all the gifts of the Holy Spirit, which are tongues and interpretation of tongues, the working of miracles, discerning of spirits, the word of faith, the word of knowledge, the word of wisdom, healings, and prophecy." (1 Cor. 12:8-10.)

"I have a teachable spirit." (2 Tim. 2:24 KJV.)

Calling Those Things That Are Not As Though They Are

"I will study the Word of God; I will pray." (2 Tim. 2:15; Luke 18:1.)

"I never get tired or grow weary when I study the Word, pray, minister, or pursue God; but I am alert and full of energy. And as I study, I become more alert and more energized." (2 Thess. 3:13; Isa. 40:31.)

"I am a doer of the Word. I meditate on the Word all the day long." (James 1:22; Ps. 1:2.)

"I am anointed of God for ministry. Hallelujah!" (Luke 4:18.)

"Work is good. I enjoy work. Glory!" (Eccl. 5:19.)

"I do all my work excellently and with great prudence, making the most of all my time." (Eccl. 9:10; Prov. 22:29; Eph. 5:15,16.)

"I am a teacher of the Word." (Matt. 28:19,20; Rom. 12:7.)

"I love to bless people and to spread the Gospel." (Matt. 28:19,20.)

"I have compassion and understanding for all people." (1 Pet. 3:8.)

"I lay hands on the sick, and they recover." (Mark 16:18.)

"I am a responsible person. I enjoy responsibility, and I rise to every responsibility in Christ Jesus." (2 Cor. 11:28 KJV; Phil. 4:13.)

"I do not judge my brothers and sisters in Christ Jesus after the flesh. I am a spiritual woman and am judged by no one." (John 8:15 KJV; Rom. 14:10 KJV; 1 Cor. 2:15.)

"I do not hate or walk in unforgiveness." (1 John 2:11; Eph. 4:32.)

"I cast all my care on the Lord for He cares for me." (1 Pet. 5:7 KJV.)

"I do not have a spirit of fear; but of power, and of love, and of a sound mind." (2 Tim. 1:7 KJV.)

"I am not afraid of the faces of man. I am not afraid of the anger of man." (Jer. 1:8 KJV.)

"I do not fear. I do not feel guilty or condemned." (1 John 4:18; Rom. 8:1.)

"I am not passive about anything, but I deal with all things in my life immediately." (Prov. 27:23; Eph. 5:15,16.)

"I take every thought captive unto the obedience of Jesus Christ, casting down every imagination, and every high and lofty thing that exalts itself against the knowledge of God." (2 Cor. 10:5.)

"I walk in the Spirit all of the time." (Gal. 5:16.)

"I don't give the devil a foothold in my life. I resist the devil, and he has to flee from me." (Eph. 4:27; James 4:7.)

"I catch the devil in all of his deceitful lies. I cast them down and choose rather to believe the Word of God." (John 8:44; 2 Cor. 2:11; 10:5 KJV.)

"No weapon that is formed against me shall prosper, but every tongue that rises against me in judgment, I shall show to be in the wrong." (Isa. 54:17.)

"As a man thinketh in his heart, so is he. Therefore, all of my thoughts are positive. I do not allow the devil to use my spirit as a

garbage dump by meditating on negative things that he offers me."
(Prov. 23:7 KJV.)

"I do not think more highly of myself than I ought to in the flesh."
(Rom. 12:3.)

"I am slow to speak, quick to hear, and slow to anger." (James 1:19.)

*"God opens my mouth, and no man can shut it. God shuts my
mouth, and no man can open it."* (Rev. 3:7.)

"I do not speak negative things." (Eph. 4:29.)

*"I am purposed that my mouth shall not transgress. I will speak
forth the righteousness and praise of God all the day long."* (Ps. 17:3;
Ps. 35:28.)

"I am an intercessor." (1 Tim. 2:1.)

*"The law of kindness is in my tongue. Gentleness is in my touch.
Mercy and compassion are in my hearing."* (Prov. 31:26.)

"I do what I say I will do, and I get where I am going on time."
(Luke 16:10; 2 Peter 3:14 KJV.)

"I never bind a sister or brother with the words of my mouth."
(Matt. 18:18 KJV.)

*"I am always a positive encourager. I edify and build up; I never
tear down or destroy."* (Rom. 15:2.)

*"I cry to God Most High Who performs on my behalf and rewards
me."* (2 Chron. 16:9.)

"I take good care of my body. I eat right, I look good, I feel good, and I weigh what God wants me to weigh." (1 Cor. 9:27; 1 Tim. 4:8 TLB.)

"I cast out devils and demons; nothing deadly can hurt me." (Mark 16:17,18 KJV.)

"Pain cannot successfully come against my body because Jesus bore all my pain." (Isa. 53:3,4.)

"I don't hurry and rush. I do one thing at a time." (Prov. 19:2; 21:5.)

"I use my time wisely. All of my prayer and study time is wisely spent." (Eph. 5:15,16.)

"I am an obedient wife and no rebellion operates in me." (Eph. 5:22,24 TLB; 1 Sam. 15:23 KJV.)

"My husband is wise. He is the king and priest of our home. He makes godly decisions." (Prov. 31:10-12; Rev. 1:6 KJV; Prov. 21:1.)

"All my household members are blessed in their deeds. We are blessed when we come in and when we go out." (Deut. 28:6 KJV.)

"My children love to pray and study the Word. They openly and boldly praise God." (2 Tim. 2:15.)

"My children make right choices according to the Word of God." (Ps. 119:130; Isa. 54:13.)

"All my children have lots of Christian friends, and God has set aside a Christian wife or husband for each of them." (1 Cor. 15:33.)

"My son, David, *has a sweet personality, and he is not rebellious."* (Eph. 6:1-3.)

"My daughter, Laura, *operates in godly wisdom and discipline, and she is full of energy."* (Prov. 16:16.)

"I am a giver. It is more blessed to give than to receive. I love to give! I have plenty of money to give away all the time." (Acts 20:35; 2 Cor. 9:7,8.)

"I receive speaking engagements in person, by phone, and/or by mail every day." (Rev. 3:7,8.)

"I am very prosperous. I prosper in everything I put my hand to. I have prosperity in all areas of my life — spiritual, financial, mental, and social." (Gen. 39:3; Josh 1:8; 3 John 2.)

"All that I own is paid for. I owe no man anything except to love him in Christ" (Rom. 13:8.)

Can we confess things that we cannot find chapter and verse for?

Yes, I believe we can as long as we are reasonably sure that what we are declaring is God's will for our life and not just what we want.

Our worship leader has been with us many years. God had placed it in his heart that someday he would lead worship for our ministry before we even had much of a ministry. He said that God kept placing the desire in him, finally saying to him: "You need to declare this desire out loud."

He did as God instructed even though he felt very foolish. Into the atmosphere he spoke faith-filled words: "I will be the worship leader for Life In The Word Ministries."

What he was confessing came to pass some time later. We hired him to be our worship leader although he had no previous experience in leading worship. He was an accomplished musician in the world, but now God desired to use Him in the Kingdom. He was about to enter into God's original plan for his life, but verbalizing his faith was an important step in fulfilling that plan.

I read the confessions off of my list for six months and by then they had become part of me. To this day, almost twenty years later, when I am praying and confessing the Word I still hear many of those things come out of my mouth.

In the Old Testament, the Lord instructed Joshua to meditate on His Word "day and night." (Josh. 1:8.) In Psalm 119:148 and elsewhere the psalmist described how he meditated constantly on God's Word. In Psalm 1:2 we read of the righteous man, **...his delight and desire are in the law of the Lord, and on His law** (the precepts, the instructions, the teachings of God) he habitually meditates (ponders and studies) by day and by night.

Part of meditation is muttering,[1] conversing aloud with oneself, or declaring something.[2] Confessing the Word of God helps establish it in the heart.

I can look at my list now, and it absolutely amazes me how many of the things that I wrote on it have come to pass, and how impossible they seemed in the natural at the time.

Abraham and Sarah

> Nor shall your name any longer be Abram [high, exalted father]; but your name shall be Abraham [father of a multitude], for I have made you the father of many nations....
>
> And God said to Abraham, As for Sarai your wife, you shall not call her Sarai; but Sarah [Princess] her name shall be.
>
> And I will bless her and give you a son also by her. Yes, I will bless her, and she shall be a mother of nations; kings of peoples shall come from her.
>
> Genesis 17:5,15,16

Abraham and Sarah were not always known by those names; there was a time when they were called Abram and Sarai. They were childless and beyond child-bearing years, but they received a promise from God that He would give them a child of their own, from their own bodies.

It would take a miracle!

Apparently God changed their names because Abram and Sarai needed a new self-image before that miracle could occur. Their new names had special meaning. Each time their names were called, the future was being prophesied: Abraham would be the father of a multitude, and his princess, Sarah, would be the mother of nations.

I doubt that childless Sarai had an image of herself as a princess. She needed to see herself differently, and receiving a new name was an important part of that new self-image.

Now the right things were being spoken over Abram and Sarai. *Words* were being spoken into the atmosphere that were reaching into the realm of the spirit, where their miracle was. Those words were beginning to draw out the miracle that God had promised. Now the words on the earth were coming into agreement with God's Word, as spoken earlier in Genesis 15.

Abraham Believed God

After these things, the word of the Lord came to Abram in a vision, saying, Fear not, Abram, I am your Shield, your abundant compensation, and your reward shall be exceedingly great.

And Abram said, Lord God, what can You give me, since I am going on [from this world] childless and he who shall be the owner and heir of my house is this [steward] Eliezer of Damascus?

And Abram continued, Look, You have given me no child; and [a servant] born in my house is my heir.

And behold, the word of the Lord came to him, saying, This man shall not be your heir, but he who shall come from your own body shall be your heir.

And He brought him outside [his tent into the starlight] and said, Look now toward the heavens and count the stars — if you are able to number them. Then He said to him, So shall Your descendants be.

And he [Abram] believed (trusted in, relied on, remained steadfast to) the Lord, and He counted it to him as righteousness (right standing with God).

Genesis 15:1-6

Here we see that when God told Abram that he would have a son of his own through whom he would become the father of many nations, Abram *believed God.*

In Romans 4:18-21 we read:

[For Abraham, human reason for] hope being gone, hoped in faith that he should become the father of many nations, as he had been promised, So [numberless] shall your descendants be.

He did not weaken in faith when he considered the [utter] impotence of his own body, which was as good as dead because he was about a hundred years old, or [when he considered] the barrenness of Sarah's [deadened] womb.

No unbelief or distrust made him waver (doubtingly question) concerning the promise of God, but he grew strong and was empowered by faith as he gave praise and glory to God.

> Fully satisfied and assured that God was able and mighty to keep His word and to do what He had promised.

Like Abraham, we will never receive a miracle unless we believe that God can do the impossible and that He will do it for us.

In Abram's case, the promised miracle did not occur immediately. Many years passed by between the time that God told him that he would be the father of many nations and the birth of his son Isaac.

I believe it is important to note that not only did Abraham and Sarah believe God, but the words of their mouths were being used to release their faith.

Remember, *The Amplified Bible* version of Romans 4:17 says that we serve a God Who **...speaks of the non-existent things that [He has foretold and promised] as if they [already] existed.** The cross-reference given is Genesis 17:5 quoted above, which tells how God changed Abram's and Sarai's names.

Speaking in agreement with God's Word, His written Word or a specific word He has given us, helps keep our faith strong until our manifestation arrives.

In Amos 3:3 we read, **Do two walk together except they make an appointment and have agreed?** We cannot walk with

God concerning His plan for our lives unless we are willing to agree with Him — in our hearts and with our words.

The Choice Is Ours

> I call heaven and earth to witness this day against you that I have set before you life and death, the blessings and the curses; therefore choose life, that you and your descendants may live.
> Deuteronomy 30:19

I believe God is looking for people in whom to plant His "dream seeds." But in order to carry God's dreams for our lives, and the lives of others, we must be willing to "conceive." We must be willing to mentally agree with God; in other words, to believe what He tells us.

Believing is the first important step, because what is in our hearts will come out of our mouths: **...For out of the fullness (the overflow, the superabundance) of the heart the mouth speaks** (Matt. 12:34).

In the introduction I said that our mouths give expression to what is in our souls. As we have defined it, the mind is part of the soul. We draw to ourselves whatever our souls are full of. If we keep our soul and mouth full of doubt, unbelief, fear, and every negative thing, we will draw those things to ourselves. On

47

the other hand, if we keep our soul and mouth full of God and His Word and plan, that is what we will draw to us.

The choice is ours!

> ...if anyone does not offend in speech [never says the wrong things], he is a fully developed character and a perfect man, able to control his whole body and to curb his entire nature.
>
> — James 3:2

chapter 4

Prophesy Your Future

What was the first thing you said this morning when you got out of bed? What have you been talking about all day? Despite what you may think, it does matter — to you and to your well-being, as James points out in this verse.

Words are very important and powerful, and we will be held responsible for them, just as Jesus warned in Matthew 12:37: **For by your words you will be justified and acquitted, and by your words you will be condemned and sentenced.**

That's why each of us needs to learn to tame our tongue.

Taming the Tongue

> ...look at the ships: though they are so great and are driven by rough winds, they are steered by a very small rudder wherever the impulse of the helmsman determines.

> Even so the tongue is a little member, and it can boast of great things. See how much wood or how great a forest a tiny spark can set ablaze!
>
> And the tongue is a fire. [The tongue is a] world of wickedness set among our members, contaminating and depraving the whole body and setting on fire the wheel of birth (the cycle of man's nature), being itself ignited by hell (Gehenna).
>
> For every kind of beast and bird, of reptile and sea animal, can be tamed and has been tamed by human genius (nature).
>
> But the human tongue can be tamed by no man. It is a restless (undisciplined, irreconcilable) evil, full of deadly poison.
>
> **James 3:4-8**

As James tells us here in this passage, no man can tame the tongue — not by himself. In verse 8 James states that the tongue is "undisciplined." Anything undisciplined will be wild and uncontrollable, always wanting to do its own thing. A child is that way. So is a wild animal. So is appetite. The human tongue is no different.

That's why we need the help of the Holy Spirit to control our tongues. But God will not do it all for us. We must learn to discipline our own mouths and take responsibility for what comes out of them.

If our lives are not suitable, perhaps we should inventory what we talk about.

How do you talk about your future? If you are not satisfied with your life and want to see it change, you will have to begin prophesying a better future for yourself and your loved ones according to God's Word.

You can change things in your life by cooperating with God.

Without God, you cannot change anything, but in agreement with Him, all things are possible. (Matt. 17:20.) Yes, you can begin to change things in your life, if you will take the Word of God and start to speak it over your life.

Most of us don't use our mouth at all for what God gave it to us for. There is great power and authority in words. The kind of power depends on the kind of words. We can curse our future by speaking evil of it, or we can bless it by speaking well of it.

Some have learned the danger of speaking negatively, but God wants us to go a step further. He wants us to start prophesying what we desire to see happen in our lives.

Most of us have some kind of dream or vision. There is something we want out of life — personally, financially, socially, spiritually — for our families, our ministry, our health, etc.

In this life, there are material things we desire, and there are spiritual things we desire — usually it is a mixture of both. We want to grow spiritually and be used by God, and we want to be blessed in our material circumstances.

There were times in my own life when I desired things that would have come under the category of "blessings." But due to ignorance concerning the subject matter of this book, I said out of my mouth that I would probably never see these blessings come to pass. I spoke according to what my experience had been in the past, and therefore I was cursing my future with my own words. I was agreeing with the devil instead of with God.

I needed to call those things that were not as if they were. I needed to call forth from the spiritual realm what I desired, considering that I was only waiting for the manifestation.

I needed to cooperate with God's good plan for my life, but *I was deceived!* I was believing lies. That is what deception is — a lie.

Satan is called the deceiver because, as Jesus said in John 8:44, he is a liar and the father of lies and of all that is false. He strives to give us trouble and then uses it to influence us to prophesy that same kind of trouble in our future.

Bless Yourself!

> ...he who blesseth himself in the earth shall bless himself in the God of truth; and he that sweareth in the earth shall swear

by the God of truth; because the former troubles are forgotten, and because they are hid from mine eyes.

For, behold, I create new heavens and a new earth: and the former shall not be remembered, nor come into mind.

But be ye glad and rejoice for ever in that which I create....

Isaiah 65:16-18 KJV

Here in the passage in which the Lord Himself speaks to His people Israel, we see a twofold life principle that can be carried into every area in which we desire victory: 1) *No person's words have as much authority in our life as our own*, and 2) *our future cannot be blessed until we let go of the past.*

In Isaiah 43:18,19 the Lord sets forth this same principle:

Do not [earnestly] remember the former things; neither consider the things of old.

Behold, I am doing a new thing! Now it springs forth; do you not perceive and know it and will you not give heed to it? I will even make a way in the wilderness and rivers in the desert.

Careful consideration of these passages seems to me to indicate that you and I can cooperate with God's plan, for He says in the last verse, "Will you not give heed to it?"

We can release the plan of God for our lives by no longer considering (thinking about) the things of old, believing that God has a good plan for our future. Since what we think about eventually comes out of our mouths, we will never get our mouths straightened out unless we do something about our thoughts.

I believe that if we stop mentally living in the past we can begin to think in agreement with God. Then once we do that, we can begin to speak in agreement with Him. By so doing we can actually prophesy our own future.

Power Requires Responsibility

> But I tell you, on the day of judgment men will have to give account for every idle (inoperative, nonworking) word they speak.
>
> **Matthew 12:36**

Jesus taught that men will one day have to give an account for their words. Why? Because words are containers for power; they carry creative or destructive power.

Proverbs 18:21 states that in the tongue is the power of life and death. That sounds like power to me. Anytime we are given power, there must also be responsibility.

Often people want power to play with, not power to be responsible for, but God won't allow that.

God has given us words, and He expects us to be accountable for the power that is carried in them.

Words Are Containers for Power!

If we really believed that words hold power and that God holds us accountable for them, I am sure we would be more careful about what we say.

Sometimes we say totally ridiculous things. If any one of us would put a tape recorder on our belt and carry it around for a week and record everything we say, we would quickly gain revelation as to why we have some of the problems we have and why some things never change even though it is God's will to deliver us from them.

I am sure we would hear on that recording doubt, unbelief, complaining, grumbling, fear, and many negative statements. We would also likely hear a lot of confirmation of what is happening to us, but not much prophecy regarding our glorious future. We might hear statements like these:

"This kid of mine is never going to change. I may as well forget it - the more I pray the worse he acts."

"This marriage is just simply not going to work out. I absolutely cannot put up with any more of this. I am going to leave if one more thing happens. If necessary, I will get a divorce."

"It never fails. Every time I get a little money, some disaster comes along and takes it all away."

"I just can't hear from God; He never speaks to me."

"Nobody loves me. It looks like I am destined to be lonely all my life."

Yet at the same time we are making such negative statements, we claim that we are believing for our children, our marriages, and our finances, that we are believing to be led by the Spirit and to find our lifetime mate.

Here is an example from my own life of the ridiculous things we say under pressure.

One evening I was looking for something in my house and having a difficult time finding it. At the same time various family members were asking for my help with different things they were doing. I could feel the pressure mounting, and we all know that when pressure mounts up, the mouth flies open.

In my frustration, I blurted out, "This place drives me crazy! I can never find anything around here!"

Instantly, God called my attention to my words. He had me examine exactly what I had just said. First of all, I had lied, He told me, because I can and do find things that I am looking for in my house all the time. Just because I could not find something one time does not mean I can *never* find things.

We all have a great tendency to exaggerate horribly when we feel pressured. We magnify things, blowing them all out of proportion and making them sound much worse than what they really are. The careless words we speak in the heat of the moment may not mean much to us, but they definitely carry weight in the spiritual realm.

The Lord further said to me, "Joyce, not only is it a lie that you never find anything, but it is also untrue that you are going crazy! Your house is *not* going to drive you crazy. But if you keep saying it often enough, it just might."

If a person has had any mental illness in their family bloodline, the enemy would love for them to open a door to continue the curse by such foolish talk.

If you notice, a lot of people make negative statements about their mental capacity and condition:

"That just blows my mind."

"I feel like I'm losing my mind."

"Sometimes it seems like I'm going crazy."

"My brain just won't work right."

"I forget things all the time."

"I can't remember anything anymore; I must be getting Alzheimer's Disease."

"If this continues I just know I'll have a nervous breakdown."

"I am so dumb, so ignorant, so stupid!"

Just listen to other people, and yourself, and you will soon see what I mean.

One day my husband Dave and I played golf with a man who must have called himself "dummy" a dozen times in the course of four hours. I thought, "Mister, if you had any idea how you're cursing your own life, you would stop that."

If you ever do feel that you're having problems with your mind, pray about it, then prophesy good things about your mental capacity so your future can be different from the past.

What most of us have done in the past is pray about it, and then negate our own prayers with a negative confession.

Speak Life, Not Death!

It is the Spirit Who gives life [He is the Life-giver]; the flesh conveys no benefit whatever [there is no profit in it]. The words (truths) that I have been speaking to you are spirit and life.

John 6:63

When I suggest that you prophesy your future, I am not talking about telling others what you believe you are going to do or have. There may be a time for that, but not at this stage. I am talking about prophesying to *yourself* first: while driving to work, cleaning the house, doing yard work, working on the car, or going about your daily routine.

Speak out faith-filled words, believing, as Jesus said, that the words you speak are spirit and life.

Speak life into your life, not death.

When you enter a crowded restaurant, do you say, "We probably won't get a table, and if we do it will be a bad one with poor service"? Or do you say, "I believe that I have favor in this restaurant and that we will get a good table and excellent service"?

You might ask, "Joyce, does that really work for you?"

I cannot honestly say that it *always* works for me, but I would rather stay positive and get 50 percent good results, than stay negative and get 100 percent bad results.

An additional benefit is that when I am positive I am happier, and people enjoy being around me more.

Take just thirty seconds a day to declare that God gives you favor everywhere you go; the results may astound you.

I remember going in a store and looking at coats. Many of them were on sale at 50 percent off. I found one I really liked but did not see a sale sticker on it. I asked the clerk if it was on sale, and she answered, "No, it isn't." Then she looked at me and said, "But if you want it for half price, I'll let you have it. I wouldn't do that for anybody else, but I'll do it for you." I didn't know this woman, and she didn't know me, so there was no "earthly" reason for her to do what she did.

God delights in giving His children favor. What He did for me, He will do for you too. Line your mouth up with His Word and get ready to be blessed. Always remember to return the praise and thanksgiving to Him.

God is good, and several times a day we should tell Him that we realize that fact.

A Pain in the Foot

One afternoon I was lying in bed studying, when I suddenly got a pain in my foot. I have a bunion, and occasionally it will flare up and hurt. When the pain struck my foot, I said, "I rebuke this pain, in the name of Jesus. By His stripes I am healed. By the power of His blood I am made whole, and I will not have this pain."

Instantly there came another pain. Again I said, "In the name of Jesus, I am healed and made whole."

It seemed like a dueling match. I would say something positive out of the Word of God, and the pain would strike me again. I thought, "I don't care if I have to lie here and say this all day, I am going to win."

I said out loud, "I am healed by the stripes of Jesus. This pain has to leave."

I lay there on my bed, and every time the pain would hit me, I would hit the devil with the Word of God. Pretty soon the pain quit, and it did not bother me again for the remainder of the day.

Watch and Pray

> **All of you must keep awake (give strict attention, be cautious and active) and watch and pray....**
> **Matthew 26:41**

Sometimes we are guilty of not being persistent enough, or of just "putting up with the enemy's junk." Sometimes we get spiritually lazy. Instead, we must stay alert and awake.

Jesus' admonition to His disciples, "Watch and pray," should first be applied to our own lives.

Watch for the attacks of the enemy and pray immediately.

Come against Satan when he is trying to get a foothold, and he will never get a stronghold!

Life in the Word

The Lord once told me, "Until My people learn how to use My Word as the weapon against the enemy, and how to prophesy their future, they may as well forget about having very much power."

There is too much mixture in our mouths, and it causes us to operate with zero power. Mixing positives and negatives does not equal power in God's economy.

The Word of God coming out of the believer's mouth is a sharp sword against the enemy. In Revelation 19:11-15 Jesus is depicted as riding on a white horse, with a sharp sword coming forth from His mouth. That sharp sword is the Word of God.

In Hebrews 4:12 we read that **...the Word that God speaks is alive and full of power [making it active, operative, energizing, and effective]; it is sharper than any two-edged sword....** Second Corinthians 10:4 teaches us that **...the weapons of our warfare are not physical [weapons of flesh and blood]....** Since they are not natural weapons, they must be spiritual weapons.

The Word of God operates in the spiritual realm. It is a spiritual (unseen) weapon that defeats a spiritual (unseen) enemy.

We may not see the devil, but we can certainly see his effects. I can testify that I had his effects all over my life. I started applying these principles I am sharing with you, and soon I began to see the effects of the Word all over my life.

Life conquers death.

There is "Life in the Word."

Declaring the End From the Beginning

[Earnestly] remember the former things, [which I did] of old; for I am God, and there is no one else; I am God, and there is none like Me,

Declaring the end and the result from the beginning, and from ancient times the things that are not yet done, saying, My counsel shall stand, and I will do all My pleasure and purpose.

Isaiah 46:9,10

Here in this passage the Lord says, "I am the same God Who has helped you in the past, and I declare in the beginning how it will turn out in the end."

The Lord is the Alpha and Omega, the Beginning and the End. (Rev. 1:8.) He is also everything in between. He knows before trouble ever shows up that we can be victorious if we fight the battle His way. His way is not a negative way.

Romans 8:37 says that we are "more than conquerors." I believe that means that we can know before the battle ever begins that we will win. In other words, we can see the end from the beginning.

Prophesying our future is literally declaring in the beginning what will happen in the end.

Declare and Do!

> I have declared from the beginning the former things [which happened in times past to Israel]; they went forth from My mouth and I made them known; then suddenly I did them, and they came to pass [says the Lord].
>
> Isaiah 48:3

Notice the basic principle of God's method of operation: first He declares things, then He does them.

This principle explains why God sent the prophets. They came speaking forth into the earth God-inspired, God-instructed words that brought forth God's will from the spiritual realm into the natural. Jesus did not come to the earth until first the prophets had spoken about Him for hundreds of years. God operates on spiritual laws that He has set in place, and we cannot ignore them.

Sowing and reaping is another spiritual law which we see operating in the earth, but it also operates in the spirit realm. We sow material seed, and we reap material blessings of all kinds.

Words are also seeds. We sow word seeds and reap according to what we have sown.

God wanted stubborn Israel to know that it was He Who doing the great works in their lives, so He announced them ahead of time. We are created in His image, expected to follow His example and do what He does.

Prophesy and Profit!

Therefore I have declared things to come to you from of old; before they came to pass I announced them to you, so that you could not say, My idol has done them, and my graven image and my molten image have commanded them.

You have heard [these things foretold], now you see this fulfillment. And will you not bear witness to it? I show you specified new things from this time forth, even hidden things [kept in reserve] which you have not known.

They are created now [called into being by the prophetic word], and not long ago; and before today you have never heard of them, lest you should say, Behold, I knew them!

Isaiah 48:5-7

Please notice that the Lord said that the things He desired to do were called into being by the prophetic word.

That is what you and I are to do, to speak forth and declare the Word of the Lord — *before it comes to pass.*

"But I'm no prophet!" you might say.

You don't have to "stand in the office of prophet" in order to prophesy. You can prophesy (speak forth God's Word) over your own life at any time.

Declare New Things in Your Life!

Behold, the former things have come to pass, and new things I now declare; before they spring forth I tell you of them.
Isaiah 42:9

Here in this confirming verse in which God speaks to His people Israel, we see that the Lord declares new things before they happen.

If you are like me, I am sure that you are ready and waiting for some new things in your life. You need some changes, and reading this book is God's will and timing for you.

Even though I know these principles, I too need to be reminded of them occasionally. Sometimes we all need to be "stirred up" in things we already know. It encourages us to begin operating once again in powerful principles that we have let slip away.

If you are tired of the old things, then stop speaking the old things. Do you want some new things? Then start speaking some new things. Spend some time with God. Set aside some special time to study His Word. Find out what His will is for your life. Don't let the devil push you around any more.

Don't be the devil's mouthpiece.

Find out what God's Word promises you and begin to declare the end from the beginning. Instead of saying, "Nothing will ever change," say, "Changes are taking place in my life and circumstances every day."

I heard the story of a doctor who was not a believer but who had discovered the power of the principle I am sharing with you. His prescription to his patients was to go home and repeat several times daily: "I am getting better and better every day." He had such marvelous results that people traveled from all over the world to avail themselves of his services.

Amazing! God said it first, and a man gets the credit.

Do It God's Way!

Jesus said, "I am the way, follow Me." (John 14:6; 12:26.)

We never see Jesus being negative or speaking negatively.

You and I should follow His example.

Say about your situation what you believe Jesus would say, and you will open the door for the miracle-working power of God.

> So shall My word be that goes forth out of My mouth: it shall not return to Me void [without producing any effect, useless], but it shall accomplish that which I please and purpose, and it shall prosper in the thing for which I sent it. — Isaiah 55:11

chapter 5

Becoming God's Mouthpiece

The prophets were a mouthpiece for God. They were called to speak God's words to people, situations, cities, dry bones, mountains, or whatever God told them to speak to. To fulfill their God-ordained mission, they had to be submitted to the Lord, their mouth had to be His.

Those who desire to be used by God need to allow Him to deal with them concerning their mouth and what comes out of it. Usually people who have "verbal" gifts, also have some glaring weaknesses in the area of their mouth.

I speak from experience.

Speak Only When Spoken Through

> Having gifts (faculties, talents, qualities) that differ according to the grace given us, let us use them: [He whose gift is] prophecy, [let him prophesy] according to the proportion of his faith.
>
> **Romans 12:6**

As a minister of the Gospel, I am a mouthpiece in the Body of Christ. I have the awesome privilege of teaching the Word all over the world.

I teach a lot.

In Romans 12:6 and 7 the Apostle Paul wrote, in essence, "If you are called as a teacher, give yourself to your teaching," and I have done just that for many years. I believe that God told me that whatever I did should somehow make use of the teaching gift He has placed in me.

Regardless of our specific ministry within the Body of Christ, each of us is a mouthpiece for God in some way. Whether you and I have been given a worldwide teaching gift or whether we have been given the ability to witness to our co-workers, God wants us to use our mouth for Him.

A wise man once said to me, "Joyce, God has given you the ear of many. Stay broken and only speak when spoken through."

If you are a teacher of God's Word in any degree, I offer the same counsel to you: learn to speak only when spoken through. Obviously this requires intensive training by the Holy Spirit.

If we desire the words of our mouth to carry God's power, then our mouth must belong to Him.

Is your mouth God's mouth? Have you really given it to Him for His purpose?

A person's heart can become hardened as a result of making excuses for his behavior.

For a long time, I excused my "mouth problems" by blaming them on my personality, or on abuse in my past, or on the fact that I felt bad or was so tired.

Actually the list of excuses we make for our failure to conform to the will and Word of God is endless.

Finally the Holy Spirit got my full attention so that I began to become accountable for my words. I still have a long way to go, but I feel I have made much progress because I have reached the stage of true repentance.

The Responsibility of Being a Teacher

Not many [of you] should become teachers (self-constituted censors and reprovers of others), my brethren, for you know

> that we [teachers] will be judged by a higher standard and with
> greater severity [than other people; thus we assume the greater
> accountability and the more condemnation].
>
> For we all often stumble and fall and offend in many things.
> And if anyone does not offend in speech [never says the wrong
> things], he is a fully developed character and a perfect man,
> able to control his whole body and to curb his entire nature.
>
> **James 3:1,2**

We know that God deals with everyone, but I believe there is a stricter guideline for those who are teachers of the Word.

Leaders are expected to display a measure of maturity and self-control that will be an example to those God places under their leadership. They are to follow Christ themselves and to show them "the way" by their lives as well as by the Word of God.

In 1 Timothy 3:2 the Apostle Paul wrote that spiritual leaders are to be self-controlled. I am sure that one of the areas in which they are to exercise this fruit of the Spirit is the mouth.

Those who are trained in being God's mouthpiece will frequently be used to bring encouragement, comfort, and edification to others. There are times of correction and rebuke, but also times of speaking "a word in season" to the weary.

Bringing Comfort

> A man has joy in making an apt answer, and a word spoken at the right moment — how good it is!
>
> **Proverbs 15:23**

> A word fitly spoken and in due season is like apples of gold in settings of silver.
>
> **Proverbs 25:11**

> [The Servant of God says] The Lord God has given Me the tongue of a disciple and of one who is taught, that I should know how to speak a word in season to him who is weary. He wakens Me morning by morning, He wakens My ear to hear as a disciple [as one who is taught].
>
> **Isaiah 50:4**

These three passages deserve meditation. They are really great Scriptures. What a tremendous blessing it is to be used by God to cheer up others.

We can bless people with the words of our mouth. We can speak life to them. The power of life and death is in the tongue. (Prov. 18:21 KJV.) We can choose to speak life. When we edify or exhort, we are urging people forward. Just think of it, we can hold people back or urge them forward just by our words.

Parents should be very careful about how they speak to and about their children. Being a parent is an awesome responsibility. God attaches authority to the parental role. As parents, couples have authority over the lives of their children until those children are old enough to lead their own lives. Because of this authority, the parent's words can greatly encourage or discourage a child. The words of a parent can heal or wound.

When a child has been emotionally wounded by a teacher or another child, the parent can be used by God to help the child recover quickly and to restore his or her confidence. However, harsh words, or words that lack understanding, can deepen the wound even more.

When children make mistakes, which will occur thousands of times during the childhood years, parents need to know how to "train them up" (Prov. 22:6 KJV), how to **bring them up in the nurture and admonition of the Lord** (Eph. 6:4 KJV).

It is very important that parents not make a child feel stupid, or clumsy, or like a failure. If they are not wise with their words, this can easily occur.

Children are fragile. To a certain degree, they are tender in their young years. In the formative years, it is vital that parents help them feel secure and loved. Today so many parents have tremendous problems and pressures of their own that often they do not take the time to minister to their children concerning their challenges. There is a tendency to think, "That's just kid stuff, I have some real problems to attend to."

If you have children, when they are hurting, remember to speak "a word in season" to them, a word that will heal and encourage them.

The Gift of Exhortation

> Therefore encourage (admonish, exhort) one another and edify (strengthen and build up) one another, just as you are doing.
>
> **1 Thessalonians 5:11**

The "gift of exhortation" is spoken of in Romans 12:8. It is one of the ministry gifts that the Holy Spirit confers upon certain individuals.

In John 14:26, the Holy Spirit is called the "Helper." He exhorts people in their growth in God, encouraging them to be all they can be, for God's glory. As a Helper and an Exhorter, He anoints others for that ministry.

You and I need to see and realize that *exhortation is a ministry* — a much needed ministry. There are always plenty of people in the church at any given time who are ready to give up if something does not happen to encourage them. As an exhorter you and I can actually prevent someone from backsliding or giving up!

In that same verse, the Holy Spirit is also called the "Comforter." Exhorters bring comfort, they just simply make people feel better — about themselves, about their circumstances, about the past, about the present, about the future, about anything else that concerns them.

As we have seen in 1 Thessalonians 5:11, the Apostle Paul instructed the early Christians to continue in exhorting one another.

Any person who desires to be a mouthpiece for God must either be, or develop into, an exhorter.

Some people are very gifted in this area. I know several individuals who are natural exhorters. Everything that comes out of their mouth is something to make others better.

My ministry gift is not exhortation, but I have learned the importance of it and always try to remember that people are hurting and need to be encouraged.

Beware of Polluting Speech

> **Let no foul or polluting language, nor evil word nor unwholesome or worthless talk [ever] come out of your mouth,**

but only such [speech] as is good and beneficial to the spiritual progress of others, as is fitting to the need and the occasion, that it may be a blessing and give grace (God's favor) to those who hear it.

Ephesians 4:29

Some people believe they are called to correct everyone. God does give gifts that bring correction. The Apostle Paul had a strong gift in this area. He said that he corrected people by the grace gift that was upon him. (Rom. 12:3.)

However, people who only want to correct but never edify, build up, exhort, or comfort are out of balance. Anything out of balance eventually falls apart.

God desires to touch more people's mouths and have them for His own mouthpiece. There is much to be said and many who need to hear. I urge you to allow God to deal with you in these very important areas, and like Isaiah, realize that without God's cleansing power we are all people of unclean lips. (Isa. 6:5.)

chapter 6

Complain and Remain, Praise and Be Raised

Jesus therefore answered and said unto them, Murmur not among yourselves.

— John 6:43 KJV

Complaining is a sin! It is a corrupt form of conversation that causes many people a great deal of problems in their lives. It also opens many doors for the enemy.

Remember, we stated that words are containers of power. Complaining, grumbling words carry destructive power. They destroy the joy of the one doing the complaining and can also affect other people who have to listen to them.

As we have seen, in Ephesians 4:29 the Apostle Paul instructed us not to use any foul or polluting language. At one time I would not have known that included complaining, but now I have learned that it does.

Murmuring and complaining pollute our lives and probably sound like cursing to the Lord. To Him it is verbal pollution.

To pollute is to poison.

Did you ever stop to think that you and I can poison our future by complaining about what is going on right now? When we complain about our current situation we remain in it, when we praise God in the midst of difficulty, He raises us out of it.

The best way to start every day is with gratitude and thanksgiving. Get a jump on the devil. If you don't fill your thoughts and conversation with good things, he will definitely fill them with evil things.

Truly thankful people do not complain. They are too busy being grateful for the good things they do have they have no time to notice the things they could complain about.

The world is full of two forces, good and evil. The Bible teaches us that good overcomes evil (see Rom. 12:21), but that we must choose the good. If we find ourselves faced with a negative (evil) situation, we can overcome it with good.

Praise and thanksgiving are good, complaining and grumbling are evil.

The Tongue Can Bring Health or Disease

> A calm and undisturbed mind and heart are the life and health of the body, but envy, jealousy, and wrath are like rottenness of the bones.
>
> **Proverbs 14:30**

Besides poisoning the future, murmuring and complaining can also poison the present. A person who grumbles and complains may also be sick a lot. Words can affect the physical body. They can bring healing or they can open the door for disease.

Disease brings disease!

According to Proverbs 15:4, the tongue has healing power: **A gentle tongue [with its healing power] is a tree of life, but willful contrariness in it breaks down the spirit.**

Think of it, a person who has a calm and undisturbed mind has health for his body. But as we have seen in Proverbs 14:30, "willful contrariness," such as envy, jealousy, and wrath, can actually destroy the physical body.

Wrath is anger, and most people who complain are angry about something. In addition, I believe we can safely say that people who murmur, grumble, and complain do not have a calm and undisturbed mind.

Praise and thanksgiving release physical energy and healing. There have been many times in my life when I have been physically ill or feeling bad, but by praising God either at church or home, I have experienced a lifting of all the negative symptoms. The same thing has probably happened to you.

I suppose a person should feel great in the morning after a good night's sleep, but I have noticed that during times of physical attack I feel worse in the morning than at other times. Disciplining myself to spend regular quality time with the Lord in the morning, including time for praise and thanksgiving, has turned many a day around for me physically.

Murmuring and Complaining Open the Door to Destruction

We should not tempt the Lord [try His patience, become a trial to Him, critically appraise Him, and exploit His goodness] as some of them did — and were killed by poisonous serpents;

Nor discontentedly complain as some of them did — and were put out of the way entirely by the destroyer (death).

Now these things befell them by way of a figure [as an example and warning to us]; they were written to admonish and fit us for right action by good instruction, we in whose days the ages have reached their climax (their consummation and concluding period).

1 Corinthians 10:9-11

When we complain, God takes it personally. He considers that we are exploiting His goodness. God is good, and He wants to hear us tell Him and others about His goodness. When we murmur, gripe, and complain, we are giving a critical appraisal of the God we serve.

The Israelites exploited God's goodness and complained, and they were put out of the way by the destroyer. This is recorded in the Old Testament and recounted in the New Testament, the Bible says, for our instruction. In other words, so we can see their mistakes and not make the same ones. They complained and faced death and destruction. We should heed their example and not follow their pattern.

Praising and Giving Thanks Open the Door to Life

He who guards his mouth and his tongue keeps himself from troubles.

Proverbs 21:23

He who guards his mouth keeps his life, but he who opens wide his lips comes to ruin.

Proverbs 13:3

These Scriptures verify that the person who guards his words can keep himself from ruin, but the person who does not guard his words can bring destruction into his own life.

When the Israelites went into the wilderness, one of the problems God had to repeatedly deal with them about was complaining. It was an eleven-day journey from Egypt to the Promised Land (see Deut. 1:2), but after four decades the Israelites were still wandering in the wilderness of death and destruction.

On the other hand, Jesus went into the wilderness of His affliction with a great attitude. He continued to praise God no matter what, refusing to complain, and as a result God raised Him from death to new life.

That should be a lesson to us. We should guard against the temptation to complain and grumble, and instead purposely *choose* to offer up the sacrifice of praise and thanksgiving. (Heb. 13:15 KJV.)

We can complain and remain, or praise and be raised.

The Power of Thanksgiving

Do not fret or have any anxiety about anything, but in every circumstance and in everything, by prayer and petition (definite requests), with thanksgiving, continue to make your wants known to God.

Philippians 4:6

The Word of God has a great deal to say about thanksgiving, and I personally believe it is the antidote for the poison of complaining.

I probably should stress at this point that I believe that complaining is a major problem among believers. It has gotten so bad that sometimes we ask God to give us something, and when He answers our prayer, we complain about having to take care of the thing we asked Him to give us. We must treat the temptation to complain like the plague, because it has similar effects in our lives. Complaining weakens, whereas thanksgiving releases power — power to bring answers to our prayers.

It seems to me that in Philippians 4:6, the Apostle Paul is telling us that thanksgiving moves our requests through God's approval line.

I can recall once when I was asking God for something and He said, "Why should I give you more? You're already complaining about what you have."

Being thankful shows maturity. It demonstrates that we are spiritually mature enough to handle any type of promotion or increase.

Being thankful can also be a sacrifice. If we don't feel like it, or if our circumstances don't dictate it, thanksgiving can become a sacrificial offering, made by faith, in obedience, because we love the Lord and want to honor His Word.

Thanksgiving As a Sacrifice

Offer to God the sacrifice of thanksgiving, and pay your vows to the Most High.

Psalm 50:14

Oh, that men would praise [and confess to] the Lord for His goodness and loving-kindness and His wonderful works to the children of men!
And let them sacrifice the sacrifices of thanksgiving and rehearse His deeds with shouts of joy and singing!

Psalm 107:21,22

I will offer to You the sacrifice of thanksgiving and will call on the name of the Lord.

Psalm 116:17

Notice that in Psalm 116:17, the psalmist said that he would call on the name of the Lord, but only after he had offered the sacrifice of thanksgiving.

I know there have been many times when I have attempted to call on the power in the name of Jesus to help me, while at the same time my life was filled with complaining.

There is no positive power in complaining. It is filled with power — but it is negative (evil) power.

If we desire the power of God to be released in our lives, it will not occur through complaining.

Praise and Thank Him All the Time

> **Through Him, therefore, let us *constantly* and *at all times* offer up to God a sacrifice of praise, which is the fruit of lips that thankfully acknowledge and confess and glorify His name.**
> **Hebrews 13:15**

We should not just praise and offer thanksgiving when there is a reason to do so. It is easy to give thanks and praise if we have a reason. But then it is not a sacrifice.

We should, of course, offer up praise and thanksgiving at all times, being mindful to thank God for all the blessings in our lives and for the favor He has shown us. If we started making a list of blessings we would be quickly enlightened concerning just how good we really have it. There are many things we take for granted because we have an abundance of them, when people in other countries would think they were wealthy if they had them.

Clean, fresh water is an example. In India and many other parts of the world, water is a commodity that is not easy to come by. Some people must walk miles just to get a day's supply of it. We take baths in it, swim in it, do dishes in it, wash our hair in it, cook with it, etc. We can have it hot or cold, as often as we like, as much as we desire. There are times while I am taking a hot shower, especially if I am tired, when I stop to give thanks to God for hot water.

There are many things to be thankful for if we decide we are going to be a person who continually offers up thanksgiving. The flesh looks for things to complain about, but the spirit searches for reasons to give God glory.

In Philippians 2:14 the Apostle Paul warns us, **Do *all things* without grumbling and faultfinding and complaining [against God] and questioning and doubting [among yourselves].**

Then in 1 Thessalonians 5:18 he exhorts us, **Thank [God] *in everything* [no matter what the circumstances may be, be thankful and give thanks], for this is the will of God for you [who are] in Christ Jesus [the Revealer and Mediator of that will].**

Finally, in Ephesians 5:20, he writes that we should be *at all times* and *for everything* **giving thanks in the name of our Lord Jesus Christ to God the Father.**

From these Scriptures we see that not only are we to avoid grumbling, faultfinding, complaining, questioning, and doubting, we are also to give thanks "at all times," "in every circumstance," "for everything." That doesn't mean that we have to thank God *for* all the negative things in our life, but we are to give Him thanks *in* them.

It greatly honors the Lord when we refuse to complain in a situation that in the natural would produce complaining.

Go the extra mile and not only refuse to complain, but also actually choose to be thankful in the midst of your circumstances.

Remember, you will have to do it "on purpose" --you will not always feel like it. You can release power in your own life.

The praising life is the powerful life!

Don't Grieve the Holy Spirit

And do not grieve the Holy Spirit of God [do not offend or vex or sadden Him], by Whom you were sealed (marked, branded as God's own, secured) for the day of redemption (of final deliverance through Christ from evil and the consequences of sin).

Ephesians 4:30

I heard this Scripture for a long time before I realized that grieving the Holy Spirit is connected to the mouth. To properly understand this verse we need to read it in context with some of the preceding and following verses:

Let no foul or polluting language, nor evil word nor unwholesome or worthless talk [ever] come out of your mouth, but only such [speech] as is good and beneficial to the spiritual progress of others, as is fitting to the need and the occasion, that it may be a blessing and give grace (God's favor) to those who hear it.

And do not grieve the Holy Spirit of God [do not offend or vex or sadden Him], by Whom you were sealed (marked, branded as God's own, secured) for the day of redemption (of final deliverance through Christ from evil and the consequences of sin).

Let all bitterness and indignation and wrath (passion, rage, bad temper) and resentment (anger, animosity) and quarreling (brawling, clamor, contention) and slander (evil speaking, abusive or blasphemous language) be banished from you, with all malice (spite, ill will, or baseness of any kind).

Ephesians 4:29-31

Based on this passage, it certainly seems to me that it grieves the Holy Spirit when we mistreat others or talk to them in an abusive way. It also grieves Him when we speak evil, which includes *negative talk, complaining, grumbling,* and all the related types of speech.

Also based on this passage, we see that we are "sealed" in the Holy Spirit. Sometimes I envision this concept as like being in a zip-lock bag. Nothing can get to us that will destroy us as long as we respect our seal.

If we place a piece of bread in a zip-lock bag, it will stay fresh as long as we are careful not to get any air into the bag. But if we become careless and allow the seal to be broken, the bread will become stale and hard within a few hours.

I think our lives are much the same way. If we respect the Holy Spirit and do not vex, offend, or sadden Him, we are protecting our seal.

A Complaining, Critical, Faultfinding Spirit

Let there be no filthiness (obscenity, indecency) nor foolish and sinful (silly and corrupt) talk, nor coarse jesting, which are not fitting or becoming; but instead voice your thankfulness [to God].

Ephesians 5:4

What Paul is telling us here is, "Instead of vexing, offending, and saddening the Holy Spirit, *voice your thankfulness to God.*"

The complaining, critical, faultfinding spirit absolutely must be eradicated from the Church.

Have you complained today?

You may as well be honest...because God knows!

We never change and get to where we need to be unless we first face truth and admit where we are.

You may be thinking, "Well, yes, I have been complaining, but I have a good reason. If you were treated the way I am, if you led the life I lead, you would complain too."

I had to realize long ago that excuses of any kind only keep me right where I am; they prevent me from going forward.

In John 8:31,32 Jesus said, "If you continue in My Word...you will know the truth, and the truth will make you free" (author's paraphrase). The truth will make us free, but it has to be applied to home base, to us.

The Holy Spirit is in the conviction business. He is the Agent of sanctification. He works out the process of holiness in us. Jesus plants the seed in us, His own seed, and then the Holy Spirit teaches us the Word, watering the seed. He also sees us as God's garden, under cultivation, and He kindly keeps us weeded. Excuses are like weeds; if left unattended, they choke fruit.

I was a complainer, I was critical, and I was a faultfinder.

As a matter of fact, I had a major problem in this area. If I can be free, anyone can be. I had a lot of genuine negative circumstances in my life. I had an extended background of abuse and in the natural had much to complain about. But the very fact that I complained caused me to remain.

It seems to me that people who live in crisis most of the time also have addictive problems with complaining and faultfinding. These two negative traits always show up together.

The problems start a cycle. First an individual encounters some sour circumstances, so he complains, which causes him to remain in the circumstances. Then Satan adds more misery, which draws even more complaining. Now the person has two things to complain about.

As this cycle continues, soon the individual is lost in a sea of problems and complaints. It becomes a lifestyle. He feels deprived and oppressed. Often he also feels lonely.

People with a critical spirit have a difficult time maintaining friendships. They are addicted to their problems, and after a period of time other people just plain get tired of hearing about their woes and begin to avoid them — unless, of course, both complainers and listeners are alike, and then it is a case of misery loves company.

Complaining is like whistling for the devil.

Once I had a dog named Buddy. When he was outside, and I wanted him inside, I would whistle for him, calling, "Here, Buddy, here, Buddy." Soon he would come running in.

When we complain, it is the same scene. We are calling for the devil, who will quickly come in to give us more misery.

If you and I decide not to complain, I can tell you ahead of time, it will be a major challenge. Many times, we don't realize just how much we do complain until someone or something (like this book) calls our attention to it.

How quick are we to become impatient and begin to complain when stuck in traffic, or while waiting in check-out lanes in grocery or department stores? How quick are we to spot and point out all the faults of our friends or family members? Do we complain about our job, when we should be thanking God that we have one? Do we complain about high prices, when we should be thanking God that we are able to go out and shop?

I could, of course, go on and on, but I believe each one of us recognizes the areas in our own life in which we have a problem with complaining.

I have had to face the hard truth that a critical spirit often is rooted in pride. Indignation rises up in a proud person when he is inconvenienced. Indignation is an attitude that says, "I should not have to be in this situation. I should be treated better than this, by God and/or by other people." The attitude is, "Thousands of others can be in the same situation, but it shouldn't happen to me!"

Until we humble ourselves and realize how blessed we are to have anything at all, we will never stop complaining about what we do not have. Let us learn to appreciate what people do for us, and stop complaining about what they do not do.

My husband, for example, is not the type to buy me flowers on special days, but he is very adaptable and extremely easy to get along with. There were many birthdays, anniversaries, and Valentine's days when I found fault with him that he did not do more. He would always say, "If you want something, I'll take you out and get you anything we can afford." But, of course, being a woman, I wanted him to walk the malls looking for something and come home and surprise me. I grumbled to the Lord about it, seethed inwardly over it — got angry, offended, and hurt by it — and felt sorry for myself. All of which did me absolutely no good and did not change my husband one bit.

Dave is an absolutely wonderful man, kind and generous. He lets me do almost anything I want to do and will buy me anything I desire if the money is available. He is handsome, takes good care of himself physically, tells me he loves me almost every day, and is very affectionate.

I can look at what he is not and be miserable, or I can look at what he is and be grateful!

Who says I am perfect! We are all the same. We have strengths and weaknesses, and if we are to have good relationships with one another, we must major on the positive attributes and minor on the negative ones.

An Ungrateful Generation

> But understand this, that in the last days will come (set in) perilous times of great stress and trouble [hard to deal with and hard to bear].
>
> For people will be lovers of self and [utterly] self-centered, lovers of money and aroused by an inordinate [greedy] desire for wealth, proud and arrogant and contemptuous boasters. They will be abusive (blasphemous, scoffing), disobedient to parents, *ungrateful*, unholy and profane.
>
> 2 Timothy 3:1,2

Just as Paul predicted long ago, we live in an unthankful and ungrateful generation. It seems the more people have, the less they appreciate it.

We as believers are in the world, but we must strive not to be like it. The more others around us complain, the more we should express gratitude to God.

Bright Lights in a Dark World

> Do all things without grumbling and faultfinding and complaining [against God] and questioning and doubting [among yourselves].
>
> That you may show yourselves to be blameless and guileless, innocent and uncontaminated, children of God without

**blemish (faultless, unrebukable) in the midst of a crooked and
wicked generation [spiritually perverted and perverse], among
whom you are seen as bright lights (stars or beacons shining out
clearly) in the [dark] world.**

Philippians 2:14,15

This passage emphasizes what I am sharing. We should avoid complaining because it is the spirit of the world today. We should show the world what God is like. We should imitate Jesus and follow His example by being bright lights shining out into this dark world.

There has now arisen a new generation of people, many of whom have not been taught any godly principles. They have not been taught anything about God in school, nor have they been taught to pray at home. They have seen some sad examples of spiritual leaders who have publicly fallen, and having no solid foundation, it is easy for them to conclude that "religion" is a bunch of junk.

We are to be living epistles, read of all men. (2 Cor. 3:2 KJV.)

We don't need to show the world religion, which often is hypocritical, telling others what to do, but failing to do it ourselves. We need to show them Jesus by a lifestyle that lifts up His principles. These verses in Philippians are not to be taken lightly concerning the command not to be complainers, grumblers, or faultfinders. We are commanded to be different from the world, so that we may be able to show the world a different way of living.

A Daily Challenge

Always be full of joy in the Lord; I say it again, rejoice! Let everyone see that you are unselfish and considerate in all you do. Remember that the Lord is coming soon. Don't worry about anything; instead, pray about everything; tell God your needs *and don't forget to thank him for his answers.*

Philippians 4:4-6 TLB

You and I need to make it a daily challenge not to complain or find fault with anything. This does not mean that we don't correct situations that need to be corrected. It doesn't mean that we live with our heads in the clouds and pretend that nothing negative exists. It simply means that we make it our goal in life to be as positive as possible.

Don't complain when complaining does no good.

The problem begins in the heart and comes out of the mouth. First an attitude adjustment is needed, and then the fruit of the lips will change.

Try going to bed at night pondering everything you have to be thankful for. Let it be the first thing you do in the morning.

Thank God for "little" things: a parking place that He helps you find, waking up on time for work, the fact that you can walk or see or hear, your children.

Develop an "attitude of gratitude." Make it a "one day at a time" challenge. Don't be discouraged with yourself when you fail, but don't throw in the towel and quit either. Keep at it until you have developed new habits.

We are good at praying about our needs and lifting our petitions before God. But how many of us remember to thank God when the answer arrives? We enjoy getting our children what they need and ask for, but we feel taken advantage of if they just "grab the goods and run" without stopping to show any appreciation. If they are appreciative and remember to say "thank you," and especially if they say it more than once and are really sincere, it actually motivates us to want to do more for them.

God is the same way with us.

Be generous in your gratitude, and it will sweeten your relationship with the Lord.

Complaining in Advance

> Behold, how good and how pleasant it is for brethren [family members] to dwell together in unity!
>
> **Psalm 133:1**

Complain and Remain, Praise and Be Raised

Our oldest son David and his wife sold a mobile home once and purchased a home. The only problem was they had a month between moving out of the mobile home and into their house, with no place to live. So naturally my husband and I told them they could stay with us.

Interestingly enough, David and I had, had a difficult time getting along when he lived at home. Our personalities are a lot alike, we are both strong willed, which does not always mix well in close quarters.

Since those days we had been getting along fine. He works for us, and that works out well, but living in the same house again was another story. Nothing negative had happened, but my mind kept coming up with "what ifs."

Dave and I would be driving down the road, and my mouth would want to start talking about negative things that could take place: "What if there is no hot water left for my shower in the morning after everyone else is done? What if they leave messes for me to clean up?"

Nothing bad had happened yet. David and his wife had not even moved in. Yet my mouth was wanting to declare disaster ahead of time.

Satan wanted me to prophesy my future. He wanted me to be critical of the situation in advance.

If the devil can get us to be negative, he can provide us with negative circumstances. Often we call for our own problems. We "call those things which be not as though they were," only we do it in the negative sense.

You see, these godly principles I am sharing not only work in the positive, they also work in the negative — if we sow negative seeds.

My blender works regardless of what is placed in it. If I put ice cream and milk in it, I will get a milk shake. If I put water and dirt, I will get mud. The blender works. It is created to work. It is up to me to decide what I put in it. What I put in is what I will get out.

The same is true with our minds and hearts and mouths. What goes in is what is going to come out --for good or for bad.

David and Shelly did live with us for the month, and everything worked out fine. I knew enough of these principles by then to resist the temptation to complain in advance, and I urge you to beware of this temptation also. When I was tempted to speak forth negative words, I would choose to say, "David and Shelly's living with us will work out fine, it won't be any problem. I'm sure everyone will cooperate and be sensitive to the needs of the others."

David and I made a joke out of us getting along for thirty days under the same roof. We both like to be right, so he said, "I'll tell you what, Mom. Let's take turns being right. During the thirty days we are together, you can be right fifteen days, and I will be right fifteen days." We both laughed and had a good time.

Sowing Seeds for a Future Harvest

I know how to be abased and live humbly in straitened circumstances, and I know also how to enjoy plenty and live in abundance....

Philippians 4:12

As we see from his letter to the Philippians, Paul did not complain during the kind of hard times that come to all of us, especially in the beginning.

In our own case, God has blessed our ministry and given us much favor. We are able to hold our meetings and seminars in many great churches and convention centers around the country. But it did not start that way. Like most people, we had very small beginnings. We have learned that we are not to despise and complain about those days. (Zech. 4:10.)

One of the first hotel ballrooms we rented to hold a seminar turned out to be very run down and unattractive. We were going from our home in St. Louis, Missouri, to another state to hold the meeting and had rented the space by phone, sight unseen. Of course, the people at the hotel had said that it was nice and that the service was good.

When we arrived, the wind was blowing hard and the first thing we noticed was that several of the shingles from the roof were lying in the parking lot.

The chairs in the ballroom were in very poor condition. Some had stuffing sticking through rips and tears in the upholstery. Others had food caked on them, plus many stains from spills.

The air conditioning was not working properly, and every time the temperature needed to be adjusted in the room (which seemed to be frequently, because it was either too hot or too cold), a maintenance man had to come into the conference room during the meeting, and climb up a ladder. He had to go through the ceiling and onto the roof to adjust something, because the room controls were not working.

As we considered our situation, knowing there was nothing we could do about it because the first meeting began in about five hours, *we all started to complain* — which is the "natural" thing to do in such a situation.

Immediately the Holy Spirit began dealing with me and putting it on my heart that if we would make it through the early days without complaining, we would be laying a strong foundation for the future. He showed me that eventually we would be able to go to the nicest places, but we would never be "promoted" to better things if we did not sow seeds now for our future.

Complaining would have been sowing seeds also, but seeds that would have produced more of what we were grumbling about. Sowing seeds of being thankful *in* — not *for* — the situation we faced would produce a bountiful harvest later on.

I gathered together our entire travel team (which at that time consisted of perhaps a half-dozen people) and told them what the Holy Spirit had shown me. We all agreed not to complain about anything in the hotel. We purposely looked for things we could say something nice about.

The result was that we had a very successful meeting and learned a vital lesson that would pay huge dividends in the future.

A Foretaste of Good Things To Come

And so it was that he [Abraham], having waited long and endured patiently, realized and obtained [in the birth of Isaac as a pledge of what was to come] what God had promised him.

Hebrews 6:15

In this verse the writer of the book of Hebrews states that Isaac was a pledge of what was to come.

God did not promise Abraham just one baby, He promised him that he would be the father of many nations. Many people today have a "pledge," or a little foretaste, of the good things that God has in His plans for them.

In 1 Kings 18, after a long period of drought that Elijah had prophesied, God told him to go and tell the wicked King Ahab that it was going to rain. Elijah spoke forth the Word of God by faith with no evident signs of rain. Then he went to the top of a mountain and began to pray. As he prayed he sent his servant up to a higher point to check out the sky. Six times the servant went and came back with the report of a sunny, cloudless sky. Finally the seventh time he returned and reported, "I see a cloud the size of a man's hand." In the expanse of the sky, that is not very big, but it was enough to get Elijah motivated to take the next step of faith. He sent word to Ahab, **...Hitch your chariot and go down, lest the rain stop you** (v. 44).

This cloud, even though it was very small, was a beginning of a great downpour. (v. 45.) It was a pledge or foretaste of good things to come.

Only a Seed

> Who [with reason] despises the day of small things?....
>
> Zechariah 4:10

Probably most of us who are believing God for something can find evidence of a small beginning: a little seed, a cloud the size of a man's hand.

Rejoice over that seed. It is a sign of greater things to come. Don't curse your seed by complaining over it.

God gives us seed, something that causes us to hope, a little thing perhaps, but something is better than nothing. We should say, "Lord, this is only a little thing, but thank You for giving me some hope, something to hold on to. Thank You, Lord, for a beginning."

Take that seed and plant it by believing over it.

The Holy Spirit showed me that I was throwing away a lot of my seed.

When we despise something we regard it lightly. We take no notice of it and count it as nothing. We do not take care of it. If we don't take care of what God gives us, we lose it.

If we lose the seed, we will never see the harvest.

Part of Hebrews 13:5 says, in essence, "Be content with what you have."

Let us be like Paul: let us *learn* how to be abased and how to abound — and how to be content either way, knowing that every part is a portion of the whole picture.

That Scripture goes on to say, **For He [God] Himself has said, I will not in any way...let [you] down.**

That is why we can be content — by faith — during the small beginning. We know that the Lord is the Author and the Finisher. (Heb. 12:2.) What He begins, He completes. (Phil. 1:6.) He will do that for us — *if* we will hold our faith firm until the end. (Heb. 3:6.)

I will not talk with you much more, for the prince (evil genius, ruler) of the world is coming. And he has no claim on Me. [He has nothing in common with Me; there is nothing in Me that belongs to him, and he has no power over Me.] — John 14:30

chapter 7

Cross Over to the Other Side

He was oppressed, [yet when] He was afflicted, He was submissive and *opened not His mouth;* like a lamb that is led to the slaughter, and as a sheep before her shearers is dumb, so *He opened not His mouth.* —Isaiah 53:7

One of the most difficult times for us to discipline our minds, mouths, moods, and attitudes is during the storm. We all experience the storms of life in varying degrees, we all have our faith tested and tried, and *we all must learn how to behave in the storm!*

Scriptures such as John 14:30 and Isaiah 53:7 have always intrigued me. I had no real understanding of the message they were conveying, until the Holy Spirit revealed to me that they related to the mouth and the storm.

When Jesus was experiencing the most intense pressure, He "decided" that it would be wise not to open His mouth. Why? I believe it was because in His humanity He would have been tempted to do the same thing you and I would be tempted to do: doubt, question God, complain, say something negative, etc.

When under pressure, even a very mature believer will say things he shouldn't, if the pressure is intense enough and lasts long enough.

Jesus is the Son of God, Himself God, but He came to us in the form of a human being. The writer of Hebrews 4:15 KJV says that He **...was in all points tempted like as we are, yet without sin.**

I believe that when our Lord was faced with trying situations in which He knew He might be tempted to say things that would not be fruitful, He purposely decided and declared that He was going to be quieter than usual.

This is a wise decision for anyone to make during times of stress. Instead of speaking out of upset emotions or wounded feelings, it is always best to be quiet and allow the emotional storm to subside.

Blessings Are Coming

> On that same day [when] evening had come, He said to them, Let us go over to the other side [of the lake].
>
> Mark 4:35

It is always exciting when Jesus says to us, "Let's do a new thing." To me this phrase, "Let us go over to the other side," is equivalent to saying, "Promotion is coming," or, "Blessings are on their way," or "Come up higher," or any variety of phrases the Lord uses to communicate to us that it is time for a change.

I am sure the disciples were excited to see what would happen on "the other side." What they did not expect or foresee was a raging storm on the way!

Faith Is for the Middle

> And a furious storm of wind [of hurricane proportions] arose, and the waves kept beating into the boat, so that it was already becoming filled.
>
> But He [Himself] was in the stern [of the boat], asleep on the [leather] cushion; and they awoke Him and said to Him, Master, do You not care that we are perishing?
>
> Mark 4:37,38

The disciples probably were not nearly as excited in the middle as they may have been in the beginning.

Although God often calls us to launch out to a new destination, He usually does not let us know what is going to happen on the way to it. We leave the security of where we are and start out for the blessings of the other side, but it is often in the middle where we encounter the storms.

The middle is often a place of testing.

The storm was in full force, and Jesus was asleep! Does that sound familiar? Have you ever had times when you felt that you were sinking fast — and Jesus was asleep? You prayed and prayed and heard nothing from God. You spent time with Him and tried to sense His Presence, and yet you felt nothing. You searched for an answer, but no matter how hard you struggled against the wind and waves, the storm raged on — and you didn't know what to do about it.

We sometimes refer to those seasons as "the midnight hour" or "the dark night of the soul."

This storm the disciples found themselves facing was no little April shower or harmless summer squall, but **a storm of hurricane proportions.** The waves were not gently rolling and tossing, they were beating into the boat with such fury that it was quickly becoming filled up with water.

Now that would be enough to frighten anyone.

It is at times like this, when it looks like the boat is sinking with us in it, that we must "use" our faith. We can talk about faith, read books about it, hear sermons about it, sing songs about it, but in the storm we must *use* it.

It is also at such times when we discover just how much faith we really have.

Faith, like muscle, is strengthened by "using" it, not by talking about it. Each storm we go through equips us to handle the next one better. Soon we become such a good navigator that the storms don't disturb us at all. We have been through it before, and we already know how it will end.

Everything will be all right!

According to the Bible, we are more than conquerors. (Rom. 8:37.) To me that means that we know that we will win before the battle ever starts. In order to reach our goal, we do have to go through the storm, which is not always fun, but what a blessing to know that in Christ Jesus we have the victory.

Faith is for those times when we don't have the manifestation yet. Faith is for the middle.

It does not require tremendous faith to begin a thing, the beginning and the end are both exciting times, but oh, the middle! Yet we all have to go through the middle to get to the other side.

Jesus wanted His disciples to believe Him. He had said, "Let us go to the other side." He expected them to believe that if He said it, it would happen. But, like us, they were afraid.

Calmed Storm, Rebuked Disciples

And He arose and rebuked the wind and said to the sea, Hush now! Be still (muzzled)! And the wind ceased (sank to rest as if exhausted by its beating) and there was [immediately] a great calm (a perfect peacefulness).

He said to them, Why are you so timid and fearful? How is it that you have no faith (no firmly relying trust)?

Mark 4:39,40

Jesus calmed the storm, but He rebuked the disciples for their lack of faith.

Why does He do that?

It is vital to our future that we grow in faith, which is confidence and trust in God. If Jesus allowed us to stay in fear and continued all of our lives to calm every storm for us without correcting us, we would never learn to press on to the other side.

One of the things about us that has to change is our response to the storms of life. It is certain that we must grow in self-control and discipline of the mouth. As we have noted, we cannot "tame the tongue" without God's help, but neither will He do it all for us.

Hold On! Help Is On the Way!

So let us seize and hold fast and retain without wavering the hope we cherish and confess and our acknowledgement of it, for He Who promised is reliable (sure) and faithful to His word.

Hebrews 10:23

It is not enough to be positive and speak faith when all of our circumstances are positive.

It is time to cross over to the other side, time to come up higher.

It is time for us to hold fast our confession of faith (Heb. 10:23 KJV), and ride out the storms, knowing that God has His eye on everything, including us and the storm. He is faithful, and we can hold to His hand, knowing that He will not allow us to sink.

A Fountain With Bitter Water and Sweet

Out of the same mouth come forth blessing and cursing. These things, my brethren, ought not to be so.

Does a fountain send forth [simultaneously] from the same opening fresh water and bitter?

James 3:10,11

We should strive to eliminate "double talk" — saying one thing in good times and another in hard times.

We should strive not to be fountains who send forth sweet water in sweet times, and bitter water in bitter times.

113

Jesus was subject to the same pressures and temptations we are, and yet He always stayed the same. (Heb. 13:8.) He had to discipline His mouth and conversation during the storms of life, and so must we.

Control of the tongue should be our goal. It is a sign of maturity. It is one way we glorify God.

Bridle the Tongue

> **If anyone thinks himself to be religious (piously observant of the external duties of his faith) and does not bridle his tongue but deludes his own heart, this person's religious service is worthless (futile, barren).**
>
> **James 1:26**

My friend, this is a strong statement. We can do all types of "good works" that would be said to be a result of our religious convictions, but if we do not "bridle the tongue," they are all worthless.

I don't know about you, but that makes me even more serious about the entire issue of words, the tongue, and the mouth.

A bridle is defined by Webster as, "A harness consisting of a headstall, bit, and reins, which fits a horse's head and is used to restrain or guide."[1]

In the midst of the storms of life, if we don't bridle the tongue, we may never experience deliverance. The Holy Spirit will be our bridle if we accept His leadership and guidance.

Put a Bit in the Mouth!

If we set bits in the horses' mouths to make them obey us, we can turn their whole bodies about.

Likewise, look at the ships: though they are so great and are driven by rough winds, they are steered by a very small rudder wherever the impulse of the helmsman determines.

Even so the tongue is a little member, and it can boast of great things. See how much wood or how great a forest a tiny spark can set ablaze!

James 3:3-5

These Scriptures indicate that the tongue gives direction to all the rest of our life. One might say that our words draw borders for us, and we must live inside those borders.

The tongue is such a small member of the body, but it can accomplish major things. It would be wonderful if they were all good things, but they are not. Relationships are ruined by the tongue. The tongue can, and frequently does, cause divorce. People are emotionally wounded by someone else's tongue, and not all of them recover. Some elderly people are still hurting from things that were spoken to them and about them when they were children. Yes, the tongue may be a little member, but oh, how powerful it is!

The bit that is set in a horse's mouth is also very small, but it gives direction. Webster defines the bit as, "The metal mouthpiece of a bridle that controls and curbs an animal.... Something that controls...."[2]

We need a bit in our mouths, but it will not be forced on us, we must choose it. The Holy Spirit will function as that bit if we choose His leadership. When we begin to say the wrong thing, we will sense Him trying to pull us in the right direction. He is always working in our lives, striving to keep us out of trouble. His ministry is to be greatly appreciated.

The Holy Spirit as Bit and Bridle

Be not like the horse or the mule, which lack understanding, which must have their mouths held firm with bit and bridle, or else they will not come with you.

Psalm 32:9

A horse either follows the pull of the bridle, which controls the bit in his mouth, or he experiences great pain.

It is actually the same way with us and our relationship with the Holy Spirit. He is our bridle and the bit in our mouths. He should be controlling the reins of our life. If we follow His promptings we will end up at the right place and stay out of all the wrong places. But if we don't follow Him, we will end up with a lot of pain.

The Mouth Has a Mind of Its Own

...refute arguments and theories and reasonings and every proud and lofty thing that sets itself up against the [true] knowledge of God; and...lead every thought and purpose away captive into the obedience of Christ (the Messiah, the Anointed One).

2 Corinthians 10:5

In times of trial, the mouth just seems to have a mind of its own. Sometimes I feel that mine has a motor on it and that someone flipped the switch before I knew what was going on.

It is also very important to be accountable for our thoughts, because the root source of our words is our thoughts. Satan offers a thought like, "I just can't go on like this anymore." The next thing we know, the mouth has engaged and is verbalizing the thought.

Since the problem starts with thoughts, the remedy must begin there also. We are to lead every wrong thought captive unto the obedience of Jesus Christ. We are to "cast down" wrong imaginations. (2 Cor. 10:5 KJV.)

The mind is the battlefield,[3] and it must be renewed completely in order to ever experience God's good plan. (Rom. 12:1,2.)

117

The mouth will never be controlled unless the mind is controlled.

Speaking of mind control, it is interesting to note that people operating in witchcraft seek to control other people's thoughts. Learning to project wrong thoughts toward unsuspecting people is one of their top priorities.

What I get from this is that *Satan wants to control our mind.*

The Holy Spirit also wants to control our mind, but He never forces Himself on us. It is our choice. He leads us in the right direction by convicting us when we are thinking wrong thoughts. We then choose to cast down the wrong thought and think on something that will bear good fruit, as we are instructed to do in Philippians 4:8:

> ...whatever is true, whatever is worthy of reverence and is honorable and seemly, whatever is just, whatever is pure, whatever is lovely and lovable, whatever is kind and winsome and gracious, if there is any virtue and excellence, if there is anything worthy of praise, think on and weigh and take account of these things [fix your minds on them].

In Psalm 19:14, the psalmist prays, **Let the words of my mouth and the meditation of my heart be acceptable in Your sight, O Lord, my [firm, impenetrable] Rock and my Redeemer.** Notice that he mentions both the mind and the mouth. This is because they work together.

I think some people try to control their mouth, but they do nothing about their thoughts. That is like pulling the top off of a weed; unless the root is dug up, the weed always comes back.

Order Your Conversation

Blessed (happy, fortunate, to be envied) are the undefiled (the upright, truly sincere, and blameless) in the way [of the revealed will of God], who walk (order their conduct and conversation) in the law of the Lord (the whole of God's revealed will).

Psalm 119:1

We must order our conversation in accordance with God's will.

When you find yourself in a time of trial, try not to just look at where you are right now and at what is happening to you at the moment, but rather see yourself and your circumstances through the eye of faith.

You have cast off from the shore, and now you are out in the middle of the sea with the storm raging, but *you will get to the other side.* There are blessings waiting for you there, *so don't jump overboard!*

Many people backslide during challenging times, and part of the reason they do so is because they have never learned how to talk.

A trial is discouraging enough in itself; we don't need to add insult to injury by depressing ourselves through negative speech.

In Deuteronomy 26:14 the Israelites were commanded to bring their offerings to the Lord and say to Him, **I have not eaten of the tithe in my mourning....** Sometimes when people are mourning they begin to eat their own tithe instead of giving it to the Lord, thereby backsliding in their giving. Why? Because it is harder to be obedient to the Lord during times of personal difficulty.

The devil whispers in the ear, "This tithing business isn't working, so you'd better hold on to what you've got instead of giving it away." The mouth goes into gear and verbalizes, "This isn't working; I'd better use my money to meet my own needs, because nobody else is helping me."

Remember, Satan does not want you to get to the other side. He does not want you to make any progress at all. He wants to see you turn around and go back to where you came from.

In Mark 4 when Jesus told the parable about the sowing of the seed, the image of the ground represented different kinds of hearts which receive the Word. In verse 17 when He came to the seed that was sown on stony ground, He said of those it represented, **And they have no real root in themselves, and so they endure for a little while; then when trouble or persecution arises on account of the Word, they immediately are offended** (become displeased, indignant, resentful) and they stumble and fall away.

People can backslide during times of trial and tribulation. According to Jesus in John 16:33 we should take courage during such times, for He has overcome the world for us: **I have told you these things, so that in Me you may have [perfect] peace and confidence. In the world you have tribulation and trials and distress and frustration; but be of good cheer [take courage; be confident, certain, undaunted]! For I have overcome the world. [I have deprived it of power to harm you and have conquered it for you.]**

These are the things we need to remember and to say.

Can These Bones Live?

The hand of the Lord was upon me, and He brought me out in the Spirit of the Lord and set me down in the midst of the valley; and it was full of bones.

And He caused me to pass round about among them, and behold, there were very many [human bones] in the open valley or plain, and behold, they were very dry.

And He said to me, Son of man, can these bones live? And I answered, O Lord God, You know!

Again He said to me, Prophesy to these bones and say to them, O you dry bones, hear the word of the Lord.

Ezekiel 37:1-4

You may feel as if your life is no more than dead, dry bones. Your circumstances may be so dead that they stink. Your hope may seem lost, but let me show you God's way out.

As this passage continues, the prophet does as God instructs, and he sees God totally revive and bring breath and spirit back into what was once only dead, dry bones.

The same thing can happen to you and me. But not unless we become God's mouthpiece and prophesy His Word. We can no longer speak with our own idle words and under pressure allow our mouths to take the lead role.

Lazarus, Come Forth!

> Now a certain man named Lazarus was ill. He was of Bethany, the village where Mary and her sister Martha lived.
>
> This Mary was the one who anointed the Lord with perfume and wiped His feet with her hair. It was her brother Lazarus who was [now] sick.
>
> So the sisters sent to Him, saying, Lord, he whom You love [so well] is sick.
>
> John 11:1-3

In John 11 the illness and death of Lazarus are recorded. By the time Jesus arrived on the scene, Lazarus had been dead for four days. Going out to meet Jesus, his sister Martha said to Him, ...**Master, if You had been here, my brother would not**

have died (v. 21). Later her sister Mary said exactly the same thing to Him: **...Lord, if You had been here, my brother would not have died** (v. 32).

We all feel like that sometimes. We feel that if Jesus had only shown up sooner maybe things would not be so bad. I am sure that the disciples felt that their situation would have been different if Jesus had not been asleep in the back of the boat.

In John 11:23-25 we see how Jesus responded to these words of hopelessness and despair:

> **Jesus said to her, Your brother shall rise again.**
> **Martha replied, I know that he will rise again in the resurrection at the last day.**
> **Jesus said to her, I am [Myself] the Resurrection and the Life. Whoever believes in (adheres to, trusts in, and relies on) Me, although he may die, yet he shall live.**

You know the rest of the story. Jesus called Lazarus, a man who had been dead for four long days, to come forth from the tomb, and he did so, totally restored. If Jesus can raise a dead man, surely He can raise a dead circumstance.

We can see from Ezekiel's experience with the bones, and from the account of Lazarus, that no matter how bad things seem, God will make a way. But remember, there are spiritual laws that we must respect in order to see the miracle-working power of God.

One of these spiritual laws is illustrated by the story of the woman with the issue of blood.

Keep Saying to Yourself

> And there was a woman who had had a flow of blood for twelve years.
> And who had endured much suffering under [the hands of] many physicians and had spent all that she had, and was no better but instead grew worse.
> She had heard the reports concerning Jesus, and she came up behind Him in the throng and touched His garment.
>
> **Mark 5:25-27**

What about the woman with the issue of blood? She had been having the same problem for twelve years. She had suffered greatly, and no one had been able to help her.

Surely this woman was being attacked with thoughts of hopelessness. When she thought about going to Jesus, surely she must have heard, "What's the use?" But she pressed on past the crowd that was so thick on all sides that it was suffocating. She touched the hem of Jesus' garment, and healing virtue flowed to her, and she was made well. (Paraphrase vv. 29-34 AMP, KJV.)

But there is a part we don't want to miss: **For she kept saying, If I only touch His garments, I shall be restored to health** (Mark 5:28).

She kept *saying!* She kept *saying!* Do you get it? She kept *saying!*

No matter what she felt like, no matter how much others tried to discourage her, even though the problem was twelve years old, and the crowd looked impossible to get through, this woman got her miracle. Jesus told her that it was her faith that had made her whole. (v. 34.) Her faith was released through her words.

Faith has to be activated if it is to work, and one of the ways we activate it is through our words.

Keep saying — and don't give up hope!

Prisoners of Hope

Return to the stronghold [of security and prosperity], *you prisoners of hope;* even today do I declare that I will restore double your former prosperity to you.

Zechariah 9:12

We have just seen three situations: dry bones restored, the dead brought back to life, and an incurable disease totally cured. All three of these "storms" were impossible to man, but with God all things are possible. (Matt. 19:26.)

Recently when we were in a storm ourselves, the Holy Spirit led me to this Scripture in Zechariah that I had never seen before. It was as if He had it hidden like a treasure just waiting for a time when I would really need it.

As "prisoners of hope," we must be filled with hope, we must think hope, and we must talk hope. Hope is the foundation on which faith stands.

Some people try to have faith after having lost all hope.

It won't work.

Refuse to stop hoping no matter how dry the bones may seem, how dead the situation may appear, how long the problem has been around.

God is still God, and this Scripture tells us that if we will remain positive and be "prisoners of hope," He will restore to us double everything we have lost.

Prayer for Control of the Mouth

Set a guard, O Lord, before my mouth; keep watch at the door of my lips.

Psalm 141:3

I pray this Scripture very often, because I know that I need help with my mouth, and I need it daily. I want the Holy Spirit to convict me when I am talking too much, or when I am saying things I shouldn't, when I am speaking negatively, when I am complaining, when I am sounding harsh or engaging in any of the other kinds of "evil speaking."

Anything that offends God in our conversation needs to be eliminated. That's why we need to pray continually: **Set a guard, O Lord, before my mouth; keep watch at the door of my lips.**

Another important Scripture on this subject is Psalm 17:3, **...I have purposed that my mouth shall not transgress.**

As I have said previously, we have to *purpose* to do the right thing in this area. Whatever we do in this life of faith, we must do it on purpose.

Discipline is a choice. It is not necessarily easy, but it begins with a quality decision.

When we are crossing over to the other side and suddenly find ourselves in the middle of the journey with the storm raging, we will definitely have to purpose to keep our mouth from transgressing.

That's when we should pray this verse.

Another Scripture that I pray regularly is Psalm 19:14: **Let the words of my mouth and the meditation of my heart be**

acceptable in Your sight, O Lord, my [firm, impenetrable] Rock and my Redeemer.

Pray the Word. Nothing gets God's attention any quicker. It is His Word that carries the power of the Holy Spirit.

Let these Scriptures be the cry of your heart. Be sincere in your desire to gain victory in this area, and as you seek God for His help, you will begin to notice that you are changing.

This is what the Lord has done for me, and He is no respecter of persons. (Acts 10:34.) All those who follow God-ordained guidelines get God-ordained results.

Pray this prayer of commitment to exercise control over your mouth:

> Lord, I pray that You will help me to develop sensitivity to the Holy Spirit concerning all of my manner of conversation. I do not want to be stubborn like a horse or mule that will not obey without a bridle and bit. I want to move in Your direction with only a gentle nudge from You.
>
> During the storms of life, while I am crossing over to the other side, I ask for Your help. I always need Your help, Lord, but these times are special times of temptation.

Place a guard over my lips and let all the words of my mouth be acceptable in Your sight, O Lord, my Strength and my Redeemer.

In Jesus' name I pray, amen.

chapter 8

Is Your Mouth Saved?

...work out (cultivate, carry out to the goal, and fully complete) your own salvation with reverence and awe and trembling (self-distrust, with serious caution, tenderness of conscience, watchfulness against temptation, timidly shrinking from whatever might offend God and discredit the name of Christ).

— Philippians 2:12

I remember when God spoke to my heart and said, "Joyce, it is time for your mouth to be saved."

That may sound strange, but it was true.

It is possible to be saved and not sound like it. An individual can be a child of God, and yet not talk like one.

I know, because I was such a person.

It is not enough to be saved, the mouth must be saved also. That is part of the process which the Apostle Paul referred to as "working out" one's own salvation.

What does it mean exactly to "work out your own salvation"?

In Ephesians 2:8,9 Paul, who wrote this phrase to the Philippians, clearly stated that salvation cannot be earned, that it is given by God's grace and received through faith, that it is not the reward for good works, lest anyone should boast.

Without some understanding, these two passages in Philippians and Ephesians can almost seem conflicting.

The New Birth, God's sending His Son Jesus Christ to live in us, imparting to us His Spirit, and creating within us a new heart, is something that only He can do by His grace, mercy, love, and goodness. He does all the work, and we receive the free gift by faith.

Working out the salvation that He has freely given us is just another phase of our walk with Him. We might say that He deposits a seed in us, and we then must cooperate with the work of the Holy Spirit to see that the seed He has placed in us grows into a plant that occupies our entire life.

Cultivating the Seed

Now to Abraham and his seed were the promises made. He saith not, And to seeds, as of many; but as of one, And to thy seed, which is Christ.

Galatians 3:16 KJV

The Bible refers to Jesus Christ as "the seed." I like that, because it means that if I have a seed I can have a harvest.

Jesus is the Seed of everything good that God desires for us to have. The Seed is planted by God, but it must be cultivated, nurtured, watered, and cared for. The ground it is planted in must be kept plowed up and weed free.

Our hearts and lives are the ground. Everything that needs to be changed or removed is not taken care of all at once. There is a great work to be done, and only the Holy Spirit knows the proper "when and how." As He deals with us about certain issues, we are to submit to Him our wills, which means submitting the flesh to the leadership of the spirit.

If any one of us would go back in our thinking to the beginning of our walk with God and take an inventory of all the things that He has changed in us since then, we would be amazed at how different we are now from what we were when we began.

I remember that God dealt with me in the beginning about independence and how I could not do anything by myself. Then He went on to motives and starting teaching me that what I did was not as important as why I did it. He dealt with me about my attitudes, about my TV and movie viewing, about my manner of dress, about my thoughts — and, of course, about my mouth.

To be honest, He probably has dealt with me more consistently about my mouth than about any other issue.

When God wants to use something, the devil will try to steal it for sure. Since I am called to teach God's Word, Satan is always making a bid for the Lord's property.

Of course, I learned many things about my mouth over the years, but the day came when God said to me, "It is time for your mouth to be saved." I knew it was serious business this time, not just a little teaching from the Holy Spirit on the importance of words, but a life-changing revelation on *the mouth!*

Get Your Mouth Straight!

Hear, for I will speak excellent and princely things; and the opening of my lips shall be for right things.

For my mouth shall utter truth, and wrongdoing is detestable and loathsome to my lips.

All the words of my mouth are righteous (upright and in right standing with God); there is nothing contrary to truth or crooked in them.

Proverbs 8:6-8

When I read Scriptures like the one above, I knew I had a long way to go. I was praying for a stronger anointing on my teaching and ministry, and God had to show me three men in the Bible who were called but who had a mouth problem. He revealed to me that He had to do something about their words, about their mouths, before He could use them the way He had planned.

Jeremiah's Fearful Mouth

Then the word of the Lord came to me [Jeremiah], saying,

Before I formed you in the womb I knew and approved of you [as My chosen instrument], and before you were born I separated and set you apart, consecrating you; [and] I appointed you as a prophet to the nations.

Then said I, Ah, Lord God! Behold, I cannot speak, for I am only a youth.

But the Lord said to me, Say not, I am only a youth; for you shall go to all to whom I shall send you, and whatever I command you, you shall speak.

Be not afraid of them [their faces], for I am with you to deliver you, says the Lord.

Then the Lord put forth His hand and touched my mouth. And the Lord said to me, Behold, I have put My words in your mouth.

See, I have this day appointed you to the oversight of the nations and of the kingdoms to root out and pull down, to destroy and to overthrow, to build and to plant.

Jeremiah 1:4-10

God called Jeremiah as "a prophet to the nations," and immediately he began to say things that God had *not* told him to say. God had to straighten out Jeremiah's mouth before He could use him.

It will be no different with us.

First we must understand that when God calls us to do something, we should not say that we cannot do it. If God says we can, then we can! So often we speak out of our insecurities, or we verbalize what others have previously said about us, or what the devil has told us.

We need to say about ourselves what God says about us!

Jesus said, "I speak not My own words, but the words of the One Who sent Me. I say only what I have heard My Father say." (John 8:28; 12:50, author's paraphrase.)

God is calling us up higher. He is challenging us no longer to speak with our own words. He wants us to speak, not out of the soul, but out of the spirit.

God is preparing His people to be used by Him in the end-time harvest. No one is ever used without preparation. That means that God must deal with us, and that we must submit to His dealing.

God wants to "fine tune" us. He has been working in our lives in a general way for years, but now it is time for some precise final adjustments.

You have probably heard messages about the mouth before, so this word may not be a new revelation to you. But it is also likely that, like many of the rest of us, you still have been taking some liberties that you cannot afford to take anymore.

New Level, New Devil

> Therefore thus says the Lord God of hosts: Because you [the people] have spoken this word, behold, I will make My words fire in your mouth [Jeremiah] and this people wood, and it will devour them.
>
> Jeremiah 5:14

God is calling you and me up higher, to a new level, and on every new level of God's power and blessings we experience new opposition.

In the past, Jeremiah may have been talking the way we talk now, but God was calling him to a new level. On this new level, that kind of talk would get Jeremiah into serious trouble.

We must realize that wrong words can open doors for the enemy that we don't want to open.

For years God spoke to me about not opening doors, but then one day He said, "Joyce, forget about doors; Satan is looking for any tiny crack he can crawl through in your life."

Whatever Jeremiah had been doing previously, it was not as aggressive against the kingdom of darkness as what God had planned.

I believe the same thing holds true in your life and mine. Things that God winked at in the past, He will have to deal with now. We cannot walk in the flesh until it is time to exercise our ministry gift, and then quickly try to get in the Spirit. There will be no power, no anointing, released through such a life.

Later in the story of Jeremiah, we see that God told him that He would make His Word like fire in his mouth, and the people like wood.

I am believing for that same thing to be true in my life and ministry. When I speak God's Word, I want it to have a dramatic effect on people, changing them radically.

So should you.

We no longer have time for a little here and a little there. (Isa. 28:10,13.)

It is time to get on with God's work.

I have read books that spoke of past revivals and explained how the anointing of the Lord would be so strong on the preaching that hundreds of people would fall out of their chairs onto the floor and begin crying out for deliverance and salvation. I believe that is a manifestation of God, making the words of the speakers' mouths like fire, and the people like wood.

But that will not happen to us as long as we allow a mixture of words in our mouths. We may never experience complete perfection in this area, but it is time to approach it in a much more serious manner.

I had been praying about a stronger anointing, and God was about to give it to me, but first He said, "Joyce, it is time for your mouth to be saved."

Usually when we ask God for something, there are things that must be moved out of the way in order for it to be ushered in.

If you purchase a new bedroom suite that is larger than the previous one, you may have to move some things out of the bedroom in order to make room for the new furniture.

Don't grieve over what has to go; rejoice over what is coming!

Moses' Slow and Awkward Mouth

And Moses said to the Lord, O Lord, I am not eloquent or a man of words, neither before nor since You have spoken to Your servant; for I am slow of speech and have a heavy and awkward tongue.

Exodus 4:10

When God called Moses to be His spokesman to Pharaoh and the Israelites, Moses claimed that he wasn't eloquent enough to do what God wanted done because he had a "mouth problem."

God's response was, **...Who has made man's mouth?...Is it not I, the Lord?** (v. 11).

We think sometimes that God does not know about all of our weaknesses — but He does.

When I began to realize that God was calling me to minister His Word on a large scale, I reminded Him that I was a woman. I doubt that He had ever forgotten that fact. I did not have a problem with it myself, but I knew others who did, and it created a certain amount of doubt in me.

That doubt had to go before I could go.

In verse 12 God told Moses, **Now therefore go, and I will be with your mouth and will teach you what you shall say.**

The next time God tells you to speak for Him, and fear rises up within you, remember; if He has sent you, He will be with your mouth and will teach you what to say.

Isaiah's Unclean Mouth

In the year that King Uzziah died, [in a vision] I saw the Lord sitting upon a throne, high and lifted up, and the skirts of

His train filled the [most holy part of the] temple.

Above Him stood the seraphim; each had six wings; with two [each] covered his [own] face, and with two [each] covered his feet, and with two [each] flew.

And one cried to another and said, Holy, holy, holy is the Lord of hosts; the whole earth is full of His glory!

And the foundations of the thresholds shook at the voice of him who cried, and the house was filled with smoke.

Then said I, Woe is me! For I am undone and ruined, because I am a man of unclean lips, and I dwell in the midst of a people of unclean lips; for my eyes have seen the King, the Lord of hosts!

Then flew one of the seraphim [heavenly beings] to me, having a live coal in his hand which he had taken with tongs from off the altar;

And with it he touched my mouth and said, Behold, this has touched your lips; your iniquity and guilt are taken away, and your sin is completely atoned for and forgiven.

Also I heard the voice of the Lord, saying, Whom shall I send? And who will go for Us? Then said I, Here am I; send me.

And He said, Go and tell this people, Hear and hear continually, but understand not; and see and see continually, but do not apprehend with your mind.

                                                            Isaiah 6:1-9

The calling of Isaiah is an excellent example of God needing to cleanse the mouth before using the man.

This Scripture passage teaches me that when we come into the presence of God, He is going to deal with us.

In this case Isaiah realized that he had an unclean mouth. I believe the cry of his heart was for change, so God sent help.

The coming forward of the seraphim with a coal of fire is recorded here as an instantaneous happening, but it may not always happen that way with us. We all would prefer miracle deliverance, but often (I believe even most of the time), the Lord has to put us through a cleansing process.

What we need to glean from these verses is the principle set forth in them.

Verse 7 states that Isaiah's sin was forgiven; therefore, we can assume that his unclean mouth was sinful and needed to be dealt with as such.

Then in verse 8 we see Isaiah's call: God said, "Who will go for Me?" and Isaiah responded, "Here am I; send me." His heart was to serve the Lord, which God already knew before He drew him into His Presence.

God will always look for someone who has a perfect heart toward Him, not necessarily someone who has a perfect performance before Him. When the Lord has the heart, He can always change the behavior.

This truth should encourage those of us who want to be used by God, but who often feel that we just have too many flaws. God uses cracked pots! We come to Him as we are, and He molds and make us into vessels fit for His use. (Isa. 6:8; 2 Tim. 2:21.)

After Isaiah's mouth had been cleansed, then in verse 9 God said to Him, "Go and tell this people." The call, the anointing, and the appointment are sometimes separate, even occurring in different time periods.

Called, Anointed, and Appointed — To Lay a Foundation Before Building

> For no other foundation can anyone lay than that which is [already] laid, which is Jesus Christ (the Messiah, the Anointed One).
>
> **1 Corinthians 3:11**

God called me and anointed me, but that anointing increased as I gained experience in ministry and submitted to the work of the Holy Spirit in my soul. He appointed me, or released me, to go forth and begin building His Kingdom only after a proper foundation had been laid.

If you want to build the Kingdom of God, you must take time to lay the proper foundation. One of the first steps in laying that foundation is getting the mouth in line.

"Lord, Save My Mouth!"

And you will know the Truth, and the Truth will set you free.

John 8:32

Jeremiah, Moses, and Isaiah all realized that God had to change some things about their mouths if they were to fulfill their divine call.

The same will be true for you and me.

God will heal our mouths, but first we must realize that we need healing.

Jesus said that it is the truth that sets us free. The truth is that we need to say to the Lord, "My mouth needs to be saved!"

chapter 9

Fasting Includes Your Mouth

[The facts are that] you fast only for strife and debate and to smite with the fist of wickedness. Fasting as you do today will not cause your voice to be heard on high.

—Isaiah 58:4

Isaiah chapter 58 is a powerful portion of God's Word that teaches us what He considers to be "true fasting." I suggest that you read the entire chapter at this point before going on with this book.

Is This What You Call a Fast?

Is such a fast as yours what I have chosen, a day for a man to humble himself with sorrow in his soul? [Is true fasting merely mechanical?] Is it only to bow down his head like a bulrush and to spread sackcloth and ashes under him [to indicate a condition of heart that he does not have]? Will you call this a fast and an acceptable day to the Lord?

Isaiah 58:5

The scene we are encountering here is an exchange between the Israelites and their God. The people had been fasting, and they felt that God was taking no notice of it. He told them they were fasting with wrong motives, and that they had things in their lives that needed to be dealt with.

True fasting is supposed to be for the purpose of breaking the power of the flesh. It is meant to be a time of special prayer in which God's people seek Him in a more serious manner for breakthrough for themselves or for others.

My purpose in this chapter is not to teach on all the principles of fasting food, but I will say that there are many varieties of ways that people are led to fast. If you are beginning a fast on your own, or if you are being called to begin one by God, He will lead you in your particular commitment.

These people in Isaiah 58 had been abstaining from food, but they had missed the real point. God told them they were fasting for the wrong reasons and that such a fast would not cause their voices to be heard. In this verse He asks them, "Is true fasting merely mechanical — just something to be gone through like an exercise with no real meaning?" Then in verses 6 through 9 the Lord shares with them what His chosen fast is.

Get Free To Set Free

> [Rather] is not this the fast that I have chosen: to loose the bonds of wickedness, to undo the bands of the yoke, to let the oppressed go free, and that you break every [enslaving] yoke?
>
> Isaiah 58:6

I believe that means that not only are you and I to be busy setting others free, we are also not supposed to sit around and allow ourselves to remain in bondage.

Jesus said, **...if the Son liberates you [makes you free men], then you are really and unquestionably free** (John 8:36). The more familiar *King James Version* reads: **If the Son therefore shall make you free, ye shall be free indeed.**

I believe that we need to cooperate with the Spirit of God in order to break the yokes of bondage in our lives and the lives of those around us. If we are to be able to set others free, we must first be set free ourselves.

Fast To Share

> Is it not to divide your bread with the hungry and bring the homeless poor into your house — when you see the naked, that you cover him, and that you hide not yourself from [the needs of] your own flesh and blood?
>
> Isaiah 58:7

Some people get so involved in ministry that they forget about their own family members and relatives. In this verse the Lord makes it clear that we are not to neglect one in order to attend to the other.

Here we are told by the Lord that not only are we to meet the needs of those around us in the world, the poor and the naked, but that we are also to meet the needs of our flesh and blood, our own family and relatives.

I have a widowed aunt whom I minister to quite often. I used to think that I was too busy for that kind of thing. But the Lord showed me that she is my "flesh and blood," and that it is my responsibility to minister to her needs just as it is my responsibility to minister to the needs of others. If I ignore that responsibility, then I am going to pay the price of seeing part of the anointing of God lifted from my life.

It is not enough just to be called. It is not enough just to pray. It is not enough just to read the Word of God. We also have to *do* what the Word says. And the Word says that we are to feed the poor, clothe the naked, and hide not ourselves from our own flesh and blood.

After we have done all these things, *then* verse 8 will work for us.

Receiving Grace Requires Giving Grace

Then shall your light break forth like the morning, and your healing (your restoration and the power of a new life) shall spring forth speedily; your righteousness (your rightness, your justice, and your right relationship with God) shall go before you [conducting you to peace and prosperity], and the glory of the Lord shall be your rear guard.

Isaiah 58:8

I have studied the fifty-eighth chapter of Isaiah quite a bit because there are some pretty bold promises in it. But there are also some pretty clear requirements laid out in it.

One depends upon the other.

I thank God for His grace. I am grateful that I don't have to try to do everything on my own. I am thankful that whatever He tells me to do, He gives me the grace to accomplish. That way He gets the credit and the glory, not me.

But that does not mean that I have nothing to do, that I can just sit in a chair and wait for the Lord to do it all.

No, I have to cooperate with the grace of God.

So do you.

In this chapter there are many promises of peace and prosperity for us as God's people, but they are all dependent upon our doing certain things, as we see in this verse.

Judge Not, Scorn Not — and Watch Your Mouth!

Then you shall call, and the Lord will answer; you shall cry, and He will say, Here I am. If you take away from your midst yokes of oppression [wherever you find them], the finger pointed in scorn [toward the oppressed or the godly], and every form of false, harsh, unjust, and wicked speaking.

Isaiah 58:9

If our prayers are not being answered, it may well be because we are not doing what God has plainly told us to do.

One of the things He has told us to do is to take away the yokes of oppression in our midst and to stop pointing the finger of scorn toward the oppressed or the godly.

That is judgment.

When you and I stop judging one another, things will begin to improve in our own lives.

Another one of the things we are to do is to stop speaking falsely, harshly, unjustly, and wickedly. The *King James Version* of this verse translates this last phrase as "speaking vanity." What is vain speech? It is useless speech, nonsense talk.

If I am not careful I can be particularly guilty of speaking vainly. I can get started talking and just go on and on forever. Sometimes in my personal life and ministry I am speaking from the time I get up in the morning until I go to bed late at night. By that time I have talked so much that my insides are rattled, and my brain is mincemeat. I am just physically and mentally exhausted.

Do you know what the Lord told me about that? He said, "The reason you are so tired all the time is because you talk too much!"

So I have had to do as this Scripture says and learn to bring my speech under control. As a minister of the Gospel, I have been called into the service of His Majesty, the King. As a royal ambassador (2 Cor. 5:20.), I am required and expected to exercise careful control over my words.

The same is true for you and for all who serve the Lord.

Bless, Not Curse

And if you pour out that with which you sustain your own life for the hungry and satisfy the need of the afflicted, then shall your light rise in darkness, and your obscurity and gloom become like the noonday.

And the Lord shall guide you continually and satisfy you in drought and in dry places and make strong your bones. And you shall be like a watered garden and like a spring of water whose waters fail not.

And your ancient ruins shall be rebuilt; you shall raise up the foundations of [buildings that have laid waste for] many generations; and you shall be called Repairer of the Breach, Restorer of Streets to Dwell In.

Isaiah 58:10-12

What wonderful promises!

When can you and I expect all these blessings of the Lord to come upon us and overtake us?

When we stop judging each other and put away from ourselves every form of vain, false, harsh, unjust, and wicked speaking.

We must stop expecting God to pour out blessings on us while we pour out of our mouths curses on others.

Isn't It Worth It?

If you turn away your foot from [traveling unduly on] the Sabbath, from doing your own pleasure on My holy day, and call the Sabbath a [spiritual] delight, and the holy day of the Lord honorable, and honor Him and it, not going your own way or seeking or finding your own pleasure or speaking with your own [idle] words,

Then will you delight yourself in the Lord, and I will make you to ride on the high places of the earth, and I will feed you with the heritage [promised for you] of Jacob your father; for the mouth of the Lord has spoken it.

Isaiah 58:13,14

Basically, what the Lord is saying here in this passage is: "If you really want to enjoy My blessings in this life, then don't run around doing your own thing. Instead, find out what I want you to do — and then do it. Don't seek your own pleasure, but seek first My will. Don't speak your own idle words, but speak My powerful words, for they will not come back void, without producing any effect, useless." (Isa. 55:11.)

If you and I really want the blessing of God to be upon our lives, we can't just say whatever we want to say, anytime we want to say it. We have got to use our mouths to bless God, to bless others, and to bless ourselves.

We have got to bring God's blessings into our churches, into our homes, into our jobs, into our society. We don't need to preach to people nearly as much as we need to live godly lives before them. We don't need to "stir up a stink," we need to bring forth a sweet-smelling aroma, pleasing to others and pleasing to God. (2 Cor. 2:14,15.)

The Lord has been telling me, "Don't be stinky, be oozy. Just ooze with the fruit of the Spirit, with kindness, gentleness, goodness, love, joy, peace, and all the other fruit."

As you and I go through life, there is an aroma that comes from us. Although we may not smell it ourselves, the Lord does. He has a very sensitive nose. When I pray, I don't want my prayers to be a stench in the nostrils of the Lord because of the words I have spoken outside of my prayer time.

The Bible says that God knows every word that is still unuttered on our lips. **For there is not a word in my tongue [still unuttered], but, behold, O Lord, You know it altogether** (Ps. 139:4). He knows not only what we said yesterday, and what we are saying today, but also what we are going to say tomorrow — even what we are thinking. That's why our prayer needs to be that of the psalmist, **Let the words of my mouth and the meditation of my heart be acceptable in Your sight, O Lord, my [firm, impenetrable] Rock and my Redeemer** (Ps. 19:14).

chapter 10

The Slanderous Mouth

Death and life are in the power of the tongue, and they who indulge in it shall eat the fruit of it [for death or life]. —Proverbs 18:21

If you have heard or read any teaching on the mouth, you have probably come across this Scripture several times. We have already mentioned it in this study, but it is so vital to this subject that I think it is worth reviewing.

Think about it for a moment: **Death and life are in the *power* of the tongue.**

Do we have any idea what that means? It means that you and I go through life with an awesome power — like fire or electricity or nuclear energy — right under our noses, one that can produce death or life, depending on how it is used.

With this power we have the capacity for great good or for great evil, for great benefit or great harm. We can use it to create death and destruction, or we can use it to create life and health. We can speak forth sickness, disease, dissention, and disaster, or we can speak forth healing, harmony, exhortation, and edification.

The choice is ours.

Sowing and Reaping

Be not deceived; God is not mocked: for whatsoever a man soweth, that shall he also reap.

For he that soweth to his flesh shall of the flesh reap corruption; but he that soweth to the Spirit shall of the Spirit reap life everlasting.

Galatians 6:7,8 KJV

Notice that the second part of Proverbs 18:21 says that we will eat the fruit of our lips.

That recalls the spiritual principle that whatever we sow is what we will reap. If we sow to the flesh, we shall reap from the flesh ruin and decay and destruction. But if we sow to the Spirit, we will reap from the Spirit life and health and abundance.

Do you know that you have the power to do something about your future? That power is located right under your nose.

Recently I was reading in a little book about how in this day and hour God is looking for soaring eagles, men and women of integrity who will take a stand, keep their word, honor their commitments, and live holy lives. The statement was made, "It's awfully hard to be a soaring eagle when you're surrounded by so many turkeys."

Sometimes it is hard to maintain control of our mouths, to be positive, and to praise and glorify the Lord when all those around us seem to be giving in to griping and complaining and every other kind of negativism.

Are you using your mouth to exhort and edify, or are you using it to discourage and destroy? Are you using it to build up yourself and others, or are you using it to tear down? Do you have any idea how important the words of your mouth are?

As we have emphasized, if there is any place in our life that we need to exercise discipline and self-control, it is in the choice of our words.

I have shared with you how the Lord once told me that my worst problem was that I just talked too much. What I was saying was not necessarily bad, it was just blabber. Do you know what the Bible says about this kind of activity? It says that if we are a blabbermouth, we are going to get into trouble. (Eccl. 5:1-7 TLB.)

That's what I have learned in my years of ministry. If I talk too much I get unsettled and lose my peace — not necessarily because I am saying something evil, but simply because I need to be quiet and listen.

Speaking a Word in Season

> [The Servant of God says] The Lord God has given Me the tongue of a disciple and of one who is taught, that I should know how to speak a word in season to him who is weary. He wakens Me morning by morning, He wakens My ear to hear as a disciple [as one who is taught].
>
> Isaiah 50:4

You and I need to train ourselves to keep one ear tuned to God. We also need to do as James instructs and be quick to hear and slow to speak. (James 1:19.)

What do you think would happen if we thought about what we were going to say before we said it? Do you think we might not say some of the things we say?

The prophet said that the Lord had given him the tongue of a disciple — a learner, one who is taught — so that he would know how to "speak a word in season" to the weary.

Do you see any weary people in the Body of Christ? Yes, the world has serious problems. But there are also many who are born again and filled with the Spirit of God who are needy.

As a minister, I am not seeing the joy that should be in evidence among God's people. According to the Bible, the joy of the Lord is our strength. (Neh. 8:10.) Joy is not found in our circumstances, it is found in Christ, the Mystery of the Ages, Who dwells within us. You and I are learning to find our joy in Christ alone. While we are in the process, speaking words in due season to one another will keep us from growing weary.

These Things Ought Not So To Be

> But the tongue can no man tame; it is an unruly evil, full of deadly poison.
>
> Therewith bless we God, even the Father; and therewith curse we men, which are made after the similitude of God.
>
> Out of the same mouth proceedeth blessing and cursing. My brethren, these things ought not so to be.
>
> James 3:8-10 KJV

During the years of my life and ministry I have learned a great deal about gossip, judging, criticism, and faultfinding. For one thing, I have learned that these things are disgusting to God. It disturbs Him that with the same mouth we use to bless and praise Him, we curse and condemn our fellow man, made in His image just as we are.

That is an easy thing to do, isn't it? Do you know why? Pride. Pride is the attitude that we are clean and if others don't agree with us, they must have something wrong with them.

The Bible says that **all the ways of a man are clean in his own eyes** (Prov. 16:2 KJV).

It would do us good to choose about three of our friends, sit down with them several times a year, and ask them, "How do you see me?" Because we see ourselves a whole lot different from the way others see us.

I think one of the biggest favors we can do God and ourselves is to realize that we have a way to go before we become perfect. Now there is nothing wrong with being less than perfect, *if* we have a perfect heart toward God. The Lord looks upon our heart and counts us as perfect while we are on the way to becoming so.

But if we were humble enough to see ourselves as we really are, then we wouldn't be so quick to criticize everyone else. Nor would we be so quick to spread that criticism, that slander.

Spreading Slander

In a Greek dictionary I found a definition of the word "slanderers" as those who are guilty of finding fault with others and spreading criticism.[1]

After reading this definition, I began to think about that word "spreading." Spreading doesn't necessarily mean going out and telling something to ten other people. Something can be spread if it is told to only one other person.

I once went through a period in which I had to overcome gossiping, carrying tales to other people. But I would still tell them to my husband. Although I knew that Dave would not repeat what I had shared with him in confidence, I came to realize that by exposing him to these stories (whether they were true or not), I was running the risk of poisoning his spirit.

Do you know that once we are told something about another person, even if we decide not to believe it, that thing is still lodged inside of us. The next time we meet that individual we may look at him or her a bit differently. Why? Because our spirit has been poisoned.

According to Webster the word "slander" is derived from the Latin word s*candalum*, meaning "scandal," which itself is derived from the Greek word *skandalon*, meaning "trap."[2] The Greek word translated "slanderers" in the *King James Version* of 1 Timothy 3:11 is *diabolos*, which Strong defines as "a *traducer:* spec. Satan...false accuser, devil, slanderer."[3]

As I have noted, the Greek dictionary states that this Greek word is an adjective meaning "slanderous, accusing falsely," and that its noun form is translated "'slanderers' ...where the reference is to those who are given to finding fault with the demeanor and conduct of others, and spreading their innuendos and criticisms in the church." For more information, "see ACCUSER" or "DEVIL."[4] The word translated "devil" in English is the exact same Greek word, *diabolos,* meaning "an accuser, a slanderer."[5]

Do you realize what that means? It means that when you and I slander someone or accuse another person falsely, we are allowing the devil to use our mouths. As James tells us, **These things ought not so to be** (James 3:10 KJV)!

Now please understand. I am not bringing this message because I have no problems in this area. I do. So there is no need to feel guilty if you do too. The reason the Lord is revealing this message to all of us is because He wants to do something good in our lives, but our mouths are affecting our anointing.

Many of us have probably received revelation about not judging others or about talking harshly to others. Although harshness is not exactly slandering, it has the same flavor.

If I have the ability to speak life to you, to encourage you, to help you, to make you feel good, to cause you to believe that you can make it, but I choose instead to discourage you, to tear you down, to make you feel miserable, to cause you to want to give up and quit, then there is something wrong with my mouth.

There are many people in the Body of Christ who use their mouths for the wrong purposes, to slander and criticize, to depress and discourage others.

It grieves me to see numbers of people flocking to the altar seeking comfort and release from pains that were inflicted on them by others ten, fifteen, even twenty years ago.

Too often such people can't lay hold of the good things of God because somebody wounded or even broke their spirit so that they ended up with a failure image. Sometimes these people are so depressed and despondent, they are never able to rise above their state in life.

You have no idea how it hurts me to see people who can hardly stand to approach and talk to those in spiritual authority like me, simply because of the way they have been treated in the past — often by those in the home or the Church.

My brother, my sister, these things ought not so to be!

Don't Break Their Spirit!

Fathers, do not provoke or irritate or fret your children [do not be hard on them or harass them], lest they become discouraged and sullen and morose and feel inferior and frustrated. [Do not break their spirit.]

Colossians 3:21

I did this to my oldest son. I was ignorant and didn't know any better. I wish I had known how to raise my first two children correctly, the way I raised the last two.

All of us are products of our environment, of what we came from. Thank God, Jesus opens those doors, and we can go free. He is the Healer of the brokenhearted. (Luke 4:18 KJV.) The Bible says that He is so gentle that **a bruised reed He will not break...** (Isa. 42:3). He has the healing balm for broken bodies and broken spirits. (Jer. 8:22; Mal. 4:2.)

If you come to Jesus hurt and wounded, He will heal you so you can go forth and bring that healing to someone else. Those whom you have hurt will also forgive you and receive healing.

Today my oldest son works for Life In The Word. We have a great relationship. We love one another. But I had wounded him by doing the very things described in this verse. I had nagged and harassed and aggravated him. I was constantly on him, harping at him, telling him the same thing over and over again.

Before my son and I could both be set free from that bondage, I had to learn the lesson set forth in this passage. I hope you will learn it quicker than I did.

Don't break another person's spirit!

"Be a Sweetheart!"

Wives, be subject to your husbands [subordinate and adapt yourselves to them], as is right and fitting and your proper duty in the Lord.

Husbands, love your wives [be affectionate and sympathetic with them] and do not be harsh or bitter or resentful toward them.

Colossians 3:18,19

In this passage, which immediately precedes the verse we just read, we see how wives and husbands are to regard and treat one another in the Lord.

Wives are told to "adapt" themselves to their husbands. Now I know that no one likes to adapt to anyone else. That is just not part of our nature. But that is part of our calling in Christ Jesus: **Be subject to one another out of reverence for Christ (the Messiah, the Anointed One)** (Eph. 5:21).

Likewise, husbands are to be affectionate and sympathetic. That word "sympathetic" doesn't mean that husbands are to feel sorry for their mates; it means that they are to be considerate of them, not harsh or unkind or bitter toward them.

So here we see a two-way relationship. The wife adapts to her husband, she becomes a sweetheart to him. The husband in turn loves his wife and is thoughtful toward her. They learn to treat and speak to one another with love, dignity, and respect.

When I learned that God wanted me to be a sweetheart to my husband, I didn't know how to do that, and I resisted. For a full week He kept repeating, "Be a sweetheart, be a sweetheart, be a sweetheart." But I just couldn't comprehend it.

Near the end of the week, a lady gave me a bracelet with the letters K-U-I-P-O on it. When I asked her what it meant, she said, "Oh, it's the Hawaiian word for 'sweetheart.'"

I said, "Ohhh." I realized then that God meant what He had been telling me all week long! The gift was a strong confirmation.

If I have learned anything about God, it is that He doesn't quit! He is more determined than anyone I've ever known.

I suddenly knew that in His perfect timing, God was delivering me from harshness. The Lord kept the "be a sweetheart" message ever before me in an unusual way. The bracelet was so small that once I got it on my wrist, I couldn't get it off!

I had to use soap and lotion and work and work to remove it. In a year and a half I had it off only two or three times. So for years, I had God's sign hung on me day and night: "Sweetheart!"

Now that may not seem to be the manly word to use, but in this passage this is exactly what God is saying to husbands as well as to wives: "Be a sweetheart!"

If you want to have a sweetheart of a husband, be a sweetheart of a wife. If you want to have a sweetheart of a wife, be a sweetheart of a husband.

Try it!

It works!

I didn't know how to be a sweetheart at first. I am still learning how, but I am doing much better. Just be sweet, kind, nice, and encouraging!

The Spirit Is the Key

The strong spirit of a man sustains him in bodily pain or trouble, but a weak and broken spirit who can raise up or bear?
Proverbs 18:14

Do you realize what this verse is saying? It is saying that regardless of what comes into a person's life, he can bear up under it if he has a strong spirit within him to sustain him in those times of trouble. But if his spirit is weak or wounded, he is going to have a hard time bearing anything in life.

Do you know what is wrong with many in the Body of Christ today, why they can't seem to handle their problems? It's not because their problems are any worse than those of anybody else. It's because they are weak — weak in spirit.

The Bible says that we are to bear with the failings and the frailties of the weak. (Rom. 15:1.) We are to lift them up and support them. (1 Thess. 5:14.)

We have seen in Romans 12:8 that one of the ministry gifts to the Church is the encourager or exhorter. Such people are usually easy to recognize because every time we get around them, they make us feel better by the things they say and do. It just seems to come natural to them to uplift, encourage, and strengthen others by their very presence and personality.

Now you and I may not "stand in the office of encourager or exhorter," but we can all encourage. We can all exhort. We can all build up, edify, lift up, and speak life. We can all refuse to be slanderers. We can all refuse to do the work of the devil with the words of our mouth.

Encourage and Strengthen Yourself in the Lord

> David was greatly distressed, for the men spoke of stoning
> him because the souls of them all were bitterly grieved, each
> man for his sons and daughters. But David encouraged and
> strengthened himself in the Lord his God.
>
> 1 Samuel 30:6

Now, you may be thinking, "Well, Joyce, that's a fine message,
but the truth is that I need someone to exhort and encourage *me.*"

Let me tell you what to do about that situation. I know,
because I have been there — many times. In my ministry I used
to get so discouraged and down in the dumps that I just wanted
to give up and quit. It seemed that there was no one to encourage
me at all.

I would get so "weary in well doing" — hard work, heavy
travel, still raising children at that time, laying the foundation for
a new ministry, endless decisions to be made. I would become
physically, mentally and emotionally worn out. I felt I needed
encouragement, but there wasn't always someone to give it to me.

In fact, I used to get angry because there was no one to
encourage me. I would think of all I was doing for others and
how little they did for me.

Do you know what that kind of thinking does? It fills the soul
with bitterness and resentment. It is not the way the Lord wants

us to react. He wants us to come to Him and find our strength and encouragement in Him.

I finally learned that if, instead of getting angry, bitter, and resentful, I would go to God in earnest, humble prayer, things would go much better for me. I would say, "Lord, I need to be encouraged," and within a week or two He would speak to six or seven people. The next thing I knew, I would be receiving cards, gifts, and flowers. People would seem to fall all over me with words and gestures of encouragement.

But every time I would allow myself to get resentful and start to complain about my lack of encouragement, things would just get worse.

Right now you may be feeling that nobody cares about you, that nobody appreciates you. Maybe the reason no one seems to appreciate you is because they are so self-centered they don't know how to appreciate anybody. Or perhaps they don't understand your need. If you become bitter and resentful toward them, they will never learn, and you will never receive from them what you desire most. In fact, your bitterness and resentment may end up destroying both you and your relationship.

But if you will take your burden to the Lord, He will hear you and help you. He has thousands of exhorters in the Body of

Christ, and He will send to you the very person or people you need to uplift, encourage and edify you.

First, you pray; then second, you sow.

Don't just sit around and wait for somebody to encourage you. And don't refuse to encourage others just because you are not being encouraged yourself. Don't wait for them to come to you, go to them.

Remember, the spiritual rule is: you reap what you sow. Right now you may be reaping the fruit of the seeds you have sown in the past by your refusal to encourage others. But that can change. Get busy and sow a new crop!

Start being an exhorter!

Slanderous Mouth or Soothing Mouth?

According to the concordance, the Greek word translated *exhort* is *parakaleo,* meaning "to call near."[6] It is related to the Greek word *parakletos,* translated *Comforter* in the *King James Version* and used to refer to the Holy Spirit.[7]

If you and I call a person near to us in order to strengthen and encourage that individual to press on with Jesus because God is with him to do great things through him, we are engaging in exhortation.

What happens?

The healing balm of Gilead begins to drip down into that person's wounded soul. Suddenly he begins to think, "Yes, I believe I can make it."

That is exactly what the Holy Spirit, the Comforter, does for us. He comes alongside us to comfort us, to encourage us, to urge us to press on, to propel us forward.

That is what we are to do for one another.

So what does all this mean to us? It means that we have a choice. We can either open our mouth and use it as *diabolos* to slander, accuse, find fault, and spread innuendoes and criticism. Or we can use it as *parakletos*, to encourage, strengthen, help, inspire, and comfort.

When we open our mouth, what comes out can either be the devil or the Holy Spirit.

Which will it be?

chapter 11

Angry and Impatient Words Lead to Trouble

Let all bitterness and indignation and wrath (passion, rage, bad temper) and resentment (anger, animosity) and quarreling (brawling, clamor, contention) and slander (evil-speaking, abusive or blasphemous language) be banished from you, with all malice (spite, ill will, or baseness of any kind.) — Ephesians 4:31

All the descriptive words in this verse identify the things that get us into trouble: wrath, passion, rage, bad temper, resentment, anger, animosity, quarreling, brawling, clamor, contention, slander, evil-speaking, abusive or blasphemous language, malice, spite, ill will, or baseness of any kind.

What a list!

Which of these things pose the biggest problem for you?

In my own case, I would have to say that it was rage and bad temper. I used to have a terrible temper, but not anymore.

However, the thing that was hardest for me to overcome and receive healing in was my tendency to be harsh and hard. It was quite a struggle for me to give that up and learn to become gentle. If the Lord can do a miracle in that area for me, He can do it for you too.

You and I do not have to have bad tempers. We don't have to get mad every time something doesn't go our way. We have the ability in the Holy Spirit to be adjustable and adaptable. (Rom. 12:16.)

Slow To Speak and Slow To Get Angry

> Understand [this], my beloved brethren. Let every man be quick to hear [a ready listener], slow to speak, slow to take offense and to get angry.
>
> **James 1:19**

James tells us to be quick to hear, but slow to speak, slow to take offense, and slow to get angry. Of these, the most important — and often the hardest part — is being slow to speak. Once we let that tongue start flying, other things are going to start flying with it.

All of us get upset when we have our plans all made, then something comes along to upset them. When that happens to me, I have learned to take a deep breath, shut my mouth for a minute, get control of myself, then go on with my life.

I say, "Okay, Lord, with Your help I can do this. I don't have to have everything my way. According to Romans 12, I can be adaptable. I can change my plan. It has been changed anyway, so I may as well go with the flow."

"Go With the Flow"

"Go with the flow" has a double meaning for me because of an incident that used to happen quite often when my children were very young.

It seemed to me that almost every time we sat down to a meal, somebody would spill a glass of milk. Whenever that happened, the devil would use it to upset me. I would immediately fly into a rage:

"I don't believe it! Look what you did! I spent all afternoon fixing that meal, and you have just ruined it!"

But it wasn't my family who was ruining every meal, it was someone else — and it wasn't Satan! I thought my problem was the spilled milk, but it was actually the spoiled me.

In those days we had big meals with lots of dishes and utensils all over the table. When that milk spilled, it would invariably start running right under all those dishes and utensils and head straight for the "crack" in the table top where you expand it by adding a leaf.

174

In fact, I used to think that the devil designed dinner tables with a crack in them just to drive me crazy. Now I think that perhaps it was God Who designed them that way (at least mine) to help crucify the impatient spirit in me.

The reason I was so concerned about the milk reaching the crack is because I knew that if it did, it would then run down the table legs and under everybody's feet. So I would have to take the table apart, clean in the crack (where there was usually a lot of accumulated dirt anyway, which really made a mess), and then get down on my hands and knees and crawl under the table to clean it and the floor.

Since our children were small, this spilling routine seemed to happen several times a week. One of them would spill something, and the minute it happened, they knew that a fit was coming.

I would jump up in a rage and run to get a rag. I would get down on all fours and crawl under the table with the kids kicking me in the head, and I would *not* be a "happy homemaker"! In fact, I would be so mad that I would nearly explode.

Do you know that when we get that mad, when we are caught in a situation we cannot change no matter what we do, that's when we need to learn acceptance with joy.

"Acceptance with joy." That's a handy little phrase I have learned.

In such situations, the Lord has taught me to say, "Well, I've got it again, and only God can take it away. If He doesn't, then I may as well accept it with joy."

But I didn't know how to do that when I first started diving under tables to chase down milk spills. I would be under there having a fit and screaming and yelling — acting like an adult brat.

During one of these scenes, the Holy Spirit spoke to me right there under the table and said, "You know, Joyce, all the fits in the world are not going to get this milk to run back up the table legs, across the table top and back into that glass."

In other words, He was telling me that the temper tantrum I was throwing was not going to reverse the situation in which I found myself.

That is the lesson, one of several, that I want to share with you in this chapter.

No matter how mad you get, no matter how angry you become, no matter how impatient you may be, no matter what kind of a rage you may get into, or what kind of fit you may pitch, it is not going to reverse your bad situation.

If you are caught in a traffic jam, you can sit there and fuss and fume and rant and rave for a solid hour, and it will not get you out one second sooner. What it will do is give you a headache, a neck ache, a backache, an upset stomach, a rash, high blood pressure, possibly an ulcer, and eventually a nervous breakdown, if not a heart attack or stroke.

Is it worth it?

So the Lord said to me under the table that night, "You know, Joyce, you may as well learn to go with the flow. If the milk goes down the table legs, just go with it, and don't lose your peace."

So that's when I began to learn to "go with the flow." Much nicer things come out of my mouth when I go with the flow rather than against it.

Be Adaptable and Adjustable

> Live in harmony with one another; do not be haughty (snobbish, high-minded, exclusive), but readily adjust yourself to [people, things] and give yourselves to humble tasks. Never overestimate yourself or be wise in your own conceits.
>
> **Romans 12:16**

According to the Apostle Paul, we can learn to be adaptable and adjustable. We can also be pliable and moldable.

That does not mean, of course, that there are not certain things we need to resist or to change. Neither does it mean that we are just to lie down and let the world and the devil run all over us.

But there are little minor issues that come up every day in our lives that steal our peace, things that we can do absolutely nothing about. We need to learn how to handle those minor irritations, how to calm down and stop having a fit every time the slightest thing goes wrong.

As we have seen, in Ephesians 4:31, Paul lists some of the kinds of things that get us into trouble, things like bad temper, resentment, anger, animosity, quarreling, brawling, clamor, and contention. I believe that each one of these issues has a root cause and a cure. I believe that the root cause is pride and self-concern or self-centeredness. In other words, these things arise because we want what we want when we want it.

As Paul points out in Romans 12:16, we have such an inflated opinion of ourselves that we think we are entitled to have everything our way. That's why we get so mad when things don't go as we want or expect them to. Anger generates angry words, and we usually end up hurting others.

Where Does Strife Come From?

What leads to strife (discord and feuds) and how do conflicts (quarrels and fightings) originate among you? Do they not arise from your sensual desires that are ever warring in your bodily members?

You are jealous and covet [what others have] and your desires go unfulfilled; [so] you become murderers. [To hate is to murder as far as your hearts are concerned.] You burn with envy and anger and are not able to obtain [the gratification, the contentment, and the happiness that you seek], so you fight and war. You do not have, because you do not ask.

[Or] you do ask [God for them] and yet fail to receive, because you ask with wrong purpose and evil, selfish motives. Your intention is [when you get what you desire] to spend it in sensual pleasures.

James 4:1-3

If we would admit it, we have a tremendous problem with selfishness, don't we? One reason I call attention to this sin is because I was as guilty of it as anyone, so I needed this message as much as anybody else.

I don't know if you are like me, but my flesh (that is, my carnal nature) just loves itself. It always wants its own way. But I just can't let it have its way all the time.

And that denial causes conflict.

Do you know the two main reasons people argue? First, to prove that they are right, because we all want to be right. And

179

second, to have their way, because we all want to have our own way in everything.

We need to learn that God is the only One Who can get us our way. When things don't go as we want them to, we need to just calm down and exercise a bit more humility, realizing that the minor things we fuss and argue over don't make that much difference in life anyway. The thing that is important is God's anointing, and the only thing that is going to maintain that anointing is our willingness to dwell together in peace and harmony.

If we want God's anointing, we must dwell together in peace and harmony with our brothers and sisters in Christ!

Love Is Not Self-Centered

Love endures long and is patient and kind; love never is envious nor boils over with jealousy, is not boastful or vainglorious, does not display itself haughtily.

It is not conceited (arrogant and inflated with pride); it is not rude (unmannerly) and does not act unbecomingly. Love (God's love in us) does not insist on its own rights or its own way....

1 Corinthians 13:4,5

The solution to the problem of arguing is love. We have got to learn to love peace and harmony, and to love them with all of our being. We have got to love them so much that we would rather have them than to be right or to have our own way.

That is what Paul meant when he said, **I die daily** (1 Cor. 15:31). Dying to self is something that you and I are going to have to do on a daily basis if we are to maintain peace and harmony.

I recall an argument Dave and I got into a few years ago over what color stripes we should put on a van we own. Is it really going to matter to me six months or six years from now whether the stripes on the van are the way I wanted them to be, if they have started a war between me and my husband? I am not going to be hanging out the window looking at them all the time. Even if I were, pretty soon they would be covered up with dirt so that neither I nor anyone else can see the color of them.

Why do we start wars over such petty things, such trifles? Two reasons: because we want to be right, and because we want our way, which is selfishness. What is the solution to the problem of selfishness? Love, which is caring more for the opinions and desires of others than for our own.

In this study, the Lord is asking you and me, by the power of the Holy Spirit, to make some choices. We must choose to come up higher, to give up trying to have everything our own way all the time, and to remember that whatever is in your heart eventually comes out of your mouth. (Matt. 12:34.)

Peace does have a price, but if we are willing to pay it, the rewards are worth it.

Follow After Peace

[After all] the kingdom of God is not a matter of [getting the] food and drink [one likes], but instead it is righteousness (that state which makes a person acceptable to God) and [heart] peace and joy in the Holy Spirit.

He who serves Christ in this way is acceptable and pleasing to God and is approved by men.

So let us then definitely aim for and eagerly pursue what makes for harmony and for mutual upbuilding (edification and development) of one another.

Romans 14:17-19

The *King James Version* of verse 19 says, **Let us therefore follow after the things which make for peace, and things wherewith one may edify another.**

One of the things I believe the Lord is revealing to us in this passage is the vital necessity of walking in peace. According to Ephesians 6:15, peace is part of the armor of God with which we are to clothe ourselves.

God has blessed our ministry. One reason is because it is based on certain principles revealed to us by the Lord and prescribed for us at the time of its beginning.

When Jesus sent out the disciples two by two to preach and heal, He told them to go into each city, find in it a suitable house in which to stay, and to say to the people, "Peace be unto you." He went on to say that if they were accepted, they should stay there and minister, but if they were not accepted they were to leave, shaking the very dust of that place off their feet. (Matt. 10:11-15.)

I used to wonder why Jesus said that. Then the Lord revealed to me that if the disciples remained in a house or city that was in strife, they could not do any real work there. Do you know why? Because strife grieves the Holy Spirit. When peace leaves, the Holy Spirit leaves, and He is the One Who does the real work.

When you picture Jesus going about ministering to others, how do you see Him? Certainly not with the hurry-up attitude we often have. Don't you instead get an image of Him ministering in quiet, tranquil peace?

One Easter season I watched part of the film, *Jesus of Nazareth*. The thing that struck me most was Jesus' response to those He met and dealt with. Some of them would react violently against Him, cursing Him and even throwing things at Him. But no matter how they treated Him, He never lost His temper or became upset or struck back. I thought then what a wonderful job those film makers did in portraying the inner peace and stability that our Lord maintained regardless of His outward circumstances.

That is a trait you and I need to develop. As ambassadors for Christ, we need to be more like our Master. If we want to do anything for our Lord and Savior, we need to learn to hunger and thirst after peace, because it is in this area that Satan is stealing from God's people. If we have a peaceful spirit we will have a peaceful mouth.

Watch Your Language!

It's true that moral guidance and counsel need to be given, but the way you say it and to whom you say it are as important as what you say.

1 Timothy 1:8 MESSAGE

Gestures, voice tone, and facial expressions all convey a message, just as much as words do. It is possible to say all the right things and still deliver a totally wrong message.

In the early days of our marriage, when my husband would ask me to do something I really didn't want to do, I would say, "Yes, honey." But I would say it in such a sarcastic tone that he knew what I really meant. He knew I wasn't saying, "Yes, honey. You are such a wonderful husband that although I don't want to do what you ask, I will do it because I love you." Rather he knew that what I was really saying was, "Yes, honey, I will do as you ask, but only because I have to."

The words said yes, but the voice tone and facial expression delivered quite a different message.

Two Kinds of Anger

> For man's anger does not promote the righteousness God [wishes and requires].
> So get rid of all uncleanness and the rampant outgrowth of wickedness, and in a humble (gentle, modest) spirit receive and welcome the Word which implanted and rooted [in your hearts] contains the power to save your souls.
> **James 1:20,21**

Here in this passage James tells us that man's anger does not promote the righteousness of God, and that is true. That is why we are to control our anger and other dangerous emotions.

But, there is a righteous anger. I believe that there are times when it is all right to get mad and to display anger.

For example, Jesus became angry and cleaned out the temple because the people were defiling the house of God by buying and selling in it (John 2:13-17) and not genuinely caring for the people. He went through that place overthrowing tables, driving animals out before Him with a whip, and speaking out against what was taking place, and I don't believe He was whispering when He did it. He was mad, and He had every right to be. His was a righteous anger, and we have the same right to display the same kind of anger that Jesus did.

God gave us our emotions, anger being one of them. Without anger, we could not discern if someone was abusing us. If I were to preach that we are never to get angry, I would be prescribing something that is impossible. The emotion of anger should submit to the spiritual fruit of self-control.

That difference may be decided by what is called in the Bible "the law of kindness."

The Law of Kindness

> **She opens her mouth in skillful and godly Wisdom, and on her tongue is the law of kindness [giving counsel and instruction].**
>
> **Proverbs 31:26**

One of my biggest problems in learning to control my anger and my words was the fact in the earlier years of my life I had been mistreated and abused. As a result, I ended up with a harsh, hard spirit. I was determined that nobody was ever going to hurt me again, and that attitude influenced my words and speech.

Although I tried to say things that were right and pleasing to others, by the time they had passed through my soul and picked up the hardness and bitterness that were hidden there, they came out harsh and hard.

No matter how right your heart may be before the Lord, if you have pride or anger or resentment in your spirit, you cannot open your mouth without expressing those negative traits and emotions.

Why is that? Because, as Jesus told us, it is out of the abundance of the heart or spirit that the mouth speaks.(Matt. 12:34.)

So the Lord had a work to do in me. Gentleness became a key issue in my life. Part of what God revealed to me in His Word on this subject was this Scripture in Proverbs 31, the chapter that speaks of "the virtuous woman." In it the writer says that on her tongue is the law of kindness.

When I read that, I thought, "Oh, God, I've got anything in my mouth but the law of kindness." It seemed to me that I was so hard inside that whenever I opened my mouth, out came a hammer.

You may relate to that situation. You may have been mistreated and abused as I was so that you are full of hatred, resentment, distrust, anger, and hostility. Instead of kindness and gentleness, you are filled with harshness and hardness.

Instead of the law of kindness, you live by the law of the jungle.

The Yoke of Kindness

Take My yoke upon you and learn of Me, for I am gentle (meek) and humble (lowly) in heart, and you will find rest (relief and ease and refreshment and recreation and blessed quiet) for your souls.

For My yoke is wholesome (useful, good — not harsh, hard, sharp, or pressing, but comfortable, gracious, and pleasant), and My burden is light and easy to be borne.

Matthew 11:29,30

Before the Lord did a work in my mouth, I sounded terrible. I couldn't even tell the kids to take out the trash without sounding like a drill sergeant. Who wants to live with a person like that? I didn't want to be that way, always so irritable and impatient.

Are you like that? If so, I can tell you that you are making yourself more miserable than anybody else. I don't say this to bring condemnation on you, but to shed some light on the root cause of many of our worst problems.

Our main problem is right under our noses — in our mouths. As we have seen, James tells us that no man can tame the tongue. But there is something we can do about the tongue. We can submit it to God, asking that His Spirit take command of our tongue and bring it into submission to His will and way.

That is part of what Jesus was talking about when He told us to take His yoke upon us.

Be Gentle — But Firm!

> But the wisdom from above is first of all pure (undefiled); then it is peace-loving, courteous (considerate, gentle). [It is willing to] yield to reason, full of compassion and good fruits; it is wholehearted and straight-forward, impartial and unfeigned (free from doubts, wavering, and insincerity).
>
> James 3:17

I remember sitting in my home looking up the word "gentle" in Strong's concordance and saying, "Lord, You've got to help me!"

I thought I could never be gentle.

Finally, the Lord began to do a work in me in the area of gentleness.

The only problem was that, like so many other people in the Body of Christ, I was such an extremist that I couldn't "strike a happy medium." Once I saw that I was overbalanced in one area, I thought I had to go totally in the other direction. I "adjusted" and "adapted" far too much. I became so "gentle" and "kind" and "patient" that I wouldn't exercise any discipline over my youngest son, who was born after my other children were grown.

I also went overboard in my relationship with others. I let things get out of hand in my marriage, my home, and my ministry.

The problem was that I was so accommodating and understanding I was ineffective when dealing with people or situations that called for a firm hand. I kept telling myself after each encounter, "Oh, Joyce, you have come so far! You handled that situation so well! You were so *sweet!*"

It made me feel good to think that I was so "sweet" — especially when dealing with my son. The only problem was that he wasn't changing, at least not for the better. In fact, he was getting worse.

Finally, I got mad, and I told him so. I warned him, "Look, don't you ever do that again!" And he didn't. Always seek the balance in tough love and displaying a mild or lenient attitude.

Now my son is precious to me, but there comes a time when I have to say to him in a strong way, "Enough! I love you, but I am not going to put up with this kind of attitude and behavior."

I learned from my experiences that one extreme is just as bad as the other. What we must learn in all this is *balance.*

On one hand, we must not be harsh and hard. But on the other hand, we must not be weak and excessively soft. We must not be irritable and impatient, flying off the handle and acting out of emotion. On the other hand, we must not be so mild mannered that we become doormats and whipping posts for those who will take advantage of us if we give them a chance.

There is a time to be patient and forbearing, and there is a time to be firm and decisive. There is a time to "be not angry," and there is a time to display righteous indignation. It is wisdom to know when to do which.

Sown in Peace by Those in Peace

And the harvest of righteousness (of conformity to God's will in thought and deed) is [the fruit of the seed] sown in peace by those who work for and make peace [in themselves and in others, that peace which means concord, agreement, and harmony between individuals, with undisturbedness, in a peaceful mind free from fears and agitating passions and moral conflicts].

James 3:18

This is such an important Scripture.

Do you know why Satan tries so hard to get you and me upset before we go to church? Do you know why the devil tries his best to get the preacher upset before he steps up behind the pulpit?

Because he does not want us to gather together in an attitude of peace. He knows that if we are in turmoil inside, the words that we hear will bounce right off of us. They will not take root. Our words should carry life and not turmoil.

This verse says that the harvest of righteousness is the fruit of the seed sown in peace by those who work for and make peace in themselves and in others.

No wonder the Lord told me not to try to sow peace in the lives of others if I did not get the strife out of my own life.

Have you ever wondered why you can hear a message preached by different people at different times, and it will have no effect, and then suddenly you hear it again, and it has great meaning to you? It is because of the anointing that is on the message when preached by one who is sowing the seed while living in peace, someone who has no strife in his life.

That doesn't mean that the one who preaches the message is perfect. But it does mean that in order for the Word of the Lord to take root, it must be sown in a ground of peace by someone who is walking in peace.

That's why, if you intend or plan to work for the Lord, you must get the strife out of your life.

It's just that simple.

We Have a Choice!

....choose you this day....

Joshua 24:15 KJV

Although the devil tries everything he can to upset us, if we actually do get upset, it is not because he has forced us to do so; it is because we have chosen to do so.

The choice is always ours.

Do you know that how you and I react in every situation is a choice? Each of us has attitudes. Attitudes produce responses to situations. We are all responding all day every day.

But not always in the same way.

Why is it that two different people can be caught in the same traffic jam, and one will react one way, and the other will react in a totally different way? It's because of their different attitudes, which lead them to make different choices.

That's why sometimes we may say something to two different people, and one of them will get upset and offended while the other one won't be bothered at all.

I have a very straightforward personality. Some people like that, and some don't. One person may think what I have just said is wonderful, while another person may think it is terrible. Why? Because one may be secure, and the other may be insecure.

In the same way, you and I have a choice about the responses that we make to the various situations of life.

"Oh, but Joyce, it can't be as simple as making a choice. Surely you realize that, just as you say, people are different and therefore they have different ways of perceiving, experiencing, and relating to outside influence."

Yes, I know each of us has a different psychological makeup, and that each of us has been exposed to different experiences in life which have formed and shaped us in different ways. I know in most of us there are hurts and other kinds of mental, emotional, and spiritual wounds, and that no two of us are exactly alike. But the truth is that, regardless of our differences, we all have the power to make a choice about how we will respond to outward situations and circumstances.

Our past hurts and wounds may cause us to react negatively, but we overcome those negative responses by learning the Word of God and choosing to act upon it rather than to *re*-act to circumstances.

God has created us with a free will, with the ability and freedom to make our own decisions in life. I think the word He is sharing with us in our time is the same one He told the children of Israel in the days of Joshua: **Choose you this day** (Josh. 24:15 KJV).

In other words, "Grow up!"

chapter 12

Speak
No Evil

A gentle tongue [with its healing power] is a tree of life, but willful contrariness in it breaks down the spirit.

—Proverbs 15:4

This verse mirrors the same message as Proverbs 18:21, which says that out of the mouth we minister either life or death.

That's why throughout the Word of God we are told to be careful how we use our mouths, to pay attention to our words. As Paul told us in Ephesians 4:29, **Let no foul or polluting language, nor evil word nor unwholesome or worthless talk [ever] come out of your mouth, but only such [speech] as is good and beneficial to the spiritual progress of others, as is fitting to the need and the occasion, that it may be a blessing and give grace (God's favor) to those who hear it.**

You and I are never to speak things that are going to make people want to give up or quit. We are not to pollute ourselves or each other with the negative words that issue from our lips.

The writer of Proverbs tells us that willful contrariness breaks down the spirit. Notice that the word "spirit" is spelled with a small "s." So this verse is not talking about the Holy Spirit, it is referring to our own human spirit. Depression of the human spirit is another problem created and magnified by wrong thoughts and words — our own or those of others.

We are not to use our mouths to hurt, break down, or depress, but rather to heal, restore, and uplift.

Magnify the Good Over the Bad

Do not let yourself be overcome by evil, but overcome (master) evil with good.

Romans 12:21

The thing I believe the Lord wants us to get out of this study is that in every situation there is good and there is bad, just as in every person there is good and there is bad.

Every day that you and I live there are going to be some things that please us, and there are going to be some things that we would just as soon do without.

Because we are children of light, in addition to magnifying Him, the Lord wants us to learn how to magnify the good in life, in others, and in ourselves.

In this sense, to magnify means to make larger. When we lift up our voices and say, "Oh, Lord, we magnify You," what we are saying is that we are making God larger than all our problems. That's what He wants us to do with the good in our lives — to make it larger than the bad.

Again, this is a choice, one that we need to make constantly and continually so that it becomes a habit with us.

Overcoming the Stronghold of Negativism

> For the weapons of our warfare are not physical [weapons of flesh and blood], but they are mighty before God for the overthrow and destruction of strongholds.
>
> **2 Corinthians 10:4**

The Bible speaks about the strongholds that are built up within us — especially in our minds. Until such strongholds are destroyed, they are going to cause us trouble.

The Lord has shown me that a stronghold is like a brick wall. It is built up one brick at a time by rotating certain kinds of thoughts in the mind. We could say that by thinking the same thoughts again and again over a period of time we wear ruts in our mind. Once established, those ruts, or habitual ways of thinking and viewing things, become very difficult to change.

I once counseled with a young woman who had a terrible self-image. It was because throughout her life she had been told repeatedly that she was no good and would never amount to anything. When she got older, she began to replay that message herself: "I'm no good. I'll never amount to anything. There must be something wrong with me. Otherwise, people would love me and treat me right."

I understand how strongholds like that are built up in a person's life because I had them in my own life. As I have said, I was very negative in my thinking and in my speaking. The reason there was such a stronghold of negativism in my life was because so many negative things had happened to me and so many negative things had been said to me and about me.

I grew up in a rather negative environment — surrounded by negative people who looked at things in a negative way. I learned to be the same way, so by the time I was grown I felt that I was protecting myself by having a negative outlook on life. I thought that if I didn't expect anything good to happen to me, I wouldn't be disappointed when it didn't.

But keep in mind that I was also depressed and hard to get along with. In addition, I had a lot of physical ailments associated with people who are negative.

In my ministry, I meet people like that all the time. Like me, they were raised in a negative atmosphere, so they have a negative spirit within them. Such people are not a joy to be around. They are also no joy to themselves. But there is a way to avoid becoming negative — or to overcome it if you already are.

A Negative Report

> **So they brought the Israelites an evil report of the land which they had scouted out, saying, The land through which we went to spy it out is a land that devours its inhabitants. And all the people that we saw in it are men of great stature.**
>
> **Numbers 13:32**

Here in this passage is a truth that I would like for you to lay hold on:

Evil reports God considers negative reports.

That's why the title of this chapter is "Speak No Evil."

Not only are we not to talk negatively about our circumstances, as the Hebrew spies did and came under correction from the Lord; we are also not to talk negatively about other people.

Do you know anybody who is perfect? Have you found the perfect pastor or the perfect church or the perfect workplace? Do you live in a perfect neighborhood? Does everyone in your area keep his house and car and yard in perfect condition?

Everything connected with this natural realm is going to have a bit of decay in it. The Apostle Paul tells us that when Jesus returns to receive us unto Himself, we are going to take off the corruptible and put on the incorruptible. (1 Cor. 15:51-55.) But while we are here in this earthly realm, we are always going to have to contend with corruption — including other people.

Like us, most people are a "mixed bag." Most of them have some good and some bad in them, just as we do. God doesn't want us to magnify the bad in others or in ourselves. He wants us to magnify the good.

The Apostle Peter says love covers a multitude of sins. (1 Peter 4:8.) That's what you and I are to do. We are to cover — not expose — people's imperfections.

Now I am not talking about closing our eyes to all the bad in this life and never acknowledging it or dealing with it. What I am talking about in this study is not our outward actions, but the thoughts that occupy our minds and the words that come out of our mouths.

No matter how badly someone is acting toward you or me, our going around repeating to everyone we meet what is happening to us is not going to make the situation any better. There is only one thing that is going to make it better, and that is turning our faces toward the Lord and crying out to Him to help us.

The reason we need to stop running to others, complaining about our situation, is because every time we do so we add another brick to the stronghold that is being built up in our lives.

That doesn't mean that we should never talk about our situation or problems. If we need counseling in that area, we should seek it out. If we can talk out the problem with someone who has the power to change it or us, then by all means we ought to do so. But just carrying idle tales about a negative situation is not going to make it better, only worse.

I am not saying that we should never talk about our problems. I am saying that we need to *speak with purpose.*

In Matthew 12:36 Jesus said that we are going to be held accountable for our vain, useless conversation, what the *King James Version* calls **every idle word.** We need to keep that truth in mind before we open our mouth. That was the mistake the Hebrew spies made that caused them to be corrected by the Lord for delivering a negative, evil report to Moses and the people of Israel.

Evil Report or Good Report?

And they returned from scouting out the land after forty days.

They came to Moses and Aaron and to all the Israelite congregation in the Wilderness of Paran at Kadesh, and brought them word, and showed them the land's fruit.

They told Moses, We came to the land to which you sent us; surely it flows with milk and honey. This is its fruit.

But the people who dwell there are strong, and the cities are fortified and very large; moreover, there we saw the sons of Anak [of great stature and courage]...

Caleb quieted the people before Moses, and said, Let us go up at once and possess it; we are well able to conquer it.

But his fellow scouts said, We are not able to go up against the people [of Canaan], for they are stronger than we are.

So they brought the Israelites an evil report of the land which they had scouted out, saying, The land through which we went to spy it out is a land that devours its inhabitants. And all the people that we saw in it are men of great stature.

There we saw the Nephilim [or giants], the sons of Anak, who come from the giants; and we were in our own sight as grasshoppers, and so we were in their sight.

Numbers 13:25-28,30-33

As we remember, when the twelve Hebrew spies came back from their scouting expedition into the land of promise, only

Joshua and Caleb gave a favorable report. The other ten gave an evil or negative report.

Didn't all twelve spies go to the same place and experience the same things? Then why this discrepancy in their reports?

Do you know that five people can be confronted with the same trial? Four of them can be totally defeated by it, simply because of the way they look at it, and one can come through it victoriously, for the very same reason!

Why the difference? Because the one chooses to magnify the good, while the others choose to magnify the bad.

Remember, like the giants in the land of Canaan, whatever is magnified becomes bigger and bigger in the eyes of the one doing the magnifying.

Whatever you and I talk about is what is going to become most real to us — whether negative or positive.

Keep the Vessel Clean and Fit for the Master's Use!

> But in a great house there are not only vessels of gold and silver, but also [utensils] of wood and earthenware, and some for honorable and noble [use] and some for menial and ignoble [use].

So whoever cleanses himself [from what is ignoble and unclean, who separates himself from contact with contaminating and corrupting influences] will [then himself] be a vessel set apart and useful for honorable and noble purposes, consecrated and profitable to the Master, fit and ready for any good work.

2 Timothy 2:20,21

It is hard not to talk about our problems. Do you know why? Because we want pity. But if we continue to tell everyone else how we feel and how terrible things are in our life, it won't be long before we won't have anybody to tell it to. It is possible to wear people out with our negative report — even those who care the most about us.

No matter how much others may love us, they do not want to hear that same negative report day after day. One reason is because they have problems of their own — they don't want or need to take on ours.

That's understandable.

How many of us can truthfully say that we want to listen to someone else's problems all the time? If we do, then maybe *we* need counseling and prayer!

You and I have two responsibilities in regard to "evil reports." One is not to give them, and the second is not to receive them.

Each of us has a responsibility not to talk to the other negatively, and not to let the other talk to us that way.

It is our responsibility to help one another in a godly way to get out of the mode of thinking and speaking negatively about others, about ourselves, or about the situations we all have to face and deal with in this life.

At one time when people would come to me to gossip about others, I thought I was obligated to listen to what they had to say. I have to admit that there was also a part of me that still wanted to hear it, so I hid behind the excuse, "Well, I can't tell these people not to share these things with me because I don't want to hurt their feelings."

That's not what the Apostle Paul has told us in the verses we have seen in Ephesians 4. He has said that we are not to be involved in polluting our own minds or the minds of those around us.

According to what Paul wrote to his young disciple Timothy, you and I are supposed to be clean vessels. We are to keep ourselves pure, and to help others to keep themselves pure as well.

One of the ways we do that is by thinking and speaking the way that God wants us to think and speak. We should always be aware of our thoughts and words because God hears them and records them in His book of remembrance.

God's Book of Remembrance

Then those who feared the Lord talked often one to another; and the Lord listened and heard it, and a book of remembrance was written before Him of those who reverenced and worshipfully feared the Lord and who thought on His name.

Malachi 3:16

I believe it makes God's heart glad when He hears us saying the right things. But I also think it makes Him very unhappy when He hears us using our mouths to gossip, complain, find fault, slander, and cause trouble for ourselves and for others by magnifying our problems rather than magnifying Him.

Just think of it. You and I have an opportunity to make glad the heart of God. One way we do that is by magnifying Him in our conversation. We can walk as children of the light, being salt and light to the world, magnifying the name of the Lord to all those around us. Or we can magnify the enemy and his work.

I remember how I used to be before the Lord revealed to me many of these truths I am sharing with you in this book. I was so negative and critical.

I could walk into someone's home that had been newly redecorated, and instead of appreciating all the fine work that had been done, all I could see was one tiny area where the wallpaper was not just perfect.

"Well, you ought to get that fixed," I would say, totally ignoring all the good things that had been done.

I just happen to have one of those personalities that spots problems. That's not entirely bad, because if nobody spotted problems in my life or ministry, we would be in trouble.

But the Lord has shown me that I cannot go around magnifying problems and still walk in peace and joy. Even though there are problems in my life and ministry, it is not going to bless or help or edify or encourage me or anyone else if I magnify all the negatives I see.

That doesn't mean that I ignore problems and never deal with them. It just means that I have to keep them in proper perspective.

Now when I go into someone's newly decorated home, although I may still see the minor imperfections, I don't focus on them or call attention to them. Instead I say something like, "I love your carpet!" I find something to be positive and encouraging about. Then later in private I may point out the minor problem with the wallpaper, saying, "Oh, you may want to have this little tear fixed."

You see, there are proper ways to deal with sensitive issues. The Bible says that God is listening to see how we handle ourselves in all the circumstances we encounter in this life.

Give the Good Report — Not the Evil Report!

> **Amalek dwells in the land of the South (the Negeb); the Hittite, the Jebusite, and the Amorite dwell in the hill country; and the Canaanite dwells by the sea and along by the side of the Jordan [River].**
>
> **Numbers 13:29**

When the Hebrew scouts came back with their reports after spying out the land that the Lord had promised to give to them, they told about the different peoples who occupied it: the Amalekites, the Hittites, the Jebusites, the Amorites, and the Canaanites.

Each of these "ites" represented a different problem to the Children of Israel.

That's why ten of the twelve reported, "Yes, it is a land flowing with milk and honey, *but....*" And it is always the "buts" in life that get us into trouble.

These ten stirred up the whole of the millions of Israelites who were waiting for a decision about whether they should cross over Jordan and take possession of their inheritance. When they started listening to the "evil report" of the ten, they picked up the same spirit that was within them, and they began to murmur and doubt and fear.

As we have seen in verse 30, Caleb saw what was happening and immediately jumped up and tried to quiet the people, assuring them that with the Lord's help they were well able to go in and subdue the land.

But instead of listening to the good report of the two, Caleb and Joshua, the people of Israel listened to the evil report of the ten.

Every day you and I have the opportunity of giving the good report or the evil report, of magnifying the Lord or magnifying the enemy. That is why the Lord has given us this message from His Word, so we will choose to use our mouths not to speak evil, but to speak good.

A Time To Keep Silence and a Time To Speak

> To everything there is a season, and a time for every matter or purpose under heaven...

...a time to keep silence and a time to speak.

Ecclesiastes 3:1,7

As we see in this passage from Ecclesiastes, there is a time and a season for everything. That means that there is a time to deal with problems and a time to leave them alone. There is a time to point out to someone that his wallpaper is peeling off the wall, and a time to keep quiet about it.

It is wisdom to be able to know when to speak and when not to. But as a general rule, it is always timely to exhort and encourage others.

Mark Twain used to say that he could live for two months on one good compliment. I believe that is true for just about everybody.

The devil is doing a great job of tearing down and beating up everybody. He doesn't need our help. We need to be on God's side, not the enemy's.

That is part of our problem. Our fallen nature naturally gravitates toward the wrong side of things. It wants to find fault with others and magnify problems. But our born-again nature wants to bless others and to magnify the good.

As always, the final choice is up to us.

Forget the Past and Press On!

> I do not consider, brethren, that I have captured and made it my own [yet]; but one thing I do [it is my one aspiration]: forgetting what lies behind and straining forward to what lies ahead,
> I press on toward the goal to win the [supreme and heavenly] prize to which God in Christ Jesus is calling us upward.
> Philippians 3:13,14

The devil wants each of us to concentrate on how far we have fallen, rather than how far we have risen. He wants us to focus our attention on how far we still have to go, rather than how far we have come. He wants us to think about how many times we have failed, rather than how many times we have succeeded.

But the Spirit of God wants us to focus on our strengths and not our weaknesses, our victories and not our losses, our joys and not our problems. Those are the things we should be magnifying — the works of the Lord and not the works of the devil.

And we need to help others learn to do that too.

Often people come to me and say, "Joyce, I don't know what my ministry is."

I tell them, "Well, until the Lord reveals it to you, why don't you try the ministry of exhortation, encouragement, and edification?"

These things are always our ministry. It is always our calling to urge others to keep being all that they can be in Christ Jesus and to encourage them to keep on straining forward toward the prize.

Let's not magnify the bad — let's magnify the good! Let's make it larger by talking about it, by being positive in our thoughts, in our attitudes, in our outlook, in our words, and in our actions.

As I have shared with you, I was once so negative that I couldn't even see the positive anymore. I struggled and struggled and struggled until finally the Lord said to me, "Joyce, if you will give Me your mind, someday you will be as positive as you are negative now."

The Lord was wanting me to quit trying all my works of the flesh and just start trusting Him to help me.

If you are negative, I am not suggesting that you draw up a ten-point plan on how you are going to change yourself into a positive person. Instead, I am suggesting that you surrender your will to the Lord, Who is all positive. Say to Him, "O Lord, I want to be like You. Help me to be positive and not to be negative anymore." Ask God to change you! (Phil. 1:6.)

Do whatever God tells you to do. Cooperate with His Spirit and follow His leadership and guidance as you move from darkness to light, from negativism to positivism, from death to life.

God's Part, Our Part

My covenant [on My part with Levi] was to give him life and peace, because [on his part] of the [reverent and worshipful] fear with which [the priests] would revere Me and stand in awe of My name.

The law of truth was in [Levi's] mouth, and unrighteousness was not found in his lips; he walked with Me in peace and uprightness and turned many away from iniquity.

Malachi 2:5-7

This passage deals with priests and the kind of mouth that they are supposed to have. Since I am a minister of the Gospel, naturally this subject is of great interest to me.

But in reality, according to Revelation 1:6, all of us are kings and priests because Jesus Christ has **...formed us into a kingdom (a royal race), priests to His God and Father — to Him be the glory and the power and the majesty and the dominion throughout the ages and forever and ever. Amen (so be it).**

So that is why each of us needs to pay careful attention to this verse which tells us that God has a covenant with His priests.

Now whenever there is a covenant between two individuals, each has a part to play in that agreement or contract. In our covenant with the Lord, He has a part to play, and we have a part to play. He covenants to give us life and peace; our part is to give Him reverence and worshipful fear, to revere Him, and to stand in awe of His name.

Now if we have reverential and worshipful fear of the Lord, if we revere Him and stand in awe of His name, then we are not going to use our mouths to speak evil against His people for whom we serve as His priests.

The Root of Evil Speaking

Therefore you have no excuse or defense or justification, O man, whoever you are who judges and condemns another. For in posing as judge and passing sentence on another, you condemn yourself, because you who judge are habitually practicing the very same things [that you censure and denounce].

Romans 2:1

Do you know that gossip, slander, backbiting, and talebearing have a root, just like a tree or a flower or a weed? The root of these things is judgment. And the root of judgment is pride.

So when we speak evil of other people, it is because we think we are better than they are.

One time I was talking about somebody and the Spirit of the Lord spoke to me and said, "Who do you think you are?"

In God's eyes, sin is sin, and wrong is wrong. All of it is equally displeasing and distasteful to Him. It is also dangerous. That's why Jesus warned us in Matthew 7:1,2:

> Do not judge and criticize and condemn others, so that you may not be judged and criticized and condemned yourselves.
>
> For just as you judge and criticize and condemn others, you will be judged and criticized and condemned, and in accordance with the measure you [use to] deal out to others, it will be dealt out again to you.

Then in verses 3-5 in *The Living Bible* He goes on to say:

> And why worry about a speck in the eye of a brother when you have a board in your own? Should you say, "Friend, let me help you get that speck out of your eye," when you can't even see because of the board in your own? Hypocrite! First get rid of the board. Then you can see to help your brother.

My paraphrase of this passage: "Why try to get the toothpick out of your brother's eye when you have a telephone pole in your own?"

I understood what the Lord meant when He said to me, "Who do you think you are?" because He went on to say, "That's My child you are talking about!"

So from that experience I learned to be very careful about criticizing and judging and condemning other people —

especially other believers — because as a minister, a priest, that is a violation of my divine calling. Since you are also a priest unto our God, it is also a violation of your divine calling.

Keep the Law of Truth in Your Mouth!

The law of truth was in [Levi's] mouth, and unrighteousness was not found in his lips; he walked with Me in peace and uprightness and turned many away from iniquity.

For the priest's lips should guard and keep pure the knowledge [of My law], and the people should seek (inquire for and require) instruction at his mouth; for he is the messenger of the Lord of hosts.

Malachi 2:6,7

Since you and I are priests and kings to our God, we need to keep the law of truth in our mouths.

As we have seen, that means many things: not judging or criticizing or condemning, not being a gossip or a busybody.

And Don't Be a Busybody!

But let none of you suffer as a murderer or a thief or any sort of criminal, or as a mischief-maker (a meddler) in the affairs of others [infringing on their rights].

1 Peter 4:15

The Living Bible translation of this verse reads: **Don't let me hear of your suffering for murdering or stealing or making trouble or being a busybody and prying into other people's affairs.**

What is a *busybody?* One version of Webster's defines *busybody* as "One who concerns himself with other people's affairs."[1] Another Webster's dictionary says, "a nosy, meddlesome person."[2] My definition of a busybody is one who digs up evil reports and makes it his business to spread them by gossip, slander, whispering, and so forth.

Webster defines *gossip* as *"n.* ...one who habitually repeats intimate or private rumors or facts," *"vi.* ...To engage in or spread gossip."[3] My definition of a gossip is one who magnifies and sensationalizes rumors and partial information.

A *slanderer* we have already defined (from Vine). *Slanderers* are "those who are given to finding fault with the demeanor and conduct of others, and spreading their innuendos and criticisms in the church."[4] *Slander* from Webster's, *"n.* ...Utterance of defamatory statements injurious to the reputation or well-being of a person. A malicious report or statement," *"vt.* ...To utter damaging reports about."[5]

Whisper is defined in Webster's dictionary as *"n.* ...A surreptitiously or secretly expressed belief, rumor, or hint <a *whisper* of impropriety>," *"vt.* ...To speak quietly or privately, as when imparting gossip, slander, or intrigue."[6] A *whisperer* speaks quietly or privately to surreptitiously or secretly impart gossip, slander or intrigue.

When we think about these definitions, being a busybody or a gossip or a whisperer — or even a slanderer — does not seem to be as bad as being a murderer or a mischief-maker or a thief or a criminal. Yet the Apostle Peter links all these together as being sin in the eyes of God. Another great scriptural instruction to mind our own business is found in 1 Thessalonians 4:11, **To make it your ambition and definitely endeavor to live quietly and peacefully, to mind your own affairs, and to work with your hands, as we charged you.**

The Sin of Exaggeration

The Lord has revealed to me that even the seemingly harmless habit of exaggerating is as much a sin as any of these others.

Why do we always want to exaggerate? Because we want things to sound better than they are when they are good, and worse than they are when they are bad. It just seems to be the nature of the flesh to exaggerate and blow things all out of proportion.

In this passage, the Lord says that the lips of His priests are to guard and keep pure the knowledge of His law. Why? Because the people seek, inquire, and require instruction at the mouth of the priest, who is the messenger of God.

As God's messengers, His mouthpiece, you and I need to make sure that both the law of truth and the law of kindness are in our mouths and that we speak no evil with our lips.

Hear, for I will speak excellent and princely things; and the opening of my lips shall be for right things.

For my mouth shall utter truth, and wrongdoing is detestable and loathsome to my lips.

All the words of my mouth are righteous (upright and in right standing with God); there is nothing contrary to truth or crooked in them.

They are all plain to him who understands [and opens his heart], and right to those who find knowledge [and live by it]. —Proverbs 8:6-9

chapter 13

A Soothing Tongue

This passage should be not only our confession and testimony, but also our reputation. That is, it should be not only what we say about ourselves, but also what others say about us.

Unfortunately, all of us have learned in this life to speak in circles. When we get through speaking, often others still don't have the slightest idea of what we have said. We need to learn how to engage in plain, straightforward, honest, truthful communication.

As James has told us, blessings and cursings ought not both issue from our mouths. Instead, we ought to be like the virtuous woman in Proverbs 31: in our mouths should be the law of kindness.

As children of God, filled with His Spirit, we are to manifest the fruits of the Spirit, especially kindness, gentleness, meekness, and humility.

That is to be our disposition.

What Is Your Disposition?

As a roaring lion, and a ranging bear; so is a wicked ruler....
Proverbs 28:15 KJV

Webster defines the word *disposition* as "one's usual mood: TEMPERAMENT," "habitual tendency or inclination," or "usual manner of emotional response."[1]

What kind of disposition do you have? Are you basically happy and good-natured, or are you grouchy or grumpy? Are you sweet and kind, or are you sour and mean? Are you even-tempered, or do you get mad easily? (If so, do you stay mad for a long time?) Are you positive and upbeat, or are you negative and depressed? Are you easy-going and easily pleased, or are you harsh and demanding?

As I have shared, I seemed to be surrounded by people with a negative disposition. It is difficult to please a person who has that kind of disposition. If you have ever been around someone like this, I'm sure you know what I mean. They always seem to want something other than what they have — like sitting down to a meal of fried chicken and expressing their disappointment that the chicken was fried instead of baked. That's a very simple example, I know, but I'm sure you get the point.

A person with that kind of disposition is often called "grumpy," "a grouch" or "a bear."

What is your disposition? Are you "a grumpy bear" or are you "a teddy bear"?

The Proud Disposition

> Everyone proud and arrogant in heart is disgusting, hateful, and exceedingly offensive to the Lord; be assured [I pledge it] they will not go unpunished.
>
> Proverbs 16:5

People with a proud disposition are hard to deal with because they are so arrogant. They can't be told anything because they already know everything. Since they are so opinionated, they are always on the defensive, which makes it hard for them to receive correction because to them that would seem to be an admission that they are wrong — and that is something they find almost impossible to do.

In my ministry the Lord uses me to bring correction from His Word. Generally, the flesh doesn't care for that, but it is what makes us grow up in the Lord. Although I try to do it in a loving way, sometimes it still causes people to react against me because, being proud, they resist the truth. Yet Jesus told us that it is the truth that sets us free. (John 8:32.)

Remember, *it is free people who are happy people.*

Besides always being on the defensive, proud people are also usually busy trying to convince others how they need to change or what they need to do.

It was amazing to me to learn that it isn't my job to convince anybody. That is the job of the Holy Spirit. In John 16:8 Jesus said that it is the Holy Spirit Who convicts and convinces people of the truth. That means that you and I don't have to try to "play God" in other people's lives.

I have described how I used to do that with my children. I didn't know how to do as my husband did — tell them what they should do and not do based on the Word of God, and then go on about my business, allowing the Holy Spirit to convict and convince them of the truth.

If they needed to be corrected, I thought it was my job to try to convince them that they were wrong and I was right. I would lecture and preach to them for hours on end, trying to get them to agree with me. That kind of repetitious, overbearing approach did nothing but produce a couple of kids who were so frustrated they could hardly stand me. I am thankful that God has healed and restored our relationships.

Proud people feel that they have to convince others that they are right and others are wrong. As this verse from Proverbs tells us, that kind of domineering, superior approach is not pleasing to God Who wants His children to walk in kindness and humility, not arrogance and pride.

Proud people are also usually very rigid, which explains why they are often such strict disciplinarians. They have their own way of doing things, and if anyone doesn't do it their way, they react strongly, sometimes even violently: "This is it! This is the way it has to be done — or else!"

That's the way I was with my children — which is why my husband, who had been in the military, told me that I would make a good army drill sergeant. But my attitude and behavior toward my own family were not producing the kind of results I wanted or expected. In fact, they were having just the opposite effect.

Finally, proud people are often complicated people. Although the Bible calls us to a life of simplicity, they feel that they have to make a big deal out of everything, to make a mountain out of every molehill. Part of the reason is because they think they have to figure out everything, that they have to know the ins and outs of every situation and know the reason for everything that happens in life.

All these things help to explain why proud people are usually not very happy people. And unhappy people do not make very many other people happy either.

So that brings us to the question: what kind of disposition does God want us to have in order to be a blessing to ourselves and to others? Has He given us an example we can model ourselves after?

A Soothing Disposition

Behold, My Servant Whom I have chosen, My Beloved in and with Whom My soul is well pleased and has found its delight. I will put My Spirit upon Him, and He shall proclaim and show forth justice to the nations.

> He will not strive or wrangle or cry out loudly; nor will anyone hear His voice in the streets;
>
> A bruised reed He will not break, and a smoldering (dimly burning) wick He will not quench, till He brings justice and a just cause to victory.
>
> And in and on His name will the Gentiles (the peoples outside of Israel) set their hopes.
>
> Matthew 12:18-21

As believers, as God's beloved children created in His image, He wants us to have the same soothing disposition that His Son Jesus displayed.

Many of us believe that if Jesus walked into a room full of strife, it would only take Him a few minutes to bring peace to that situation. He had that kind of soothing nature about Him. He was clothed with meekness. He wasn't out to prove anything. He wasn't concerned about what people thought about Him. He already knew Who He was, so He didn't feel the need to defend Himself. Although others would get upset with Him and start all kinds of arguments with Him, His response was always peaceful and loving.

That is the kind of soothing disposition God wants you and me to have. That is the kind of tongue He wants us to have in our mouths — one that brings encouragement and edification and exhortation everywhere we go.

Is that the way we are, or are we grouches and soreheads? Are we humble and simple and agreeable, or are we proud and complicated and rigid?

My husband is one of the few people I have ever known who truly has a soothing disposition. He is so easy-going, it is amazing to me. He can be ready to lie down and take a nap, and I can ask him to go to the grocery store for me. He will say, "Sure, I'll go right now."

Now if that were me, I can assure you that the reaction would be quite different!

Often people with this kind of soothing disposition are encouragers and exhorters. No matter what is going on around them or what others are saying or doing, they always seem to have a word of encouragement and kindness to share with everyone.

That is the way God intends for us to be. That is what He gave us our mouths for — not to cut people to pieces or to judge others or to criticize and condemn those who disagree with us.

As God's messengers, His mouthpiece, His ambassadors of peace, you and I are not to be harsh and hard, proud and arrogant, rigid and unbending. Instead, we are to be soothing and kind, simple and humble, pliable and adaptable.

To do that, to be the way God wants us to be as His representatives on this earth, we are going to have to put off our old nature and put on the new nature — which is the nature of His beloved Son Jesus Christ.

A New Nature

Strip yourselves of your former nature [put off and discard your old unrenewed self] which characterized your previous manner of life and becomes corrupt through lusts and desires that spring from delusion;

And be constantly renewed in the spirit of your mind [having a fresh mental and spiritual attitude],

And put on the new nature (the regenerate self) created in God's image, [Godlike] in true righteousness and holiness.

Ephesians 4:22-24

In the *King James Version* the opening statement of verse 22 reads, **That ye put off concerning the former *conversation* the old man....**

Although the Greek word *anastrophe* in this passage is no longer translated "conversation" in more modern versions because the meaning of that English word has changed from the time of King James when it meant "behavior,"[2] I still believe there is a vital link between our conversation and our behavior, which is a reflection and expression of our nature.

The Lord has revealed to me that our nature is seen through our conversation. That is to say that the kind of person we are is revealed by our speech.

Our nature comes out of our mouth.

If we have a soothing disposition, our words will bring that soothing to troubled waters.

Doesn't the Bible say that a soft answer turns away wrath? (Prov. 15:1 KJV.) That is true — if we are willing to lay aside our pride and allow the Holy Spirit to work through us as He wills in every situation.

If we are willing to humble ourselves before the Lord in meekness and obedience, as Jesus did, then the same nature that motivated His words and actions will become our nature and will bring soothing to our lives and the lives of all those with whom we come in contact. Jesus called it taking His yoke upon us.

The Nature of Jesus

Come to Me, all you who labor and are heavy-laden and overburdened, and I will cause you to rest. [I will ease and relieve and refresh your souls.]

Take My yoke upon you and learn of Me, for I am gentle (meek) and humble (lowly) in heart, and you will find rest (relief and ease and refreshment and recreation and blessed quiet) for your souls.

For My yoke is wholesome (useful, good — not harsh, hard, sharp, or pressing, but comfortable, gracious, and pleasant), and My burden is light and easy to be borne.

Matthew 11:28-30

If we are to have and display the nature of Jesus, then we need to know what that nature is.

Each of us has a different nature. No two of us are exactly alike. Our nature also changes as we go through the various experiences and cycles of life.

Through the years I have seen the difference in my nature and my husband's. I am the type that has a warring personality. People with my type of disposition are hard to please. Nothing ever suits them. They have to make a big deal out of everything. Such people are not very happy.

Those who are the happiest are those who take things in stride, those who are easy to please and get along with, those who just sort of "go with the flow," those who are adjustable and adaptable. Such people usually bring soothing to troubled waters.

I have to admit that during the first twenty-one years of our marriage, until I was filled with the Holy Spirit, my husband was much happier than I was. Since that time I have finally begun to catch up to him, because I have more of the Word of God in me now than I did then. But even after I was baptized in the Holy Spirit, there was no instantaneous, overnight change in me.

Real change just doesn't come easily or quickly.

Have you learned yet that if you are going to change, you must want to change — and want it badly enough to put some effort into it?

Many people would like to just take a pill or utter some magic words one night and wake up the next morning totally different, completely transformed. It just doesn't work that way.

There are no overnight saints or instant ministries.

If you and I are to be different from the way we are now, then we are going to have to endure some suffering. We are going to have to cooperate with the Lord as step by step He brings us into conformity to His will and way, gradually transforming us into the image of His Son Jesus.

In verse 29 of this passage, Jesus describes His nature. He says that He is gentle, meek, humble, and lowly of heart. Then He goes on to say that if we will take His yoke — His nature — upon us and learn of Him, we will find rest.

When you and I begin to take on the gentleness, the meekness, and the humility that marked the life of Jesus, we will find His rest for our souls.

In verse 30 Jesus describes His yoke — His nature — as wholesome and good, not harsh, hard, sharp, or pressing, but comfortable, gracious, and pleasant.

Remember, if you are under pressure, that pressure is not coming from God. His yoke is not harsh, hard, sharp, or pressing — because His nature is not that way. That is not the way the Lord is, that is the way the devil is, and the way he makes those who submit to him.

Jesus has a soothing, peaceful disposition. That is why the Bible says that if we want to be led by the Spirit of God, we must learn to be led by peace. (Col. 3:15.) If you and I are led by peace, then we can be assured that we are being led by God, because He is the peace that is on the inside of us.

Too many believers go from one meeting to the next seeking a "voice," looking for a "word" from God. At the leading of the Holy Spirit, I have given words of knowledge, words of wisdom, and words of prophecy in our meetings. Everybody likes that.

But when it comes to laying aside the fleshly nature and being transformed by the Spirit into the nature of Jesus Christ, that's a different story. That's where the mature Christians are separated from the baby Christians. That's where it is revealed who really wants to be serious with God and who doesn't.

It is easy to stay the way we are. It is easy to keep being harsh and hard and sharp and pressing. But it steals our peace and joy.

We must learn that if we are ever going to be truly happy, we are going to have to be like Jesus, to take His nature upon us, even as He took our nature upon Himself. (Heb. 2:16 KJV.)

Whether we are harsh and hard or sweet and soothing determines whether we are true worshippers of God.

A Holy and Perfumed Anointing Oil

Moreover, the Lord said to Moses,
Take the best spices: of liquid myrrh 500 shekels, of sweet-scented cinnamon half as much, 250 shekels, of fragrant calamus 250 shekels,
And of cassia 500 shekels, in terms of the sanctuary shekel, and of olive oil a hin.
And you shall make of these a holy anointing oil, a perfume compounded after the art of the perfumer; it shall be a sacred anointing oil.

Exodus 30:22-25

Do you really want to be anointed? Do you want to be just dripping with the anointing of the Holy Ghost? Do you want to be saturated with the sweet fragrance of the Spirit of God?

According to the Bible, there is a spiritual aroma that goes up from our lives: **For we are the sweet fragrance of Christ [which** exhales] unto God, [discernible alike] among those who are being saved and among those who are perishing (2 Cor. 2:15).

So these things we see in the Old Testament are very relevant to the practical aspects of the New Testament.

The Ingredients of the Anointing Oil

And you shall anoint the Tent of Meeting with it, and the ark of the Testimony,

And the [showbread] table and all its utensils, and the lampstand and its utensils, and the altar of incense,

And the altar of burnt offering with all its utensils, and the laver [for cleansing] and its base.

You shall sanctify (separate) them, that they may be most holy; whoever and whatever touches them must be holy (set apart to God).

And you shall anoint Aaron and his sons and sanctify (separate) them, that they may minister to Me as priests.

Exodus 30:26-30

I happen to have in my possession a book by Hannah Hurnard called *Mountains of Spices*.[3]

When I read this passage in Exodus, I began to ask myself what these various spices represented, so I looked them up in this book.

According to this author, myrrh represents meekness.[4] Since the recipe for the anointing oil calls for 500 shekels of myrrh, that represents a great deal of meekness!

As we have seen, meekness is one of the self-described attributes of Jesus Christ.

Cinnamon represents goodness,[5] and calamus represents gentleness.[6]

So if you and I want the anointing of God upon us, then we are going to have to be imbued with a mixture of meekness, goodness, gentleness, and humility.

Grow Up in Christ and in Love

Now what I mean is that as long as the inheritor (heir) is a child and under age, he does not differ from a slave, although he is the master of all the estate;

But he is under guardians and administrators or trustees until the date fixed by his father.

Galatians 4:1,2

We are also going to have to grow up and become mature in Christ so that we may claim the full inheritance set apart for the children of God.

In the fourth chapter of Galatians the Apostle Paul tells us that when an under-age individual receives an inheritance, that inheritance is held by a trustee until the person becomes of full age.

As heirs of God and joint-heirs with Jesus (Rom. 8:17 KJV), you and I have an inheritance in Christ. But until we grow up and put away childish things, that inheritance is held for us by the Holy Spirit.

We only receive God's blessings when we are mature enough to handle them. One way we show we are mature is by demonstrating that we have control of our mouths.

As we have seen in Isaiah 58:6-9, we also have to loose the bands of wickedness, undo the bands of the yoke, let the oppressed go free, and break every enslaving yoke. We have to divide our bread with the hungry, and bring the homeless into our houses. We have to cover the naked and hide not ourselves from our own flesh and blood.

What the Lord is telling us in these passages is that He wants us to have the kind of mature disposition that His Son Jesus had, one that is not selfish and self-centered, but one that cares for others.

Then, as He has said, our light will break forth as the morning, and our healing, our restoration, the power of a new life, will spring forth speedily. Then our righteousness, our justice, our right relationship with the Lord, will go before us, conducting us to peace and prosperity. Then the glory of the Lord will be our rear guard. Then we will call upon the Lord, and He will answer.

When we take away from our midst the yokes of oppression and the finger pointed in scorn toward the oppressed, when we stop being critical and judgmental of each other, when we put away every form of false, harsh, unjust, and wicked speaking, then the blessings of the Lord will come forth in our lives.

That's when we become true worshippers — a sweet-smelling aroma unto the Lord.

A Formula for Kingdom Living

By means of these He has bestowed on us His precious and exceedingly great promises, so that through them you may escape [by flight] from the moral decay (rottenness and corruption) that is in the world because of covetousness (lust and greed), and become sharers (partakers) of the divine nature.

For this very reason, adding your diligence [to the divine promises], employ every effort in exercising your faith to develop virtue (excellence, resolution, Christian energy), and in [exercising] virtue [develop] knowledge (intelligence),

And in [exercising] knowledge [develop] self-control, and in [exercising] self-control [develop] steadfastness (patience, endurance), and in [exercising] steadfastness [develop] godliness (piety),

And in [exercising] godliness [develop] brotherly affection, and in [exercising] brotherly affection [develop] Christian love.

> **For as these qualities are yours and increasingly abound in you, they will keep [you] from being idle or unfruitful unto the [full personal] knowledge of our Lord Jesus Christ (the Messiah, the Anointed One).**
>
> 2 Peter 1:4-8

Here in this passage is a biblical formula for moving out of the flesh and into the divine nature in order to experience true Kingdom living.

We start our relationship with God in the outer court. From there we move into the inner court, and then finally into the Holy of Holies.

We begin our Christian lives as new-born infants. We pray in the flesh. We read the Bible in the flesh. We go to church in the flesh. We worship in the flesh. And God accepts that kind of worship, because He takes us where we are.

But then later He will say to us, "It is time to move into the inner court." Part of that word comes through messages on holiness which tell us that God used to allow certain things, but not anymore.

Finally, the day comes when He says to us, "Now it is time to move into the Holy of Holies." In order to come into that place, our whole lives must be placed upon the altar before the Lord. We cannot reserve the little things that we want for ourselves.

We must give it all up to God, becoming true worshippers in spirit and in truth. (John 4:23.) That means that we must be ready to live our lives before Him as He desires, trusting Him to give us the grace to do so. (Phil. 2:13.)

In this passage, the first thing we are told is that we must take the promises of God and add to them diligence.

Many people are stopped right there at the beginning. They never get beyond the promises of God. They go around quoting promises all their lives, but they never add any diligence or effort on their part, so they never see the fulfillment of those promises.

If you and I are going to grow to true Christian maturity and fulfill God's will and plan for our lives, then we are going to have to be determined to finish the course laid out before us. (2 Tim. 4:7 KJV.) There are going to be things that come against us to discourage us and cause us to give up. So we must be determined, we must be diligent.

Then we are told to add to our diligence faith, which in turn develops virtue or excellence.

There comes a time in all of our lives when the Lord says to us, "You can no longer be lazy, sloppy, and undisciplined; you have to exercise excellence, resolution, and Christian energy."

That excellence then develops knowledge, which produces self-control. This means we can no longer do whatever we feel like doing, but we must be committed as Jesus was to doing the will of the Father.

Once we have developed self-control, it in turn leads to steadfastness, which is patience or endurance. Patience is not just the ability to wait, but the ability to wait with a good attitude. As we are waiting, our lives are still giving forth that sweet aroma before the Lord.

Granted, it is easier to give off a good aroma when things are going our way. It is much more difficult to do that when everything is going against us, when those around us are having their prayers answered while our own prayers seem to be bouncing back off the ceiling. At such times it may seem that God is deaf, that for some reason we cannot understand He refuses to hear us. We all go through such times. The test is what kind of fragrance we give off while we are doing so.

Then our steadfastness, patience, and endurance develop into something called godliness. That is when we begin to be exposed to a constant barrage of messages on holiness. Why? Because God deals with each of these Christian virtues one at a time, in order. He is taking us some place. He is taking us unto Himself, making us fit to stand in His holy Presence. He is preparing us to be used by Him in the great end-time revival.

After godliness comes brotherly affection, what the *King James Version* calls **brotherly kindness.** This kind of brotherly affection or kindness produces true **Christian love,** which is *The Amplified Bible* translation of the Greek word *agape*, meaning God-like love.

Clothe Yourself With Humility

...Clothe (apron) yourselves, all of you, with humility [as the garb of a servant, so that its covering cannot possibly be stripped from you, with freedom from pride and arrogance] toward one another. For God sets Himself against the proud (the insolent, the overbearing, the disdainful, the presumptuous, the boastful) — [and He opposes, frustrates, and defeats them], but gives grace (favor, blessing) to the humble.

1 Peter 5:5

At the time I began this study on the mouth, the Lord revealed to me through this formula that I was right before *agape*.

As I looked back over my life up to that point, I could see that the Lord had brought me through every one of those stages of Christian growth. Now He was saying to me that it was time for me to do as Peter had said and clothe myself with the humility of Christ.

I believe He is saying that to each one of us in the Body of Christ. We are to take on the cloak of humility, meekness, kindness, and gentleness. We are to wear that cloak out into the world where we are to act like Jesus, giving forth a sweet-smelling aroma and having a soothing personality.

After I had received this message from the Lord, I was ministering in a meeting. At the close of the service a man came to me and said, "I feel that this will be only a confirmation to you, but I have a word from the Lord for you." He went on to quote this passage, 2 Peter 1:4-9, and then said, "The Lord says that you are at kindness, and after that comes the Kingdom."

Now as I have cautioned, I am careful about personal words from other people, but in this case there is no way that word could have been accidental. It encouraged me so much because I believed it to be a confirmation of what God had already shown me.

Be Willing To Be Changed

And all of us, as with unveiled face, [because we] continued to behold [in the Word of God] as in a mirror the glory of the Lord, are constantly being transfigured into His very own

> image in ever increasing splendor and from one degree of glory
> to another; [for this comes] from the Lord [Who is] the Spirit.
>
> 2 Corinthians 3:18

The change that needs to take place in each of us does not come by our effort or strain or good works. It comes from knowing God personally and intimately.

In this final chapter I am not going to tell you seven things to do to grow in the knowledge of the Lord. I am going to tell you what your one responsibility is.

Confession is good. It does things in the life of the believer. But it does not change the inner man.

Certain kinds of prayer programs are good. They help to develop spiritual discipline. But they do not change the inner man.

Bible reading and church attendance and many other such exercises are good. They are things that every believer ought to practice. But they do not change the inner man.

There is only one thing that changes the inner man, and that is sitting in the Presence of God and allowing Him to do a work on the inside.

Right now, the entire Church of Jesus Christ is working and struggling — trying to change. God has revealed to me that He would appreciate it so much if we would all just behold Him in His Word and allow His Spirit to transform us into His image.

We Charismatics have become so religious. In fact, we have our own religion! We have planned and programmed everything in our spiritual lives. There is nothing wrong with discipline and order, but if we plan and program God out of the picture, then we have a big problem on our hands.

The only thing that is going to truly change you and me is getting into God's presence and waiting on Him to do for us what we cannot do for ourselves.

I am not challenging you to go out and try to be kind, or humble, or gentle, or loving. If that is the message that you have received from this book, then you will only end up frustrated.

This message is not meant to bring condemnation for what you are or what you have been. It is to bring encouragement because of what you can be — if you are willing to submit to the Spirit of the Living God.

The Lord is looking for people who are willing to be changed from what they are to what only He can make them to be. The first step in that process usually involves a change in speech. That was true for Abram and Sarai who had to learn to call themselves by different names. It was true for Moses who made the excuse that he could not speak properly because of problems with his mouth. That was true for Isaiah who said that he was a man of unclean lips who lived among a people of unclean lips. It was true for Jeremiah who claimed that he was too young to be able to speak for the Lord.

It will also be true for you and me. If we are willing to be changed, the Lord will do the transforming and transfiguring of us — in His own way and in His own time — as we simply fellowship with Him in the inner man.

Experiencing the Lord

In closing, I would like to share with you this quotation from a book called *Experiencing the Depths of Jesus Christ:*

> And there in your spirit God dwells. Oh, when you have learned how to dwell there with Him. His divine presence dissolves the hardness of your soul. And as that hardness of your soul melts, precious fragrances pour forth from your soul.[7]

Think about it for a moment. God dwells there in your spirit. But you have to learn to dwell there with Him.

Fruit-bearing does not come from church attendance or prayer vigils or Bible reading or positive confession, as good as these things are. It comes from abiding in the Lord and allowing Him to abide in you. It is His divine Presence that dissolves the hardness of your soul so that sweet-smelling fragrances pour forth from you.

Do you want to change? Do you want to quit being hard, harsh, sharp, and pressing? Do you want to become humble, meek, gentle, and kind? Do you want to be like Jesus? Then learn to fellowship with Him so He can develop in you a soothing tongue and spirit.

Conclusion

> But avoid all empty (vain, useless, idle) talk, for it will lead people into more and more ungodliness.
>
> —2 Timothy 2:16

In this study I have tried to emphasize the importance of how much blessing — and how much damage — we do by the words of our mouth.

Remember, words are containers of power.

That is why there are so many passages in the Word of God about the wrong and the right use of the mouth (see the following Scripture list).

To illustrate the many Scriptures on this subject, I have shared several personal experiences highlighting the lessons I have learned in my own life and ministry. I have also shared examples of some of the personal positive confessions I use to apply the Word of God to the many situations of life that all of us encounter in our Christian walk.

It is my sincere prayer that these will be of help to you in your own effort to gain control over your words, and thus change your life and circumstances — for your own sake and for the sake of all those with whom you come in contact.

Avoid all empty, idle, vain, and useless talk. Instead, learn to speak as God speaks. It is the Word of God, spoken in truth and love from your lips, that will return to Him after accomplishing His will and purpose.

But in order to speak that Word in truth and love, your heart must be right before the Lord, for it is out of the abundance of the heart that the mouth speaks — for good or for evil.

You are bound by your words, by your declarations.

You are also judged by them.

Watchman Nee once said, "If you listen to a person, you can detect by their words the spirit that is coming forth from them."

That is why it is so important to place a guard upon your lips so that what issues forth from them is not only truthful, but also kind and positive and edifying and in line with the will of God.

You can change your action and behavior, but to do so you must first change your thoughts and words. And to do that, you need the help of the indwelling Spirit of God.

Attitude determines action.

If you truly want your life to be totally different, then submit yourself to the Lord and in humility ask Him to transform you into the image and nature of His Son Jesus Christ.

He is doing that for me, and if He can do it for me, He can — and will — do it for you too.

God bless you.

Scriptures on the Mouth

For we all often stumble and fall and offend in many things. And if anyone does not offend in speech [never says the wrong things], he is a fully developed character and a perfect man, able to control his whole body and to curb his entire nature.

If we set bits in the horses' mouths to make them obey us, we can turn their whole bodies about.

Likewise, look at the ships: though they are so great and are driven by rough winds, they are steered by a very small rudder wherever the impulse of the helmsman determines.

Even so the tongue is a little member, and it can boast of great things. See how much wood or how great a forest a tiny spark can set ablaze!

And the tongue is a fire. [The tongue is a] world of wickedness set among our members, contaminating and depraving the whole body and setting on fire the wheel of birth (the cycle of man's nature), being itself ignited by hell (Gehenna).

For every kind of beast and bird, of reptile and sea animal, can be tamed and has been tamed by human genius (nature).

But the human tongue can be tamed by no man. It is a restless (undisciplined, irreconcilable) evil, full of deadly poison.

With it we bless the Lord and Father, and with it we curse men who were made in God's likeness!

Out of the same mouth come forth blessing and cursing. These things, my brethren, ought not to be so.

251

Does a fountain send forth [simultaneously] from the same opening fresh water and bitter?

Can a fig tree, my brethren, bear olives, or a grapevine figs? Neither can a salt spring furnish fresh water.

— James 3:2-12

If anyone thinks himself to be religious (piously observant of the external duties of his faith) and does not bridle his tongue but deludes his own heart, this person's religious service is worthless (futile, barren).

— James 1:26

Even so consider yourselves also dead to sin and your relation to it broken, but alive to God [living in unbroken fellowship with Him] in Christ Jesus.

Let not sin therefore rule as king in your mortal (short-lived, perishable) bodies, to make you yield to its cravings and be subject to its lusts and evil passions.

Do not continue offering or yielding your bodily members [and faculties] to sin as instruments (tools) of wickedness. But offer and yield yourselves to God as though you have been raised from the dead to [perpetual] life, and your bodily members [and faculties] to God, presenting them as implements of righteousness.

— Romans 6:11-13

As it is written, I have made you the father of many nations. [He was appointed our father] in the sight of God in Whom he believed, Who gives life to the dead and speaks of the non-existent things that [He has foretold and promised] as if they [already] existed.

— Romans 4:17

By the word of the Lord were the heavens made, and all their host by the breath of His mouth.

— Psalm 33:6

And God said, Let there be light; and there was light.

— Genesis 1:3

A man's [moral] self shall be filled with the fruit of his mouth; and with the consequence of his words he must be satisfied [whether good or evil].

Death and life are in the power of the tongue, and they who indulge in it shall eat the fruit of it [for death or life].

— Proverbs 18:20,21

It is not what goes into the mouth of a man that makes him unclean and defiled, but what comes out of the mouth; this makes a man unclean and defiles [him].

— Matthew 15:11

Do you not see and understand that whatever goes into the mouth passes into the abdomen and so passes on into the place where discharges are deposited?

But whatever comes out of the mouth comes from the heart, and this is what makes a man unclean and defiles [him].

For out of the heart come evil thoughts (reasonings and disputings and designs) such as murder, adultery, sexual vice, theft, false witnessing, slander, and irreverent speech.

These are what make a man unclean and defile [him]; but eating with unwashed hands does not make him unclean or defile [him].

— Matthew 15:17-20

Let your speech at all times be gracious (pleasant and winsome), seasoned [as it were] with salt, [so that you may never be at a loss] to know how you ought to answer anyone [who puts a question to you].

— Colossians 4:6

Who satisfies your mouth [your necessity and desire at your personal age and situation] with good so that your youth, renewed, is like the eagle's [strong, overcoming, soaring]!

— Psalm 103:5

Peace, peace, to him who is far off [both Jew and Gentile] and to him who is near! says the Lord; I create the fruit of his lips, and I will heal him [make his lips blossom anew with speech in thankful praise].

— Isaiah 57:19

The wicked is [dangerously] snared by the transgression of his lips, but the [uncompromisingly] righteous shall come out of trouble.

From the fruit of his words a man shall be satisfied with good, and the work of a man's hands shall come back to him [as a harvest].

— Proverbs 12:13,14

Either make the tree sound (healthy and good), and its fruit sound (healthy and good), or make the tree rotten (diseased and bad), and its fruit rotten (diseased and bad); for the tree is known and recognized and judged by its fruit.

You offspring of vipers! How can you speak good things when you are evil (wicked)? For out of the fullness (the overflow, the superabundance) of the heart the mouth speaks.

— Matthew 12:33,34

Cease, my son, to hear instruction only to ignore it and stray from the words of knowledge.

— Proverbs 19:27

But I tell you, on the day of judgment men will have to give account for every idle (inoperative, nonworking) word they speak.

— Matthew 12:36

He who shuts his eyes to devise perverse things and who compresses his lips [as if in concealment] brings evil to pass.

— Proverbs 16:30

A good man eats good from the fruit of his mouth, but the desire of the treacherous is for violence.

He who guards his mouth keeps his life, but he who opens wide his lips comes to ruin.

— Proverbs 13:2,3

He who guards his mouth and his tongue keeps himself from troubles.

— Proverbs 21:23

For the Word that God speaks is alive and full of power [making it active, operative, energizing, and effective]; it is sharper than any two-edged sword, penetrating to the dividing line of the breath of life (soul) and [the immortal] spirit, and of joints and marrow [of the deepest parts of our nature], exposing and sifting and analyzing and judging the very thoughts and purposes of the heart.

— Hebrews 4:12

There are those who speak rashly, like the piercing of a sword, but the tongue of the wise brings healing.

— Proverbs 12:18

A man has joy in making an apt answer, and a word spoken at the right moment — how good it is!

— Proverbs 15:23

Let no foul or polluting language, nor evil word nor unwholesome or worthless talk [ever] come out of your mouth, but only such [speech] as is good and beneficial to the spiritual progress of others, as is fitting to the need and the occasion, that it may be a blessing and give grace (God's favor) to those who hear it.

And do not grieve the Holy Spirit of God [do not offend or vex or sadden Him], by Whom you were sealed (marked, branded as God's own, secured) for the day of redemption (of final deliverance through Christ from evil and the consequences of sin).

Let all bitterness and indignation and wrath (passion, rage, bad temper) and resentment (anger, animosity) and quarreling (brawling, clamor, contention) and slander (evil-speaking, abusive or blasphemous language) be banished from you, with all malice (spite, ill will, or baseness of any kind).

And become useful and helpful and kind to one another, tenderhearted (compassionate, understanding, loving-hearted), forgiving one another [readily and freely], as God in Christ forgave you.

— Ephesians 4:29-32

Lord, who shall dwell [temporarily] in Your tabernacle? Who shall dwell [permanently] on Your holy hill?

He who walks and lives uprightly and blamelessly, who works rightness and justice and speaks and thinks the truth in his heart,

He who does not slander with his tongue, nor does evil to his friend, nor takes up a reproach against his neighbor.

— Psalm 15:1-3

Then said I, Woe is me! For I am undone and ruined, because I am a man of unclean lips, and I dwell in the midst of a people of unclean lips; for my eyes have seen the King, the Lord of hosts!

Then flew one of the seraphim [heavenly beings] to me, having a live coal in his hand which he had taken with tongs from off the altar; And with it he touched my mouth and said, Behold, this has touched your lips; your iniquity and guilt are taken away, and your sin is completely atoned for and forgiven.

— Isaiah 6:5-7

Set a guard, O Lord, before my mouth; keep watch at the door of my lips.

— Psalm 141:3

Let the words of my mouth and the meditation of my heart be acceptable in Your sight, O Lord, my [firm, impenetrable] Rock and my Redeemer.

— Psalm 19:14

My son, attend to my words; consent and submit to my sayings.

Let them not depart from your sight; keep them in the center of your heart.

For they are life to those who find them, healing and health to all their flesh.

Keep and guard your heart with all vigilance and above all that you guard, for out of it flow the springs of life.

Put away from you false and dishonest speech, and willful and contrary talk put far from you.

— Proverbs 4:20-24

Let there be no filthiness (obscenity, indecency) nor foolish and sinful (silly and corrupt) talk, nor coarse jesting, which are not fitting or becoming; but instead voice your thankfulness [to God].

— Ephesians 5:4

A soft answer turns away wrath, but grievous words stir up anger.

The tongue of the wise utters knowledge rightly, but the mouth of the [self-confident] fool pours out folly.

The eyes of the Lord are in every place, keeping watch upon the evil and the good.

A gentle tongue [with its healing power] is a tree of life, but willful contrariness in it breaks down the spirit.

— Proverbs 15:1-4

Anxiety in a man's heart weighs it down, but an encouraging word makes it glad.

— Proverbs 12:25

Herald and preach the Word! Keep your sense of urgency [stand by, be at hand and ready], whether the opportunity seems to be favorable or unfavorable. [Whether it is convenient or inconvenient, whether it is welcome or unwelcome, you as preacher of the Word are to show people in what way their lives are wrong.] And convince them, rebuking and correcting, warning and urging and encouraging them, being unflagging and inexhaustible in patience and teaching.

— 2 Timothy 4:2

And He said to them, Go into all the world and preach and publish openly the good news (the Gospel) to every creature [of the whole human race].

— Mark 16:15

In a multitude of words transgression is not lacking, but he who restrains his lips is prudent.

— Proverbs 10:19

He was oppressed, [yet when] He was afflicted, He was submissive and opened not His mouth; like a lamb that is led to the slaughter, and as a sheep before her shearers is dumb, so He opened not His mouth.

— Isaiah 53:7

Hear, for I will speak excellent and princely things; and the opening of my lips shall be for right things.

For my mouth shall utter truth, and wrongdoing is detestable and loathsome to my lips.

All the words of my mouth are righteous (upright and in right standing with God); there is nothing contrary to truth or crooked in them.

— Proverbs 8:6-8

For I [Myself] will give you a mouth and such utterance and wisdom that all of your foes combined will be unable to stand against or refute.

— Luke 21:15

He who has knowledge spares his words, and a man of understanding has a cool spirit.

Even a fool when he holds his peace is considered wise; when he closes his lips he is esteemed a man of understanding.

— Proverbs 17:27-28

...the Lord hates...A false witness who breathes out lies [even under oath], and he who sows discord among his brethren.

— Proverbs 6:16,19

With his mouth the godless man destroys his neighbor, but through knowledge and superior discernment shall the righteous be delivered.

When it goes well with the [uncompromisingly] righteous, the city rejoices, but when the wicked perish, there are shouts of joy.

By the blessing of the influence of the upright and God's favor [because of them] the city is exalted, but it is overthrown by the mouth of the wicked.

He who belittles and despises his neighbor lacks sense, but a man of understanding keeps silent.

He who goes about as a talebearer reveals secrets, but he who is trustworthy and faithful in spirit keeps the matter hidden.

— Proverbs 11:9-13

The mouth of the [uncompromisingly] righteous utters wisdom, and his tongue speaks with justice.

— Psalm 37:30

But now put away and rid yourselves [completely] of all these things: anger, rage, bad feeling toward others, curses and slander, and foulmouthed abuse and shameful utterances from your lips!

Do not lie to one another, for you have stripped off the old (unregenerate) self with its evil practices,

And have clothed yourselves with the new [spiritual self], which is [ever in the process of being] renewed and remolded into [fuller and more perfect knowledge upon] knowledge, after the image (the likeness) of Him Who created it.

— Colossians 3:8-10

God is not a man, that He should tell or act a lie, neither the son of man, that He should feel repentance or compunction [for what He has promised]. Has He said and shall He not do it? Or has He spoken and shall He not make it good?

— Numbers 23:19

But when He, the Spirit of Truth (the Truth-giving Spirit) comes, He will guide you into all the Truth (the whole, full Truth). For He will not speak His own message [on His own authority]; but He will tell whatever He hears [from the Father; He will give the message that has been given to Him], and He will announce and declare to you the things that are to come [that will happen in the future].

— John 16:13

You are of your father, the devil, and it is your will to practice the lusts and gratify the desires [which are characteristic] of your father. He was a murderer from the beginning and does not stand in the truth, because there is no truth in him. When he speaks a falsehood, he speaks what is natural to him, for he is a liar [himself] and the father of lies and of all that is false.

— John 8:44

But as for the cowards and the ignoble and the contemptible and the cravenly lacking in courage and the cowardly submissive, and as for the unbelieving and faithless, and as for the depraved and defiled with abominations, and as for murderers and the lewd and adulterous and the practicers of magic arts and the idolaters (those who give supreme devotion to anyone or anything other than God) and all liars (those who knowingly convey untruth by word or deed) — [all of these shall have] their part in the lake that blazes with fire and brimstone. This is the second death.

— Revelation 21:8

Therefore, rejecting all falsity and being done now with it, let everyone express the truth with his neighbor, for we are all parts of one body and members one of another.

Leave no [such] room or foothold for the devil [give no opportunity to him].

— Ephesians 4:25,27

Rather, let our lives lovingly express truth [in all things, speaking truly, dealing truly, living truly]. Enfolded in love, let us grow up in every way and in all things into Him, Who is the Head, [even] Christ (the Messiah, the Anointed One).

— Ephesians 4:15

Lying lips are extremely disgusting and hateful to the Lord, but they who deal faithfully are His delight.

— Proverbs 12:22

A man who flatters his neighbor spreads a net for his own feet.

— Proverbs 29:5

You shall not witness falsely against your neighbor.

— Exodus 20:16

These are the things that you shall do: speak every man the truth with his neighbor; render the truth and pronounce the judgment or verdict that makes for peace in [the courts at] your gates.

— Zechariah 8:16

He who breathes out truth shows forth righteousness (uprightness and right standing with God), but a false witness utters deceit.

There are those who speak rashly, like the piercing of a sword, but the tongue of the wise brings healing.

Truthful lips shall be established forever, but a lying tongue is [credited] but for a moment.

— Proverbs 12:17-19

If I [can] speak in the tongues of men and [even] of angels, but have not love (that reasoning, intentional, spiritual devotion such as is inspired by God's love for and in us), I am only a noisy gong or a clanging cymbal.

And if I have prophetic powers (the gift of interpreting the divine will and purpose), and understand all the secret truths and mysteries and possess all knowledge, and if I have [sufficient] faith so that I can remove mountains, but have not love (God's love in me) I am nothing (a useless nobody).

Even if I dole out all that I have [to the poor in providing] food, and if I surrender my body to be burned or in order that I may glory, but have not love (God's love in me), I gain nothing.

— 1 Corinthians 13:1-3

Be glad and supremely joyful, for your reward in heaven is great (strong and intense), for in this same way people persecuted the prophets who were before you.

— Matthew 5:12

Finally, all [of you] should be of one and the same mind [united in spirit], sympathizing [with one another], loving [each other] as brethren [of one household], compassionate and courteous (tenderhearted and humble).

Never return evil for evil or insult for insult (scolding, tongue-lashing, berating), but on the contrary blessing [praying for their welfare, happiness and protection, and truly pitying and loving them]. For know that to this you have been called, that you may yourselves inherit a blessing [from God — that you may obtain a blessing as heirs, bringing welfare and happiness and protection].

For let him who wants to enjoy life and see good days [good — whether apparent or not] keep his tongue free from evil and his lips from guile (treachery, deceit).

— 1 Peter 3:8-10

Those who are fencing me in raise their heads; may the mischief of their own lips and the very things they desire for me come upon them.

— Psalm 140:9

And they will be made to stumble, their own tongues turning against them; all who gaze upon them will shake their heads and flee away.

— Psalm 64:8

But no weapon that is formed against you shall prosper, and every tongue that shall rise against you in judgment you shall show to be in the wrong. This [peace, righteousness, security, triumph over opposition] is the heritage of the servants of the Lord [those in whom the ideal Servant of the Lord is reproduced]; this is the righteousness or the vindication which they obtain from Me [this is that which I impart to them as their justification], says the Lord.

— Isaiah 54:17

By the blessing of the influence of the upright and God's favor [because of them] the city is exalted, but it is overthrown by the mouth of the wicked.

— Proverbs 11:11

Thank [God] in everything [no matter what the circumstances may be, be thankful and give thanks], for this is the will of God for you [who are] in Christ Jesus [the Revealer and Mediator of that will].

— 1 Thessalonians 5:18

Through Him, therefore, let us constantly and at all times offer up to God a sacrifice of praise, which is the fruit of lips that thankfully acknowledge and confess and glorify His name.

— Hebrews 13:15

I will bless the Lord at all times; His praise shall continually be in my mouth.

— Psalm 34:1

[Direct such people] to the teaching and to the testimony! If their teachings are not in accord with this word, it is surely because there is no dawn and no morning for them.

— Isaiah 8:20

Truly I tell you, whoever says to this mountain, Be lifted up and thrown into the sea! and does not doubt at all in his heart but believes that what he says will take place, it will be done for him.

— Mark 11:23

Then Jesus was led (guided) by the [Holy] Spirit into the wilderness (desert) to be tempted (tested and tried) by the devil.

And He went without food for forty days and forty nights, and later He was hungry.

And the tempter came and said to Him, If You are God's Son, command these stones to be made [loaves of] bread.

But He replied, It has been written, Man shall not live and be upheld and sustained by bread alone, but by every word that comes forth from the mouth of God.

Then the devil took Him into the holy city and placed Him on a turret (pinnacle, gable) of the temple sanctuary.

And he said to Him, If You are the Son of God, throw Yourself down; for it is written, He will give His angels charge over you, and they will bear you up on their hands, lest you strike your foot against a stone.

Jesus said to him, On the other hand, it is written also, You shall not tempt, test thoroughly, or try exceedingly the Lord your God.

Again, the devil took Him up on a very high mountain and showed Him all the kingdoms of the world and the glory (the splendor, magnificence, preeminence, and excellence) of them.

And he said to Him, These things, all taken together, I will give You, if You will prostrate Yourself before me and do homage and worship me.

Then Jesus said to him, Begone, Satan! For it has been written, You shall worship the Lord your God, and Him alone shall you serve.

Then the devil departed from Him, and behold, angels came and ministered to Him.

— Matthew 4:1-11

Therefore be imitators of God [copy Him and follow His example], as well-beloved children [imitate their father].

— Ephesians 5:1

Beat your plowshares into swords, and your pruning hooks into spears; let the weak say, I am strong [a warrior]!

—Joel 3:10

Then said the Lord to me, You have seen well, for I am alert and active, watching over My word to perform it.

— Jeremiah 1:12

Forever, O Lord, Your word is settled in heaven [stands firm as the heavens].

— Psalm 119:89

I will worship toward Your holy temple and praise Your name for Your loving-kindness and for Your truth and faithfulness; for You have exalted above all else Your name and Your word and You have magnified Your word above all Your name!

— Psalm 138:2

He is the sole expression of the glory of God [the Light-being, the out-raying or radiance of the divine], and He is the perfect imprint and very image of [God's] nature, upholding and maintaining and guiding and propelling the universe by His mighty word of power. When He had by offering Himself accomplished our cleansing of sins and riddance of guilt, He sat down at the right hand of the divine Majesty on high.

—Hebrews 1:3

By faith we understand that the worlds [during the successive ages] were framed (fashioned, put in order, and equipped for their intended purpose) by the word of God, so that what we see was not made out of things which are visible.

— Hebrews 11:3

In the beginning [before all time] was the Word (Christ), and the Word was with God, and the Word was God Himself.

—John 1:1

And the Word (Christ) became flesh (human, incarnate) and tabernacled (fixed His tent of flesh, lived awhile) among us; and we [actually] saw His glory (His honor, His majesty), such glory as an only begotten son receives from his father, full of grace (favor, loving-kindness) and truth.

—John 1:14

But what does it say? The Word (God's message in Christ) is near you, on your lips and in your heart; that is, the Word (the message, the basis and object) of faith which we preach,

Because if you acknowledge and confess with your lips that Jesus is Lord and in your heart believe (adhere to, trust in, and rely on the truth) that God raised Him from the dead, you will be saved.

For with the heart a person believes (adheres to, trusts in, and relies on Christ) and so is justified (declared righteous, acceptable to God), and with the mouth he confesses (declares openly and speaks out freely his faith) and confirms [his] salvation.

—Romans 10:8-10

And you will know the Truth, and the Truth will set you free.

—John 8:32

For this commandment which I command you this day is not too difficult for you, nor is it far off.

It is not [a secret laid up] in heaven, that you should say, Who shall go up for us to heaven and bring it to us, that we may hear and do it?

Neither is it beyond the sea, that you should say, Who shall go over the sea for us and bring it to us, that we may hear and do it?

But the word is very near you, in your mouth and in your mind and in your heart, so that you can do it.

—Deuteronomy 30:11-14

So be done with every trace of wickedness (depravity, malignity) and all deceit and insincerity (pretense, hypocrisy) and grudges (envy, jealousy) and slander and evil speaking of every kind.

Like newborn babies you should crave (thirst for, earnestly desire) the pure (unadulterated) spiritual milk, that by it you may be nurtured and grow unto [completed] salvation.

— 1 Peter 2:1,2

And now [brethren], I commit you to God [I deposit you in His charge, entrusting you to His protection and care]. And I commend you to the Word of His grace [to the commands and counsels and promises of His unmerited favor]. It is able to build you up and to give you [your rightful] inheritance among all God's set-apart ones (those consecrated, purified, and transformed of soul).

— Acts 20:32

So faith comes by hearing [what is told], and what is heard comes by the preaching [of the message that came from the lips] of Christ (the Messiah Himself).

—Romans 10:17

So shall My word be that goes forth out of My mouth: it shall not return to Me void [without producing any effect, useless], but it shall accomplish that which I please and purpose, and it shall prosper in the thing for which I sent it.

— Isaiah 55:11

And they went out and preached everywhere, while the Lord kept working with them and confirming the message by the attesting signs and miracles that closely accompanied [it]. Amen (so be it).

— Mark 16:20

Yet we have the same spirit of faith as he had who wrote, I have believed, and therefore have I spoken. We too believe, and therefore we speak.

— 2 Corinthians 4:13

And out of the ground the Lord God formed every [wild] beast and living creature of the field and every bird of the air and brought them to Adam to see what he would call them; and whatever Adam called every living creature, that was its name.

— Genesis 2:19

Now therefore go, and I will be with your mouth and will teach you what you shall say.

— Exodus 4:12

[The Lord] Who confirms the word of His servant and performs the counsel of His messengers, Who says of Jerusalem, She shall [again] be inhabited, and of the cities of Judah, They shall [again] be built, and I will raise up their ruins.

— Isaiah 44:26

Do you not believe that I am in the Father, and that the Father is in Me? What I am telling you I do not say on My own authority and of My own accord; but the Father Who lives continually in Me does the (His) works (His own miracles, deeds of power).

— John 14:10

Is not My word like fire [that consumes all that cannot endure the test]? says the Lord, and like a hammer that breaks in pieces the rock [of most stubborn resistance]?

— Jeremiah 23:29

The sky and the earth (that is, the universe, the world) will pass away, but My words will not pass away.

— Luke 21:33

For by your words you will be justified and acquitted, and by your words you will be condemned and sentenced.

— Matthew 12:37

The lips of the [uncompromisingly] righteous feed and guide many, but fools die for want of understanding and heart.

— Proverbs 10:21

This Book of the Law shall not depart out of your mouth, but you shall meditate on it day and night, that you may observe and do according to all that is written in it. For then you shall make your way prosperous, and then you shall deal wisely and have good success.

— Joshua 1:8

Talk no more so very proudly; let not arrogance go forth from your mouth, for the Lord is a God of knowledge, and by Him actions are weighed.

— 1 Samuel 2:3

May the Lord cut off all flattering lips and the tongues that speak proud boasting.

— Psalm 12:3

You have proved my heart; You have visited me in the night; You have tried me and find nothing [no evil purpose in me]; I have purposed that my mouth shall not transgress.

— Psalm 17:3

Keep your tongue from evil and your lips from speaking deceit.

— Psalm 34:13

Make me understand the way of Your precepts; so shall I meditate on and talk of Your wondrous works.

— Psalm 119:27

You are snared with the words of your lips, you are caught by the speech of your mouth.

— Proverbs 6:2

A worthless person, a wicked man, is he who goes about with a perverse (contrary, wayward) mouth.

— Proverbs 6:12

Let all those that seek and require You rejoice and be glad in You; let such as love Your salvation say continually, The Lord be magnified!

— Psalm 40:16

My whole being shall be satisfied as with marrow and fatness; and my mouth shall praise You with joyful lips

When I remember You upon my bed and meditate on You in the night watches.

— Psalm 63:5,6

Right and just lips are the delight of a king, and he loves him who speaks what is right.

— Proverbs 16:13

He who has a wayward and crooked mind finds no good, and he who has a willful and contrary tongue will fall into calamity.

— Proverbs 17:20

He who answers a matter before he hears the facts — it is folly and shame to him.

— Proverbs 18:13

Let another man praise you, and not your own mouth; a stranger, and not your own lips.

— Proverbs 27:2

A [self-confident] fool utters all his anger, but a wise man holds it back and stills it.

— Proverbs 29:11

Do you see a man who is hasty in his words? There is more hope for a [self-confident] fool than for him.

— Proverbs 29:20

To everything there is a season, and a time for every matter or purpose under heaven...

...a time to keep silence and a time to speak.

— Ecclesiastes 3:1,7

For Jerusalem is ruined and Judah is fallen, because their speech and their deeds are against the Lord, to provoke the eyes of His glory and defy His glorious presence.

— Isaiah 3:8

Then you shall call, and the Lord will answer; you shall cry, and He will say, Here I am. If you take away from your midst yokes of oppression [wherever you find them], the finger pointed in scorn [toward the oppressed or the godly], and every form of false, harsh, unjust, and wicked speaking.

— Isaiah 58:9

Let your Yes be simply Yes, and your No be simply No; anything more than that comes from the evil one.

— Matthew 5:37

Now behold, you [Zacharia] will be and will continue to be silent and not able to speak till the day when these things take place, because you have not believed what I told you; but my words are of a kind which will be fulfilled in the appointed and proper time.

— Luke 1:20

Therefore my heart rejoiced and my tongue exulted exceedingly; moreover, my flesh also will dwell in hope [will encamp, pitch its tent, and dwell in hope in anticipation of the resurrection].

— Acts 2:26

Do all things without grumbling and faultfinding and complaining [against God] and questioning and doubting [among yourselves].

— Philippians 2:14

And whatever you do [no matter what it is] in word or deed, do everything in the name of the Lord Jesus and in [dependence upon] His Person, giving praise to God the Father through Him.

— Colossians 3:17

...make it your ambition and definitely endeavor to live quietly and peacefully, to mind your own affairs, and to work with your hands, as we charged you.

—1 Thessalonians 4:11

Therefore encourage (admonish, exhort) one another and edify (strengthen and build up) one another, just as you are doing.

— 1 Thessalonians 5:11

Inasmuch then as we have a great High Priest Who has [already] ascended and passed through the heavens, Jesus the Son of God, let us hold fast our confession [of faith in Him].

— Hebrews 4:14

Understand [this], my beloved brethren. Let every man be quick to hear [a ready listener], slow to speak, slow to take offense and to get angry.

— James 1:19

[My] brethren, do not speak evil about or accuse one another. He that maligns a brother or judges his brother is maligning and criticizing the Law and judging the Law. But if you judge the Law, you are not a practicer of the Law but a censor and judge [of it].

— James 4:11

And they have overcome (conquered) him [the Devil] by means of the blood of the Lamb and by the utterance of their testimony, for they did not love and cling to life even when faced with death [holding their lives cheap till they had to die for their witnessing].

— Revelation 12:11

Prayer for a Personal Relationship with the Lord

God wants you to receive His free gift of salvation. Jesus wants to save you and fill you with the Holy Spirit more than anything. If you have never invited Jesus, the Prince of Peace, to be your Lord and Savior, I invite you to do so now. Pray the following prayer, and if you are really sincere about it, you will experience a new life in Christ.

Father,

You loved the world so much, You gave Your only begotten Son to die for our sins so that whoever believes in Him will not perish, but have eternal life.

Your Word says we are saved by grace through faith as a gift from You. There is nothing we can do to earn salvation.

I believe and confess with my mouth that Jesus Christ is Your Son, the Savior of the world. I believe He died on the cross for me and bore all of my sins, paying the price for them. I believe in my heart that You raised Jesus from the dead.

I ask You to forgive my sins. I confess Jesus as my Lord. According to Your Word, I am saved and will spend eternity with You! Thank You, Father. I am so grateful! In Jesus' name, amen.

See John 3:16; Ephesians 2:8,9; Romans 10:9,10; 1 Corinthians 15:3,4; 1 John 1:9; 4:14-16; 5:1,12,13.

Endnotes

Chapter 1

[1] *Webster's II New College Dictionary* (Boston: Houghton Mifflin Company, 1995), s.v. "wisdom."

[2] Webster's II, s.v. "prudence."

[3] Webster's II, s.v. "prudent."

Chapter 2

[1] W. E. Vine, Merrill F. Unger, William White Jr., "New Testament Section," in *Vine's Complete Expository Dictionary of Old and New Testament Words* (Nashville: Thomas Nelson, Inc., 1984), p. 121, s.v. "CONFIRM, CONFIRMATION, A. Verbs, No. 1, *BEBAIOO*.

[2] Vine, A. Verbs, No. 3, *KUROO*.

[3] Vine, B. Noun, *BEBAIOSIS*.

Chapter 3

[1] James E. Strong, "Hebrew and Chaldee Dictionary," in *Strong's Exhaustive Concordance of the Bible* (Nashville: Abingdon, 1890), p. 32, entry #1897, s.v. "meditate," Josh. 1:8.

[2] Strong, "Hebrew," p. 115, entry #7878, s.v. "meditate," Psalm 119:148.

Chapter 7

[1] Webster's II, s.v. "bridle."

[2] Webster's II, s.v. "bit."

[3] For a more complete discussion of this point, I suggest that you read my book by this title. See the book list in the back of this book.

Chapter 10

[1] Vine, "New Testament Section," p. 580, s.v. "slanderer."

[2] Webster's II, s.v. "slander."

[3] James Strong, "Greek Dictionary of the New Testament," in *The New Strong's Exhaustive Concordance of the Bible* (Nashville: Thomas Nelson, Inc., 1990).

[4] Vine, p. 580, s.v. "SLANDERER."

[5] Vine, p. 50, s.v. "DEVIL."

[6] Strong, "Greek," (Abingdon, 1890), p. 54, entry #3870.

[7] Strong, p. 55, entry #3875.

Chapter 12

[1] *Webster's New World Dictionary of the American Language* (New World Publishing Company, 1969), s.v. "busybody."

[2] Webster's II, s.v. "busybody."

[3] Webster's II, s.v. "gossip."

[4] Vine, "New Testament Section," p. 580, s.v. "slanderer."

[5] Webster's II, s.v. "slander."

[6] Webster's II, s.v. "whisper."

Chapter 13

[1] Webster's II, s.v. "disposition."

[2] Vine, "New Testament Section," pp. 128, 58, 59, s.v. "CONVERSATION," "BEHAVE, BEHAVIOR."

[3] Hannah Hurnard, *Mountains of Spices* (Wheaton: Tyndale House, Inc., 1979).

[4] Hurnard, pp. 222-229.

[5] Hurnard, pp. 168-174.

[6] Hurnard, pp. 136-144.

[7] Madame Jeanne Guyon, *Experiencing the Depths of Jesus Christ* (in France: formerly entitled *Short and Very Easy Method of Prayer*). Copyright © MCMLXXV by Gene Edwards (Gardiner, Maine: Christian Books).

Bibliography

Guyon, Madame Jeanne. *Experiencing the Depths of Jesus Christ* (in France: formerly entitled *Short and Very Easy Method of Prayer*). Copyright © MCMLXXV by Gene Edwards. Gardiner, Maine: Christian Books.

Hurnard, Hannah. *Mountains of Spices*. Wheaton: Tyndale House, Inc., 1979.

Strong, James. *The New Strong's Exhaustive Concordance of the Bible*. Nashville: Thomas Nelson, Inc., 1990.

Strong, James. *Strong's Exhaustive Concordance of the Bible* (Nashville: Abingdon, 1890.

Vine, W. E., Unger, Merrill F., White Jr., William. "New Testament Section." In *Vine's Complete Expository Dictionary of Old and New Testament Words*. Nashville: Thomas Nelson, Inc., 1984.

Webster's New World Dictionary of the American Language. New World Publishing Company, 1969.

Webster's II New College Dictionary. Boston: Houghton Mifflin Company, 1995.

Me and My Big Mouth!
Study Guide

Contents

Introduction

Words are containers for power. They have the power to be either creative or destructive. Every day we have new opportunities to say words that encourage, edify, and give hope. What we say to or about others as well as ourselves can gloriously heal or deeply hurt.

You may not realize that right speaking follows right thinking — thinking thoughts in line with the Word of God.

Our words come directly from our thoughts or mind, a part of our soul. As defined in this study, the soul consists of the mind or intellect, the will, and the emotions or feelings. We who have a personal relationship with Jesus through believing in Him have the mind of Christ, according to 1 Corinthians 2:16. This means that we hold the thoughts, feelings, and purposes of His heart. But when we operate by what *we* feel, think, or want according to the desires of our flesh, or "sinful nature" (Galatians 6:8 NIV), we're not thinking like Jesus thinks, and we say things we shouldn't say.

What we express through our mouths as what we want, think, and feel may not be in agreement with what God wants for us. We can reach the point of feeling that what we say is out of control — we say things for which we are immediately sorry. Even we believers can have a problem taming our tongue when we do not have right thinking. There is a continual struggle between the flesh and spirit. Instead of submitting to the desires of the flesh, with the help of the Holy Spirit we can learn to think God's thoughts. And as we continue to choose to submit to the Holy Spirit, eventually our desires are changed into God's desires, and our speech will begin to reflect God's heart more and more.

It is possible to master the mouth!

If your words are not producing the kinds of results or effects you want or expect and your mouth is giving expression to the wrong mindset, with the help of the Holy Spirit you can learn how to engage in uplifting conversation and purposely order what you say. The mouth can be trained to stop speaking out of the mind, feelings, and fear, but it is a process that requires time and persistence.

As you begin working in this study guide, I believe that the importance of your words will become clear to you, and you will move forward toward gaining control of your mouth. You can be saved from the destructive power of your own words. Learning how to bring your words under control will bring positive results in your life and circumstances. And when that happens, it will bless the lives of everyone around you.

Using This Study Guide

The purpose of this workbook is to reinforce the principles taught in my book, *"Me and My Big Mouth!"* You will need a copy of *"Me and My Big Mouth!"* to work through this book.

This study guide is written in a question and answer format. By reading a chapter in *"Me and My Big Mouth!"*, studying the designated Scripture verses, and answering the questions in the corresponding chapter of the study guide, you will gain a deeper understanding of the principles and learn more easily how to incorporate them into your daily life.

To use this workbook, look up and read the corresponding chapter in *"Me and My Big Mouth!"* Next look up in your Bible the Scriptures designated in the study guide and read them. This is an important step because those Scriptures are the basis of the teaching in that particular chapter and are taken directly from that chapter.

Answer the questions in the study guide by referring to the appropriate chapter in *"Me and My Big Mouth!"* Once you have finished answering the questions in each chapter, turn to the answer key in the back of this book to check your answers.

1. Work at a comfortable pace. Don't rush to finish quickly. Stay in each chapter until you have a thorough understanding of the material and how it pertains to your life.

2. Follow these steps with each chapter in this study guide.

3. Use this study guide for individual study or group discussion. When using it in a group, discuss your answers and learn how to apply the principles in a way that may not have occurred to you until you heard the experiences of others.

Consistently and steadily working through this book will help you gradually transform your mouth into verbalizing God's Word instead of expressing the wrong, negative words of the enemy, Satan. Changing your way of speaking will enable you to change things in your life that you thought you would have to live with forever. As you agree with God through your words, you will begin to experience His best for you.

Make Your Words Work for You

Proverbs 18:21 states, "Death and life are in the power of the tongue, and they who indulge in it shall eat the fruit of it [for death or life]." No subject mentioned in the Bible should be taken more seriously than the mouth. By gaining control of our words, we are making a vital move toward living in God's good plan for our life.

You may be struggling with a mouth that seems to have a mind of its own, but that can change. It is my sincere prayer that this study guide will help you to control the words you speak and make them work for you.

God bless you as you take the first step toward mastering your mouth and becoming a mouthpiece for the Lord.

1. As defined in this study, what does the soul consist of?_____
   _____
   _____.

2. Read 2 Timothy 2:21

   Why can and should the soul be purified and rendered a vessel fit for the Master's use? _____
   _____.

3. a. To what does our mouth give expression? _____
      _____
      _____.

   b. What does our mind tell us? _____
      _____
      _____.

   c. What does our will tell us? _____
      _____
      _____.

d. What do our emotions tell us?_____

_____

_____.

4. What happens as our soul is purified?_____

_____

_____

_____.

5. Read 1 Corinthians 2:16

What does the Word of God teach us in this passage? _____

_____

_____

_____.

6. What makes up what the Bible refers to as "the flesh"? _____

_____

_____.

7. Feelings can be trained to _____

_____,

but this is a process that _____

_____

_____.

8. To what does the mouth give expression? _____

_____

_____

_____

_____.

9. Review Proverbs 18:21

   Complete this Scripture: " _____
   and _____ are in the power of the tongue,
   and they who indulge in it shall _____
   _____
   _____. "

10. Why should we take the subject of the mouth as seriously as any
    subject in the Bible? _____
    _____
    _____
    _____
    _____.

Learning to Speak God's Language

*I*n the original book, "Me and My Big Mouth!", read chapter 1, then read in your Bible the Scriptures designated below, and answer the questions that follow. When you finish, check your answers in the answer key provided at the end of this book.

As you continue to follow this procedure throughout this workbook, you can be assured that you will gain insight through understanding that will help you integrate these godly principles into your daily life and win the battle to master your mouth!

1. Read Mark 11:22,23; Luke 4:1-13

   a. As we see in Mark 11:22,23, what does God's Word instruct us to do when we have mountains in our lives?_____
   _____.

   b. When we speak to the mountains, what are we to hurl at them? Why? _____
   _____
   _____.

   c. When tempted by Satan in the wilderness, according to Luke 4:1-13, how did Jesus answer every trial? _____
   _____
   _____
   _____
   _____.

d. What happens when we "try" this for a while, and then do not see quick results? _____

_____

_____

_____

_____.

e. Persistence is a vital link to victory. We must _____

_____

_____

_____.

2. Read Mark 11:24-26

a. What will happen if a person living in disobedience thinks he can speak God's Word to his mountains and get results?____

_____

_____.

b. There is no power in speaking to a mountain if the heart is full of _____.

c. Into what deception do multitudes of people fall who have accepted Christ as their personal Savior? _____

_____

_____

_____.

d. The central theme of the Bible is _____.

e. For many of us, our life is in a mess due to disobedience. The disobedience may have been the result of ignorance or rebellion, but the only way out of the mess is _____ _____ _____.

3. Read Deuteronomy 28:1,2; 1 Corinthians 1:9,10

  a. As emphasized in these passages, what two things do we often choose to ignore in the Bible? _____ _____.

  b. In 1 Corinthians 1:9 we see that God is faithful. How do we draw upon His faithfulness? _____ _____ _____.

  c. Our disobedience does not change God's faithfulness. But obedience _____ _____ _____ _____.

4. Read 1 Corinthians 3:1

When we receive Jesus as our Savior, we enter into the new life of a believer. In this passage, the Apostle Paul tells us that as "babies in Christ," we simply do not know how to talk yet. Just as natural babies must learn to speak the language of their elders, so Christians must learn _____ _____.

5. Read Hebrews 5:13,14

   a. Although many things are clearly defined in the Word, and it is obvious what God's will is, in order to make decisions about things that are not spelled out in black and white, we need to _____ _____.

   b. It takes _____ to know God, to know our own hearts, and to be able to be totally honest with ourselves and with God.

6. Read James 4:2,3,15,16; 1 Timothy 2:3,4; Proverbs 3:7

   a. _____ is a good example of something in the Word of God that is so clear that we never have to pray, "if it be Thy will."

   b. According to James 4:3, sometimes we ask God for something and yet fail to receive it because _____ _____ _____.

   c. If what we are asking for is not clearly spelled out in the Word, and we are not positive that we have heard from God about the issue, what is a wise and submissive way to pray?_____ _____.

   d. What happens if the difference between faith and confidence, and foolishness and presumption is not discerned? _____ _____ _____.

e. We do not know anything at all, at least not compared to what God knows. We must resist the temptation to play "Holy Ghost, Jr." Instead, we must _____
_____.

7. Read Proverbs 13:16; 1 Peter 5:8; Proverbs 1:1-4

a. _____ are actually the devil's playground.

b. If the devil cannot get a believer to totally ignore a truth and live in deception, his next tactic will be _____
_____
_____
_____
_____.

c. _____ is a central theme of God's Word.

d. *Webster's II New College Dictionary* defines "wisdom" as _____
_____
_____
_____.

e. Wisdom does not operate in extremes. Proverbs 1:1-4 says that wisdom is full of _____, and
_____
_____.

f. Webster's defines "prudent," the adjective form of prudence, as _____
_____
_____.

g. What might we say that "wisdom" is? _____
_____
_____.

h. The statement that "you can have what you say" means you can have what you say *if* what you say _____
_____
_____
_____.

i. What happens when you learn to cooperate with the Holy Spirit?_____
_____
_____.

The Effect of Words in the Natural Realm

A s with the previous chapter, before answering the questions below, first read the corresponding chapter in "Me and My Big Mouth!" then the Scriptures designated below. After you complete the chapter, check the answer key in the back of this book.

To gain the greatest benefit from this workbook, continue using this method throughout.

1. Read Romans 10:9,10

   a. In this passage, the Apostle Paul sets forth a spiritual truth applied to salvation, a truth that may be applied to other issues as well. What two things does the confession of a person's belief confirm? _____
   _____
   _____.

   b. What does a believer's confession declare? _____
   _____
   _____.

   c. How did the late biblical scholar W. E. Vine define two of the Greek words translated "confirm" in the *King James Version?*
   _____
   _____
   _____
   _____
   _____.

    d. How did W. E. Vine define the Greek word translated "confirmation"?_____.

    e. Based on these definitions, what does confession do for salvation?_____.

2. Read Psalm 2:7

    a. What is God's formal decree? _____.

    b. What happens when a believer declares the Word out of his own mouth, with a heart full of faith? _____.

    c. When the Royal Decree is pronounced_____!

3. Read Psalm 139:13-16; Jeremiah 29:11; review Romans 10:9,10

    a. According to the passage in Psalm 139, God's plan for our lives _____.

    b. According to Jeremiah 29:11, what kind of thoughts does God have toward us? What is their purpose? _____.

c. God has written down His will, His Word, for our lives. What happens as we believe it and speak it out loud for our lives?

_____

_____.

d. The reason some people see very little manifestation of the things they are believing for may be because they are believing but not speaking. Based on the passage in Romans 10:9,10, they would experience radical results if they would

_____

_____.

e. Some people are trying to live in the blessings of God while still _____.

f. What happens if we speak negative things? _____

_____.

g. We should remember that what we are speaking, we are

_____

_____

_____.

h. With our words, what can we draw out of Satan's realm?

_____.

i. What can we draw out of God's realm with our words?

_____.

4. Read Hebrews 1:3; 11:3; Genesis 1:26,27

a. These passages in the book of Hebrews tell us that the universe was created and upheld by_____

_____.

    b. How does that fact relate to us? _____

        _____

        _____

        _____.

5.   Read Ephesians 5:1; Romans 4:17

      As imitators of God, how are we to follow His example? _____

      _____

      _____

      _____.

6.   Read 1 Corinthians 9:19-22; 1 Corinthians 11:1;
      Galatians 5:22,23; 1 Corinthians 13:5; Galatians 5:6;
      1 Corinthians 2:14; Colossians 4:5,6

    a. In the passage in 1 Corinthians 9:19-22, the Apostle Paul said
        that he met people where they were in order to _____

        _____.

    b. According to 1 Corinthians 11:1, Paul told believers to imi-
        tate him. That is especially important when dealing with
        "those without"_____

        _____.

    c. In our conversations with others, we need to show them the
        fruit of the Spirit — especially _____

        _____ which

        Paul tells us_____

        _____.

    d. How does faith work? _____.

e. The truth is that Jesus is our Healer, and truth is more powerful than _____.

f. How can we be imitators of God in calling "those things which be not as though they were" (Romans 4:17 KJV), and yet not be offensive to people who may not understand?

_____

_____

_____

_____

_____

_____

_____

g. In the passage in 1 Corinthians 2:14, we are told that the natural man does not accept the teachings and revelations of the Spirit "because they are _____ discerned."

h. In Colossians 4:5,6 Paul was saying to the believers of his day, and to us: "Be careful how you talk to those who are not on your level spiritually. Use _____ and _____. Be led by _____ _____."

Chapter 3

Calling Those Things That Are Not As Though They Are

1. Review Romans 4:17 KJV

   a. What is one of the greatest privileges we have as God's children? _____
   _____
   _____
   _____.

   b. This practice in Romans 4:17 KJV can work against us if we are calling for things that are not God's will but the enemy's (Satan). Some people fear what has not yet taken place, and by their negative faith they are _____
   _____.

2. Read Psalm 116:10; Joshua 1:8; Psalm 119:148; 1:2

   a. What is it called when we confess the truth of God's Word?
   _____.

   b. Can we confess things that we cannot find chapter and verse for? _____
   _____
   _____
   _____.

   c. In the passage in Joshua 1:8, God instructed Joshua to meditate on His Word "day and night." Part of meditation is ____
   _____.

d. What does confessing the Word of God do? _____

_____

_____.

3. Read Genesis 15:1-6; 17:5,15,16

a. Why did God change the names of Abram and Sarai? _____

_____

_____.

b. What happened each time their new names were called? ___

_____

_____

_____

_____.

c. Each time their new names were called, *words* were being
spoken into the atmosphere that were _____

_____

_____.

d. Those words were beginning to_____

_____.

Now the words on the earth were_____

_____

_____.

4. Review Genesis 15:1-6; read Romans 4:18-21; Amos 3:3

a. What did Abram do when God told him he would have a son
of his own through whom he would become the father of
many nations?_____.

b. Like Abraham (or Abram), we will never receive a miracle unless_____

_____

_____.

c. Not only did Abraham and Sarah believe God, but the words of their mouths were being used_____

_____.

d. What does speaking in agreement with God's Word, His written Word, or a specific word He has given us, do? _____

_____

_____.

e. We cannot walk with God concerning His plan for our lives unless_____

_____.

5. Read Deuteronomy 30:19; Matthew 12:34

a. In light of the passage in Deuteronomy 30:19 that says to "choose life," in order to carry God's dreams for our lives, and the lives of others, we must be willing or choose to "conceive." In other words, we must be willing _____

_____

_____.

b. Why is believing the first important step to carrying out God's dream for our lives and the lives of others? _____

_____

_____.

c. To what do our mouths give expression? _____
   _____.

d. What do we draw to ourselves? _____
   _____.

e. If we keep our soul and mouth full of doubt, unbelief, fear,
   and every negative thing, what will happen? _____
   _____.

f. If we keep our soul and mouth full of God and His Word and
   plan, what will happen?_____
   _____.

g. Whose choice is it about what will be drawn to us? _____
   _____.

Prophesy Your Future

1. Read James 3:2; Matthew 12:37

    a. According to James 3:2, when does someone become ". . . a
        fully developed character and a perfect man. . . ."?_____

        _____

        _____

        _____.

    b. In Matthew 12:37, what did Jesus warn us about words?___

        _____

        _____

        _____

        _____

        _____.

2. Read James 3:4-8; John 8:44; Matthew 17:20

    a. According to James 3:4-8, can man tame the tongue?_____

        _____.

    b. Describe an undisciplined tongue. _____

        _____

        _____.

    c. What do we need to control our tongues? _____

        _____

        _____.

d. What else must we do to control our tongues? _____

_____

_____

_____.

e. You change things in your life by _____

_____

_____.

f. Can we curse our future? _____. If so, how? _____

_____.

Can we bless it? _____. If so, how? _____

_____.

g. When we curse our future with our words, when we agree with the devil instead of with God, we are *deceived*. What is deception? _____

_____.

h. Satan is called the deceiver because, as Jesus said in John 8:44, ". . . he is a_____

_____."

i. How does Satan try to deceive us? _____

_____

_____

_____.

3. Read Isaiah 65:16-18 KJV; 43:18,19

a. What twofold principle can be carried into every area in which we desire victory? _____

_____
_____
_____
_____.

b. How can we release the plan of God for our lives? _____
_____
_____
_____
_____.

c. If we stop mentally living in the past, we can _____
_____.

Once we do that, we can _____
_____. By so doing we can
_____.

4. Read Matthew 12:36; review Proverbs 18:21

a. Why did Jesus teach that men will one day have to give an account for their words? _____
_____
_____.

b. What does Proverbs 18:21 state about the tongue?_____
_____
_____.

c. The careless words we speak in the heat of the moment may not mean much to us, but they definitely _____
_____.

5. Read John 6:63

   a. To whom should you first prophesy your future? _____
      _____.

   b. What should you speak out? _____
      _____
      _____
      _____
      _____.

6. Read Matthew 26:41

   a. Sometimes we are guilty of getting spiritually lazy and "putting up with the enemy's junk." In this passage of Scripture, Jesus' admonition to His disciples, "Watch and pray," should first be applied to our own lives. What must we do when Satan comes against us? _____
      _____.

   b. Come against Satan when he is trying to get a foothold, and
      _____.

7. Read Revelation 19:11-15; Hebrews 4:12; 2 Corinthians 10:4

   a. Mixing _____ and _____
      does not equal power in God's economy.

   b. What is the sharp sword coming forth from the mouth of Jesus as depicted in Revelation 9:11-15? _____
      _____.

    c. Where does the Word of God operate?_____

    _____.

    d. The Word of God is a spiritual (unseen) weapon that _____

    _____.

8. Read Isaiah 46:9,10; Romans 8:37; Revelation 1:8

    a. In light of Romans 8:37 that says "we are more than conquerors," we can know before the battle ever begins that

    _____.

    b. Prophesying our future is literally_____

    _____

    _____.

9. Read Isaiah 48:3

    a. What is the basic principle of God's method of operation?

    _____

    _____.

    b. God operates on _____ that He has set in place, and we_____.

    c. How does the spiritual law of sowing and reaping apply to our words? _____

    _____

    _____.

10. Read Isaiah 48:5-7

    a. In this passage, the Lord said that the things He desired to do were called into being by the prophetic word. That is what we are to do, to_____

_____

_____.

b. How can you prophesy without "standing in the office of prophet"? _____

_____

_____.

11. Read Isaiah 42:9; John 14:6; 12:26

a. If you are tired of the old things and want some new things in your life, what should you do? _____

_____

_____.

b. How can you avoid being the devil's mouthpiece? _____

_____

_____

_____.

c. How can you follow Jesus' example, and what will be the result? _____

_____

_____

_____.

Becoming God's Mouthpiece

1. Read Isaiah 55:11

   a. The prophets were a _____
   for God. They spoke His Word to whatever God told them to
   speak to, and like this passage says, His Word accomplished
   what He pleased and purposed wherever He sent it.

   b. Those who desire to be used by God need to allow Him to
   deal with them concerning _____
   _____.

2. Read Romans 12:6,7

   a. If you are a teacher of God's Word in any degree, remember:
   _____
   _____.

   b. If we desire the words of our mouth to carry God's power,
   then _____
   _____.

3. Read James 3:1,2; 1 Timothy 3:2

   a. In light of the passage in James chapter 3, it appears that God
   has a stricter guideline for those who are teachers of the
   Word. They are to follow Christ themselves and to show
   others_____
   _____.

   b. The Apostle Paul wrote that spiritual leaders are to be self-controlled. What is one of the areas in which they are to exercise

this fruit of the Spirit? _____

_____.

c. Those trained to be God's mouthpiece will frequently be used
to bring _____

and _____ to others.

4. Read Proverbs 15:23; 25:11; Isaiah 50:4

a. According to Isaiah 50:4, why did the Lord God give the
prophet a tongue of a disciple and of one who is taught?____

_____

_____.

b. These passages of Scripture are actually saying that we can
bless people with _____

_____. We can

_____

_____.

c. If you have children, when they are hurting, what should you
remember to speak to them? _____

_____

_____.

5. Read 1 Thessalonians 5:11; Romans 12:8; John 14:26

a. According to 1 Thessalonians 5:11, what are we to do for one
another? _____

_____

_____.

b. What gift is spoken of in Romans 12:8? What is it? _____

_____

_____

_____.

c. In John 14:26, the Holy Spirit is called the _____. In this capacity, He _____

_____

_____

_____

_____.

d. You and I need to see and realize that exhortation is _____

_____ — _____.

e. As an exhorter, we can actually prevent someone from ____

_____!

f. How is the ministry of an exhorter compared to the ministry of the Holy Spirit as a "Comforter"? _____

_____

_____

_____

_____

_____

_____.

g. What were the early Christians instructed to do by the Apostle Paul in 1 Thessalonians 5:11? _____

_____.

h. Even if our ministry gift is not exhortation, we need to learn the importance of it and always try to remember that _____

_____

_____.

6. Read Ephesians 4:29; Romans 12:3; Isaiah 6:5

a. According to Ephesians 4:29, what kind of words are supposed to come out of our mouths? _____

_____

_____

_____

_____

_____.

b. How did the Apostle Paul correct people? _____

_____

_____.

c. People who only want to correct but never edify, build up, exhort, or comfort are _____

_____.

d. God desires to touch more people's _____ and have them for His own _____

_____.

e. You are urged to allow God to deal with you in these very important areas, and like Isaiah, realize that _____

_____

_____.

Complain and Remain,
Praise and Be Raised

1. Read John 6:43 KJV; review Ephesians 4:29; read Romans 12:21

    a. What is complaining? What's wrong with it?_____

    _____

    _____

    _____

    _____.

    b. What else does complaining do?_____

    _____.

    c. Words are containers of _____.

    d. Why are complaining, grumbling words said to carry destructive power? _____

    _____

    _____

    _____.

    e. What does God think of murmuring and complaining? Why?

    _____

    _____

    _____.

    f. Why should we praise God rather than complain about what is going on right now?_____

    _____

    _____

    _____

    _____.

g. The best way to start every day is with_____
_____ and_____.

h. Why do truly thankful people not complain? _____
_____
_____
_____
_____.

i. The world is full of two forces: _____
and _____.

The Bible teaches us that _____ overcomes
_____
_____.

j. If we find ourselves faced with a negative (evil) situation, we
can _____
_____.

k. Praise and thanksgiving are _____;
complaining and grumbling are _____.

2. Read Proverbs 14:30; 15:4

a. How can words affect the physical body?_____
_____
_____.

b. The tongue has _____.

    c. What effect does "willful contrariness," such as envy, jealousy, and wrath, have on the physical body? _____

        _____.

    d. Praise and thanksgiving release_____

        _____ and _____.

3.   Read 1 Corinthians 10:9-11

    a. When we complain, how does God react? Why? _____

        _____

        _____

        _____

        _____

        _____.

    b. When we murmur, gripe, and complain, we are _____

        _____

        _____.

    c. Why was the Israelites' exploitation of God's goodness recorded in the Old Testament and recounted in the New Testament? How should it affect us?_____

        _____

        _____

        _____

        _____.

4.   Read Proverbs 21:23; 13:3; Deuteronomy 1:2; Hebrews 13:15 KJV

    a. These Scriptures verify that the person who _____

        _____

but the person who _____
_____.

b. How were the wilderness experiences of the Israelites different from the wilderness experience of Jesus?_____
_____
_____
_____
_____
_____
_____
_____.

c. What lesson should we learn from these experiences? _____
_____
_____
_____
_____
_____.

d. We can _____,
or _____.

5. Read Philippians 4:6

a. What is the antidote for the poison of complaining? _____
_____.

b. Complaining _____,
whereas thanksgiving_____
_____.

c. Being thankful shows maturity. It demonstrates that we are

_____

_____

_____.

d. How can being thankful also be a sacrifice?_____

_____

_____

_____

_____

_____

_____.

6. Read Psalm 50:14; 107:21,22; 116:17

a. In Psalm 116:17 when did the psalmist say that he would call
    on the name of the Lord?_____

    _____

    _____.

b. What kind of power is complaining filled with? _____

    _____.

7. Read Hebrews 13:15; Philippians 2:14; 1 Thessalonians 5:18;
    Ephesians 5:20

a. According to Hebrews 13:15, when are we to offer up to God
    a sacrifice of praise? _____

    _____.

b. The flesh looks for _____
_____, but the spirit searches for
_____.

c. From the Scriptures listed to read above, we see that not only are we to avoid grumbling, faultfinding, complaining, questioning, and doubting, we are also to give thanks _____
_____, _____,
and _____.

d. We do not have to thank God _____ all the negative things in our life, but we are to give Him thanks _____ them.

e. The praising life is the _____ life!

8. Read Ephesians 4:29-31

a. To what is grieving the Holy Spirit connected? _____
_____.

b. Based on this passage, what does speaking evil include? ___
_____
_____
_____.

9. Read Ephesians 5:4

a. What Paul is telling us in this Scripture is, "Instead of vexing, offending, and saddening the Holy Spirit, _____
_____."

b. The _____, _____,

_____

spirit absolutely must be eradicated from the Church.

c. _____

only keep us right where we are; they prevent us from going

forward with God.

d. _____are like weeds;

if left unattended, they _____.

e. People with a critical spirit are _____

to their problems.

f. Complaining is like _____

_____. When we complain,

we are calling for _____

_____.

g. A critical spirit often is rooted in _____.

h. How do we stop complaining about what we do not have?

_____

_____

_____

_____.

i. We all have strengths and weaknesses, so if we are to have

good relationships with one another, we must_____

_____

_____.

10. Read 2 Timothy 3:1,2

    a. Just as Paul predicted long ago in this passage of Scripture, we live in an _____ and _____ generation.

    b. The more others around us complain, the more we should

    _____.

11. Read Philippians 2:14,15; 2 Corinthians 3:2 KJV

    a. We should avoid complaining because it is _____

    _____.

    b. According to 2 Corinthians 3:2 KJV, we are to be_____

    _____.

    c. We don't need to show the world religion; we need to show them Jesus. How do we do that?_____

    _____.

    d. Why are we commanded to be different from the world?

    _____

    _____.

12. Read Philippians 4:4-6 TLB

    a. You and I need to make it a daily challenge not to _____ _____ or _____ _____ with anything. What does that mean? _____

    _____.

b. When there is an attitude adjustment, then _____

_____ .

c. Be generous in your gratitude, and it will _____

_____ .

13. Read Psalm 133:1

The devil wants us to have strife, arguing, upsets, etc. in our relationships. If he can get us to be negative, he can _____

_____ .

14. Read Philippians 4:12; Zechariah 4:10

a. As we see in these passages, we can learn how not to_____
_____ during the kind of hard times
that come to all of us, especially _____

_____ .

b. We will never be "promoted" to better things if we do not

_____ .

c. Complaining is sowing seeds also, but seeds that will produce

_____ .

Sowing seeds of being thankful *in* — not *for* — the situation
we face will produce_____

_____ .

15. Read Hebrews 6:15; 1 Kings 18:44,45

a. According to Hebrews 6:15, what was Isaac?_____

_____ .

b. In the passage in 1 Kings 18, what was the small cloud that Elijah saw? _____
_____.

16. Review Zechariah 4:10; read Hebrews 13:5; 12:2; Philippians 1:6; Hebrews 3:6

a. When we are believing God for something and we find evidence of a small beginning — a little seed, a cloud the size of a man's hand — why should we rejoice over our seed even though it is little? _____.

b. How do we curse that seed? _____
_____.

c. How do we plant that seed?_____
_____.

d. If we don't take care of the seed God gives us, we lose it. If we lose the seed,_____
_____.

e. Part of Hebrews 13:5 says, in essence, _____
_____.

f. How can we be content during the small beginning? Why?
_____
_____
_____
_____
_____
_____.

Cross Over to the Other Side

1. Read John 14:30; Isaiah 53:7

   a. When is one of the most difficult times for us to discipline our minds, mouths, moods, and attitudes? _____

   _____.

   b. We all experience the storms of life in varying degrees, we all have our faith tested and tried, and we all must learn how to

   _____.

   c. According to these passages, what did Jesus do when He was experiencing the most intense pressure? Why? _____

   _____

   _____

   _____

   _____

   _____.

   d. When faced with trying situations, what did Jesus purposely decide and declare He was going to do?_____

   _____.

   e. Instead of speaking out of upset emotions or wounded feelings during times of stress, it is always best to _____

   _____.

2. Read Mark 4:35

   When Jesus says to us, "Let's do a new thing," or, "Let's go over to the other side," or any variety of phrases He uses, He is communicating to us that_____

_____.

3. Read Mark 4:37,38; review Romans 8:37

    a. When God calls us to launch out to a new thing like He did
        to the disciples in Mark chapter 4, we leave the security of
        where we are and start out for the blessings of the other side.
        But it is often in _____

        _____.

    b. The middle is often a _____

        _____.

    c. Have you ever had times when you were in a storm and you
        prayed, you spent time with the Lord, you searched for an
        answer, but it seemed as though Jesus was asleep; the storm
        raged on and you didn't know what to do about it? We some-
        times refer to those seasons as_____

        _____ or _____

        _____.

    d. It is at times like this that we must_____

        _____.

    e. It is also at such times when we discover_____

        _____.

    f. Faith, like muscle, is strengthened by_____

        _____, not by _____.

    g. Each storm we go through_____

        _____.

h. According to Romans 8:37, ". . . we are more than conquerors. . . ." That means that we _____

_____.

i. Faith is for those times when we don't have the _____

_____ yet. Faith is for the_____.

4. Read Mark 4:39,40

a. In this passage, Jesus _____ the storm, but He _____ the disciples for their lack of faith.

b. It is vital to our future that we _____

_____

_____.

c. One of the things about us that has to change is our response to the storms of life. It is certain that we must _____

_____

_____.

5. Read Hebrews 10:23

a. According to Hebrews 10:23 KJV, it is time for us to _____

_____,and ride out the storms, knowing that _____

_____

_____.

b. God is faithful, and we can hold to His hand during the storm, knowing that_____

_____.

6. Read James 3:10,11

   a. In light of this passage of Scripture, we should strive to elimi-nate "double talk." What is "double talk"? _____

   _____

   _____.

   b. _____ of the tongue should be our goal.
   It is a sign of _____.
   It is one way we _____ God.

7. Read James 1:26

   a. According to this verse, we can do all types of good works, but if we do not bridle the tongue, they are all _____

   _____.

   b. How does Webster's define the word "bridle"? _____

   _____

   _____

   _____

   _____.

   c. What may happen if we don't bridle the tongue in the midst of the storms of life?_____

   _____.

   d. Who will be our bridle?_____

   _____

   _____.

8. Read James 3:3-5

   a. What do these Scriptures indicate about the tongue? What might one say about our words? _____
   _____
   _____
   _____.

   b. How does Webster's define the word "bit"? _____
   _____
   _____
   _____.

   c. We need a bit in our mouths, but it will not be forced on us; we must choose it. How will the Holy Spirit function as the bit if we choose His leadership? _____
   _____
   _____
   _____.

9. Read Psalm 32:9

   a. Our relationship with the Holy Spirit is the same as a horse being controlled by the pull of the bridle, which controls the bit in his mouth. The Holy Spirit is our _____.
   If we follow His promptings, what results will we get?_____
   _____
   _____.

   b. What will happen if we don't follow Him?_____
   _____.

10. Read 2 Corinthians 10:5; Romans 12:1,2; Philippians 4:8; Psalm 19:14

a. What is the root source of our words? _____
_____.

b. According to 2 Corinthians 10:5 KJV, what is the remedy for the problem of wrong thinking? _____
_____
_____
_____
_____.

c. In light of Romans 12:1,2, what must happen to the mind in order to ever experience God's good plan?_____
_____.

d. Satan wants to control our mind. The Holy Spirit also wants to control our mind, but He never forces Himself on us. Who decides which one will get control? _____
_____.

e. According to Philippians 4:8, what things are we to think on?
_____
_____
_____
_____
_____.

f. In Psalm 19:14, why did the psalmist mention both the mind and the mouth? _____
_____.

11. Read Psalm 119:1; Deuteronomy 26:14; Mark 4:17; John 16:33

   a. In light of Psalm 119:1, we must order our conversation in accordance with_____.

   b. How should you see yourself and your circumstances in a time of trial? _____
   _____.

   c. Many people backslide during challenging times, and part of the reason they do so is because _____
   _____.

   d. It is harder to be obedient to the Lord during _____
   _____.

   e. Satan does not want you to get to the other side. He does not want you to make any progress at all. He wants to see you
   _____
   _____.

   f. According to Mark 4:17, what happens to people who have no root in themselves? _____
   _____
   _____
   _____
   _____
   _____.

   g. According to John 16:33, what has Jesus done for us? _____
   _____.

12. Read Ezekiel 37:1-10

   a. As we see in this passage, God can totally revive and bring breath and spirit back into what was once only dead, dry bones. He can do the same for us, but not unless _____

   _____.

   b. We can no longer speak with _____

   _____and under pressure allow

   _____.

13. Read John 11:1-44

   a. In light of this passage, if Jesus can raise a dead man, surely He can raise a_____.

   b. We can see from the account of Lazarus in this passage that no matter how bad things seem, _____

   _____.

14. Read Mark 5:25-34

   a. What did the woman with the issue of blood do to receive her healing? _____.

   b. How was her faith released? _____

   _____.

   c. What is one way we activate our faith? _____

   _____.

   d. What should we do until we receive what we're believing for?

   _____.

15. Read Zechariah 9:12

   a. What does this verse mean when it refers to us as "prisoners of hope"? What is hope? _____
   _____
   _____
   _____
   _____.

   b. God is still God, and this Scripture tells us that if we will remain positive and be "prisoners of hope," He will _____
   _____
   _____.

16. Read Psalm 141:3; 17:3; 19:14

   a. Why do we need to pray Psalm 141:3, "Set a guard, O Lord, before my mouth; keep watch at the door of my lips," continually? _____
   _____
   _____.

   b. When we are crossing over to the other side and suddenly find ourselves in the middle of the journey with the storm raging, we will definitely have to _____
   _____.

   c. In light of Psalm 19:14, why should we pray the Word of God? _____
   _____
   _____
   _____.

d. What will be the result if you are sincere in your desire to gain victory in this area and seek God for His help? _____
_____
_____.

e. All those who follow God-ordained guidelines get _____
_____.

Is Your Mouth Saved?

1. Read Philippians 2:12; Ephesians 2:8,9

    a. It is not enough to be saved; the _____ must be saved also.

    b. That is part of the process which the Apostle Paul referred to in Philippians 2:12 as _____ _____ one's own salvation.

    c. God has freely given us salvation through His Son Jesus. Although it cannot be earned, it must be "worked out." This process is just another phase of our walk with the Lord. We might say that He _____
    _____
    _____
    _____
    _____
    _____.

2. Read Galatians 3:16 KJV

    a. How does the Bible refer to Jesus Christ in this verse? _____
    _____.

    b. That means that if we have a seed we can have a _____
    _____.

    c. Jesus is the Seed of _____
    _____.

d. Who plants this Seed in us? What must be done to it?_____
_____
_____.

e. What must be done to the ground that it is planted in? ____
_____
_____.

f. What is the ground in which this seed is planted? _____
_____.

g. How do we do the work of tending the seed? _____
_____
_____
_____.

h. What would happen if any of us would go back in our thinking to the beginning of our walk with God and take an inventory of all the things He has changed in us since then? ____
_____
_____
_____.

i. When God says, "It is time for your mouth to be saved," it is not just a little teaching from the Holy Spirit on the importance of words, but_____
_____.

3. Read Proverbs 8:6-8

This passage reveals the right way to use our mouth.

What did God have to do with three men (Jeremiah, Moses, and Isaiah) in the Bible who were called but who had a mouth problem? _____

_____

_____.

4. Read Jeremiah 1:4-10; John 8:28; 12:50

a. God had called Jeremiah as a "prophet to the nations," but why did He have to straighten out Jeremiah's mouth before He could use Him? _____

_____

_____.

b. Is this any different with us? _____.

c. We need to say about ourselves_____

_____.

d. What did Jesus say about His speech? _____

_____

_____

_____

_____

_____.

e. God wants us to speak, not out of the _____,
   but out of the_____.

5. Read Jeremiah 5:14

a. In this passage, God told Jeremiah that He would make His Word like fire in his mouth. In the past, Jeremiah may have been talking the way we talk now, but God was calling him up higher, to a new level. God is calling us in the same way, but on every new level of God's power and blessings we experience _____

_____.

b. We must realize that wrong words can _____

_____.

c. In order to have God's power, His anointing, released through our life, we cannot _____

_____

_____

_____.

d. What usually happens when we ask God for something? _____

_____

_____

_____.

e. Don't grieve over what has to go; _____

_____.

6. Read Exodus 4:10-12

a. When God called Moses to be His spokesman to Pharaoh and the Israelites, what did Moses claim? _____

_____

_____.

b. We think sometimes that God does not know about all of our weaknesses — but _____.

     c. In Exodus 4:12 God answered Moses' doubt about his ability to speak to Pharaoh by telling him, _____

_____

_____

_____.

     d. The next time God tells you to speak for Him, and fear rises up within you, what should you do? _____

_____

_____.

7. Read Isaiah 6:1-9; 2 Timothy 2:21

     a. According to this passage, what does God need to do before He can use us? _____

_____.

     b. This Scripture passage teaches us that when we come into the presence of God,_____

_____.

     c. We all would prefer miracle deliverance from our "mouth problem," but often, the Lord has to _____

_____.

     d. Although Isaiah had an unclean mouth that was sinful and needed to be dealt with, what quality did he have that prompted God to choose him as His prophet?_____

_____

_____

_____.

e. What principle about what God is looking for when He calls us is set forth in these verses? _____

_____

_____

_____

_____

_____

_____.

f. God uses people who have flaws. He uses cracked pots! We come to Him as we are, and He_____

_____.

g. The _____, the _____, and the _____ are sometimes separate, even occurring in_____.

8. Read 1 Corinthians 3:11

a. In light of this passage, if you want to build the Kingdom of God, you must take time to_____

_____.

b. What is one of the first steps in laying that foundation? _____

_____.

9. Read John 8:32

a. What did Jeremiah, Moses, and Isaiah all realize that God had to change if they were to fulfill their divine call? _____

_____.

    b. God will heal our mouths, but what must we do first?_____

_____

_____.

    c. Jesus said that it is the truth that sets us free. The truth is that we need to say to the Lord, _____

_____.

Fasting Includes Your Mouth

1. Read Isaiah 58:1-14

    Isaiah chapter 58 is a powerful portion of God's Word. What does it teach us? _____

    _____.

2. Review Isaiah 58:5

    a. True fasting is supposed to be for what purpose? What is it meant to be? _____

    _____

    _____

    _____

    _____

    _____.

    b. Are all people led to fast the same way? _____

    _____

    _____.

3. Review Isaiah 58:6

    a. According to this verse, what is the fast that God has chosen?

    _____

    _____

    _____.

    b. In order to set others free, what are we not supposed to do?

    _____

    _____.

    c. What do we need to do in order to break the yokes of bondage in our lives and the lives of those around us? Why?

_____

_____

_____.

4. Review Isaiah 58:7

    a. According to this verse, what else is part of the fast that God has chosen? _____

_____

_____

_____

_____

_____.

    b. Whose needs are we to meet? _____

_____

_____

_____.

5. Review Isaiah 58:8

In this chapter of Isaiah, there are many promises of peace and prosperity for us as God's people. What are they all dependent upon?

_____

_____.

6. Review Isaiah 58:9; read 2 Corinthians 5:20

    a. According to Isaiah 58:9, what things has God told us to do?

_____

_____

_____

_____

_____

_____.

b. In light of this passage in Isaiah 58, if our prayers are not being answered, it may well be because _____

_____

_____.

c. One of the things He has told us to do is to_____

_____

_____.

d. Another one of the things we are to do is to stop speaking

_____, _____,

_____, and _____.

e. The *King James Version* of verse 9 translates the last phrase in that verse as "speaking vanity." What is vain speech? _____

_____

_____.

f. Being physically or mentally exhausted can be a sign of what?

_____.

g. In light of 2 Corinthians 5:20, as royal ambassadors, what are we required and expected to do?_____

_____

_____.

7. Review Isaiah 58:10-12

    a. When can you and I expect all the blessings of the Lord mentioned in this passage to come upon us and overtake us?

    _____

    _____

    _____.

    b. We must stop expecting God to pour out blessings on us while we _____

    _____.

8. Review Isaiah 58:11,13,14; read 2 Corinthians 2:14,15; Psalm 139:4; 19:14

    a. Basically, what is the Lord saying to us in Isaiah 58:13,14?

    _____

    _____

    _____

    _____

    _____

    _____

    _____

    _____.

    b. If you and I really want the blessing of God to be upon our lives, we have got to use our mouths _____

    _____

    _____.

c. We don't need to preach to people nearly as much as we need
   to _____
   _____.

d. We don't need to "stir up a stink"; we need to_____
   _____
   _____.

e. How do we avoid being "stinky"? _____
   _____
   _____
   _____
   _____.

f. According to Psalm 139:4, Who knows every word that is still
   unuttered on our lips? _____.

g. That's why our prayer needs to be that of the psalmist, ____
   _____
   _____
   _____
   _____.

Chapter
10

The Slanderous Mouth

1. Review Proverbs 18:21

   a. What does Proverbs 18:21 mean? _____

   _____

   _____

   _____

   _____

   _____.

   b. With this power we have the capacity for great_____

   _____ or great _____,

   for great _____ or great_____.

   c. What can we use this power to create?_____

   _____

   _____

   _____.

   d. How do we use this power?_____

   _____

   _____

   _____

   _____.

   e. Who chooses how this power will be used?_____

   _____

   _____.

2. Read Galatians 6:7,8 KJV; review Proverbs 18:21; read
    Ecclesiastes 5:1-7 TLB

    a. What spiritual principle from Galatians 6:7,8 KJV is recalled
        by the second part of Proverbs 18:21? _____
        _____
        _____.

    b. Where is the power to do something about your future locat-
        ed? _____
        _____.

    c. If there is any place in our life that we need to exercise disci-
        pline and self-control, it is in _____.

    d. What does the Bible say about talking too much?_____
        _____
        _____.

    e. What happens when we talk too much? Why? _____
        _____
        _____
        _____
        _____.

3. Review Isaiah 50:4; read James 1:19; Nehemiah 8:10

    a. In light of Isaiah 50:4, what do we need to train ourselves to
        do? _____
        _____.

  b. What does James instruct us to do in James 1:19?_____

   _____

   _____.

  c. What do you think would happen if we thought about what
   we were going to say before we said it? _____

   _____.

  d. Why did the prophet say that the Lord had given him the
   tongue of a disciple — a learner, one who is taught? _____

   _____

   _____.

  e. According to the Bible, what is our strength? _____

   _____.

  f. Where are you and I as believers learning to find our joy? ____

   _____.

  g. While we are in the process of learning, what will keep us
   from growing weary? _____

   _____.

4. Read James 3:8-10 KJV; 1 Timothy 3:11 KJV

  a. What disturbs God about our mouth? _____

   _____

   _____

   _____

   _____.

b. What is one of the biggest favors we can do God and ourselves? _____
_____
_____.

c. Why is there nothing wrong with being less than perfect, *if* we have a perfect heart toward God? _____
_____
_____.

d. What is one definition of the word "slanderers"? _____
_____
_____
_____.

e. Is criticism spread only by telling something to ten other people? Why or why not? _____
_____
_____.

f. What does the translation of the word "slanderers" as *diabolos* ("Satan . . . false accuser, devil")[2] mean in our lives?
_____
_____
_____
_____.

g. What is the reason God is revealing this message to all of us?
_____
_____
_____.

h. Too often people who have been slandered or criticized by others can't lay hold of the good things of God because

_____

_____

_____.

5. Read Colossians 3:21; Luke 4:18 KJV

a. All of us are products of our environment, of what we came from, of how we were raised. Thank God, Jesus opens those doors, and we can go free. He is the _____

_____

_____.

b. What will happen if you come to Jesus hurt and wounded?

_____

_____

_____

_____

_____.

c. What lesson is set forth in this passage in Colossians 3:21?

_____

_____.

6. Read Colossians 3:18,19; Ephesians 5:21

a. What do we see in Colossians 3:18,19? _____

_____

_____.

b. What are wives told to do as part of their calling in Christ Jesus?_____

_____.

   c. It is not part of our nature to "adapt" to anyone else, but it is part of our _____
_____.

   d. What are husbands told to do? What does this mean? _____
_____
_____
_____
_____.

   e. What can wives and husbands do to be a "sweetheart" to each other? _____
_____.

7. Read Proverbs 18:14; review Romans 12:8

   a. This verse is saying that regardless of what comes into a person's life, he can bear up under it if _____
_____
_____.

   b. In Romans 12:8, what is one of the ministry gifts to the Church?_____
_____.

   c. Why is it easy to recognize an encourager or exhorter? ____
_____
_____
_____
_____
_____
_____.

    d. What can you and I do even though we may not "stand in the office of encourager or exhorter"? _____

_____

_____

_____

_____

_____.

8. Read 1 Samuel 30:6

    a. We all have times when we need to be encouraged by others, but sometimes it seems that there is no one to encourage us. Instead of getting angry and letting bitterness and resentment come in, what can we do at those times when we feel that nobody cares about us, that nobody appreciates us?_____

_____

_____

_____.

    b. God will send you the very person or people you need to uplift, encourage, and edify you. First, you _____; then second, you _____.

    c. Remember, the spiritual rule is: you reap what you sow. How do you reap encouragement?_____

_____.

    d. What happens when we encourage and exhort an individual?

_____

_____

_____

_____.

e. In the same way, the Holy Spirit, the Comforter, comes along-side us to _____, to _____ _____, to _____, to _____.

f. We have a choice. We can either open our mouth and use it as *diabolos* to _____ _____, or we can use it as *parakletos* to _____ _____.

g. When we open our mouth, what comes out can either be _____ _____ or _____.

*Angry and Impatient Words
Lead to Trouble*

1. Read Ephesians 4:31; Romans 12:16

   a. What descriptive words are used in Ephesians 4:31 to identify the things that get us into trouble?_____

   _____

   _____

   _____

   _____

   _____

   _____.

   b. Which of these things pose the biggest problem for you? ____

   _____

   _____

   _____

   _____.

   c. Do you and I have to have bad tempers or get mad every time something doesn't go our way? Why or why not?_____

   _____

   _____.

2. Review James 1:19

   a. James tells us to be _____ to hear, but _____ to speak, _____ to take offense, and _____ to get angry.

b. Of these, what is the most important — and often the hardest part? _____.

c. When we get mad, when we are caught in a situation we cannot change no matter what we do, that's when we need to learn _____.

d. When you are in such a situation, why is it useless and pointless to get mad, angry, impatient, in a rage, or to pitch a fit?

_____

_____.

3. Review Romans 12:16; Ephesians 4:31

a. According to the Apostle Paul in this passage, we can learn to be _____ and _____. We can also be _____ and _____.

b. What is the root cause of the things listed by Paul in Ephesians 4:31? _____

_____.

c. As Paul points out in Romans 12:16, we have such an inflated opinion of ourselves that we think _____

_____.

4. Read James 4:1-3

a. If we would admit it, we have a tremendous problem with _____. Why? _____

_____

_____.

b. What are the two main reasons people argue?_____

_____

_____

_____

_____.

c. When things don't go as we want them to, we need to just ____

_____

_____

_____

_____

_____.

d. What is the only thing that is going to maintain God's anointing? _____

_____.

5. Read 1 Corinthians 13:4,5; 15:31; review Matthew 12:34

a. How does the Word of God describe love in this passage? ____

_____

_____

_____

_____

_____

_____

_____

_____.

b. What is the solution to the problem of arguing?_____

_____.

c. We have got to learn to love peace and harmony. In light of 1 Corinthians 15:31, how are we to maintain them? _____
_____
_____.

d. Why do we start wars over petty things, trifles? _____
_____
_____
_____.

e. What is the solution to the problem of selfishness? _____
_____
_____
_____.

f. In this study, what choices is the Lord asking you and me to make, by the power of the Holy Spirit? _____
_____
_____
_____
_____
_____
_____.

6. Read Romans 14:17-19; Ephesians 6:15; Matthew 10:11-15

a. What is one of the things the Lord is revealing to us in this passage? Why? _____
_____
_____
_____.

b. In Matthew 10:11-15, why did Jesus tell the disciples that if they found a suitable house in which to stay in each city where they went to preach and heal, but they were not accepted, they were to leave, shaking the very dust of that place off their feet? _____

_____

_____

_____.

c. Why does strife hinder our work? _____

_____

_____

_____

_____.

d. The Lord maintained inner peace and stability during the time He was on earth, regardless of His outward circumstances. If we want to do anything for our Lord and Savior, we need to_____

_____.

Why? _____

_____.

e. If we have a peaceful spirit, we will have a peaceful _____

_____.

7. Read 1 Timothy 1:8 MESSAGE

Why are gestures, voice tone, and facial expressions important?

_____

_____.

8. Read James 1:20,21; John 2:13-17

    a. In this passage, what does James tell us about man's anger?
        _____
        _____.

    b. Is there such a thing as righteous anger? _____
        _____
        _____.

    c. Did Jesus ever become angry? If so, give an example._____
        _____
        _____
        _____
        _____
        _____.

    d. Jesus' anger was not the wrong kind of anger; it was a right-
        eous anger, and we have the same right to display the same
        kind of anger that He did. That's why it is wrong to preach
        that we are never to get angry. However, the emotion of anger
        should submit to the spiritual fruit of self-control. How can
        the difference between the two kinds of anger be decided?
        _____
        _____
        _____.

9. Read Proverbs 31:26; review Matthew 12:34

    a. When we determine that nobody is ever going to hurt us
        again, what does that attitude influence? _____
        _____
        _____.

b. No matter how right your heart may be before the Lord, if you have _____ or _____ or _____ in your spirit, you cannot open your mouth without _____ _____ because Jesus told us, it is out of _____ _____ _____.

10. Read Matthew 11:29,30; review James 3:8

a. Where is our main problem? _____ _____.

b. As we have seen in this passage in James, who can tame the tongue? _____.

c. There is something we can do about the tongue, and it is part of what Jesus was talking about when He told us to take His yoke upon us in Matthew 11:29,30. What is that? _____ _____ _____ _____ _____.

11. Read James 3:17

a. How does this verse describe God's wisdom? _____ _____ _____ _____

_____

_____

_____

_____

_____

_____

_____.

b. It is wisdom to know when the time is to be _____
and _____, and when to be _____
and _____, to _____
_____, and to _____
_____.

12. Read James 3:18

a. Why does Satan try so hard to get you and me upset before
we go to church and get the preacher upset before he steps up
behind the pulpit? _____

_____

_____

_____

_____.

b. In light of this Scripture, we should not try to sow peace in
the lives of others if we do not _____
_____.

    c. In order for the Word of the Lord to take root, it must be sown _____ by someone who is _____.

    d. That's why, if you intend or plan to work for the Lord, you must _____.

13. Read Joshua 24:15 KJV

    a. Can the devil force us to get upset? If not, why do we do so?

_____

_____

_____

    b. How can we overcome past hurts and wounds that may cause us to react negatively? _____

_____

_____

    c. Since God has created us with a free will, with the ability to make our own decisions in life, what is the word He is sharing with us in our time? _____

_____

_____

_____

Chapter
12

Speak No Evil

1. Review Proverbs 15:4; Ephesians 4:29

   a. In these passages and others throughout the Word of God, we are told to be careful how _____ _____.

   b. We have already discussed Ephesians 4:29 about the words we speak, but it is such an important verse for this message that it is worth reviewing. What did Paul tell us to do in this passage? Why? _____ _____ _____ _____ _____ _____ _____ _____ _____.

   c. According to the writer of Proverbs, what does willful contrariness do? _____ _____.

   d. What problem is created and magnified by wrong thoughts and words — our own or those of others? _____ _____.

      e. We are not to use our mouths to _____, _____

          _____, or _____, but rather to

          _____, _____, and _____.

2. Review Romans 12:21

    a. Because we are children of light, in addition to magnifying Him, the Lord wants us to learn how to magnify the good in _____, in _____, and in _____.

    b. In this sense, "to magnify" means_____ _____.

    c. When we magnify the Lord, what are we doing?_____ _____ _____.

    d. What does God want us to do with the good in our lives? ____ _____ _____.

3. Review 2 Corinthians 10:4

    a. What happens if the strongholds that are built up within us — especially in our minds — are not destroyed? _____ _____ _____.

    b. How is a stronghold like a brick wall? _____ _____ _____ _____.

4. Read Numbers 13:32; review Matthew 12:36

   a. What truth in Numbers 13:32 should we lay hold on?_____
   _____.

   b. Not only are we not to talk negatively about our circumstances, we are also not to talk negatively about _____
   _____.

   c. Most people have some good and some bad in them, just as
   we do. God doesn't want us to magnify the bad in others or
   in ourselves. He wants us to _____
   _____.

   d. When someone is acting badly toward us, what is the only
   thing that is going to make our situation better?_____
   _____
   _____.

   e. Why do we need to stop running to others, complaining
   about our situation? _____
   _____
   _____.

   f. It is not true that we should never talk about our problems;
   we just need to _____.

   g. In Matthew 12:36, what did Jesus say about our mouth? ___
   _____
   _____
   _____
   _____.

5. Read Numbers 13:25-28,30-33

   a. According to these passages, when the twelve Hebrew spies came back from their scouting expedition into the land of promise, only Joshua and Caleb gave a _____ report. The other ten gave an _____ report.

   b. Why is it that four out of five people can be defeated by a trial, while one can come through it victoriously? What is the difference? _____

   _____

   _____

   _____.

   c. Like the giants in the land of Canaan, whatever is magnified becomes _____

   _____.

   d. What is going to become most real to us? _____

   _____

   _____.

6. Read 2 Timothy 2:20,21; review Ephesians 4:29

   a. In light of 2 Timothy 2:20,21, how can we keep ourselves "fit and ready for any good work"? _____

   _____

   _____

   _____.

b. What two responsibilities do you and I have in regard to "evil reports"? _____

_____.

c. Each of us has a responsibility not _____

_____and not

_____.

d. As we have already seen, what has the Apostle Paul said in Ephesians 4:29? _____

_____

_____.

e. According to what Paul wrote to his young disciple Timothy, you and I are supposed to be clean vessels. We are to keep ourselves pure, and to help others to keep themselves pure as well. What is one way we do this? _____

_____

_____.

f. Why should we always be aware of our thoughts and words?

_____

_____.

7. Read Malachi 3:16

a. You and I have an opportunity to make glad the heart of God. In light of this Scripture, what is one way we do that? _____

_____

_____.

    b. There are proper ways to handle sensitive issues. The Bible says that God is listening to see _____

_____

_____.

8. Read Numbers 13:29

    a. Each of the "ites" in this Scripture represented a different problem to the children of Israel. How did the evil report of the ten spies affect the millions of Israelites who were waiting for a decision about whether they should go cross over Jordan and take possession of their inheritance?_____

_____

_____.

    b. What opportunity do you and I have every day?_____

_____

_____

_____.

    c. Why has the Lord given us this message from His Word?_____

_____

_____.

9. Read Ecclesiastes 3:1,7

    a. It is wisdom to be able to know _____

_____.

    But as a general rule, it is always timely to _____

_____.

b. Our fallen nature wants to_____

_____.

But our born-again nature wants to _____

_____.

10. Read Philippians 3:13,14; 1:6

a. The devil wants us to concentrate on our past and on our weaknesses, our losses, our problems. The Spirit of God wants us to focus on our strengths, our victories, our joys. In light of these passages of Scripture, what things should we be magnifying?_____

_____.

b. What things are always our ministry? _____

_____

_____.

c. What is always our calling?_____

_____

_____

_____

_____.

d. How do we magnify (make large) the good? _____

_____

_____

_____

_____.

    e. If you are negative, what should you do?_____

_____

_____

_____

_____

_____

_____

_____

_____

_____

_____

_____.

11. Read Malachi 2:5-7; Revelation 1:6

    a. This Scripture in Malachi chapter 2 deals with priests and the kind of mouth that they are supposed to have. But according to Revelation 1:6, all of us are _____ and _____ because Jesus has ". . . formed us into a kingdom (a royal race), _____ to His God and Father. . . ."

    b. In our covenant with the Lord, what is His part? _____ _____.

    c. What is our part? _____ _____ _____.

    d. If we have reverential and worshipful fear of the Lord, if we revere Him and stand in awe of His name, then we are not going to _____

_____

_____.

12. Read Romans 2:1; Matthew 7:1,2; 7:3-5 TLB

   a. What is the root of gossip, slander, backbiting, and talebearing? _____.

   b. What is the root of judgment? _____.

   c. Why do we speak evil of other people? _____

_____

_____.

   d. In light of the passages in Matthew chapter 7, why should you be very careful about criticizing and judging and condemning other people — especially believers? _____

_____

_____.

13. Read Malachi 2:6,7

   a. Since you and I are priests and kings to our God, what do we need to keep in our mouths? _____

_____.

   b. What does that mean? _____

_____

_____.

14. Read 1 Peter 4:15; 1 Thessalonians 4:11; review Malachi 2:7

   a. One version of Webster's dictionary defines a "busybody" as

   _____

   _____.

   Another version of Webster's dictionary defines "busybody"
   as _____

   _____.

   The author defines "busybody" as _____

   _____

   _____.

   b. Webster's dictionary defines "gossip" as _____

   _____

   _____.

   The author defines "gossip" as _____

   _____

   _____.

   c. According to Vine, what are "slanderers"? _____

   _____

   _____

   _____.

   d. How does Webster's define "slander"? _____

   _____

   _____

   _____

   _____.

e. How is "whisper" defined in Webster's dictionary? What does a "whisperer" do? _____

_____

_____

_____

_____

_____

_____.

f. How does the Apostle Peter link all these together?

_____

_____.

g. What scriptural instruction do we find in 1 Thessalonians 4:11? _____

_____

_____.

h. How does God view exaggeration? _____.

i. Why does the Lord say that the lips of His priests are to guard and keep pure the knowledge of His law? _____

_____

_____

_____.

j. As God's messengers, His mouthpiece, you and I need to make sure that both _____
and _____
are in our mouths and that we _____

_____.

Chapter
13

A Soothing Tongue

1. Read Proverbs 8:6-9

   a. This passage should be not only our confession and testimony, but also our _____. That is, it should be not only what we say about ourselves, but also what _____.

   b. Unfortunately, all of us have learned in this life to speak in circles. We need to learn how to engage in _____ _____.

   c. As children of God, filled with His Spirit, what are we to manifest as our disposition?_____ _____ _____.

2. Read Proverbs 28:15 KJV

   a. How does Webster's define the word "disposition"? _____ _____ _____ _____ _____.

   b. What kind of disposition do you have? Are you a "grumpy bear" or are you a "teddy bear"? _____ _____ _____.

3. Read Proverbs 16:5

   a. What does this passage say about the Lord's view of everyone who has a proud disposition? What will be their fate? _____

      _____

      _____

      _____

      _____.

   b. Why are people with a proud disposition hard to deal with?

      _____

      _____.

   c. What are the characteristics of proud people? _____

      _____

      _____

      _____

      _____

      _____

      _____

      _____

      _____.

   d. Besides being on the defensive, proud people are also _____

      _____

      _____

      _____

      _____

      _____

      _____

_____
_____
_____
_____.

   e. Proud people are usually not very happy people. How does this affect others? _____
_____.

4. Read Matthew 12:18-21

   a. As believers, as God's beloved children created in His image, what kind of disposition does He want us to have? _____
_____
_____.

   b. What kind of tongue does God want us to have in our mouths?_____
_____
_____.

   c. As God's messengers, His mouthpiece, His ambassadors of peace, how are we to be? _____
_____
_____.

   d. To do that, to be the way God wants us to be as His representatives on this earth, what are we going to have to do?
_____
_____
_____.

5. Read Ephesians 4:22-24; 4:22 KJV; Proverbs 15:1 KJV

   a. Our nature is seen through our _____.
      That is to say that the kind of person we are is revealed by our

      _____.

   b. Our nature comes out of our _____.

   c. Proverbs 15:1 KJV is true for us — if we are willing to _____

      _____

      _____

      _____.

6. Read Matthew 11:28-30; Colossians 3:15; Hebrews 2:16 KJV

   a. Each of us has a different nature. No two of us are exactly
      alike. Our nature also changes as we go through the various
      experiences and cycles of life. Real change just doesn't come

      _____ or

      _____.

   b. There are no _____ saints or
      _____ ministries.

   c. If you and I are to be different from the way we are now, then
      we are going to have to _____

      _____. We are going

      to have to _____

      _____

      _____

      _____

      _____.

d. In Matthew 11:29, how does Jesus describe His nature?____

_____

_____.

e. What does He say will happen if we will take His yoke — His nature — upon us and learn of Him? _____

_____.

f. In verse 30 how does Jesus describe His yoke — His nature?

_____

_____.

g. The Bible says that if we want to be led by the Spirit of God, we must learn to be led by _____.

h. If we are led by peace, then we can be assured that we are being led by God, because He is _____

_____.

i. If we are ever going to be truly happy, we are going to have to

_____

_____

_____.

j. What determines whether we are true worshippers of God?

_____

_____

_____.

7. Read Exodus 30:22-25; 2 Corinthians 2:15

    According to the Bible, there is a spiritual aroma that goes up
    from our lives when we are anointed with the Holy Ghost. What
    is it? _____
    _____.

8. Read Exodus 30:26-30

    a. According to Hannah Hurnard, the author of *Mountains of
        Spices,*[2] what does myrrh represent? Cinnamon? Calamus? ___
        _____
        _____.

    b. If you and I want the anointing of God upon us, then we are
        going to have to be imbued with_____
        _____
        _____.

9. Read Galatians 4:1,2; Romans 8:17 KJV; review Isaiah 58:6-9

    a. Why are we going to have to grow up and become mature in
        Christ?_____
        _____
        _____.

    b. When do we receive God's blessings? _____
        _____.

    c. What is one way we show we are mature?_____
        _____
        _____.

d. What is the Lord telling us in the passage in Isaiah 58:6-9?

_____

_____

_____

_____

_____.

10. Read 2 Peter 1:4-8; John 4:23; Philippians 2:13;
2 Timothy 4:7 KJV

a. In the passage in 2 Peter 1:4-8 is the biblical formula for moving out of the flesh and into the divine nature in order to
experience true Kingdom living. What are the three stages we
go through as we develop our relationship with God? _____

_____

_____

_____

_____.

b. We begin our Christian lives as newborn infants. We pray,
read the Bible, go to church, and worship _____,
or in the outer court. God accepts that kind of worship,
because He _____.

c. When God says to us, "It is time to move into the inner
court," part of that word comes through messages on holiness
which tell us that _____

_____.

d. Finally, God tells us that it's time to move into the Holy of Holies. In order to come into that place, our whole lives must be _____

_____

_____

_____

_____

_____

_____

_____

_____

_____ .

e. In 2 Peter 1:4-8, what is the first thing we are told? _____

_____

_____ .

f. Then what are we told to add to our diligence? _____

_____

_____ .

g. What does excellence develop? _____

_____ .

h. What does knowledge produce? _____

_____ .

i. What does self-control lead to? _____ .

j. What is steadfastness? _____

_____ .

k. What is patience? _____
_____
_____.

l. What is happening as we are waiting? _____
_____
_____.

m. What do our steadfastness, patience, and endurance develop
into?_____
_____.

n. What comes after godliness? What does it produce? _____
_____
_____.

11. Read 1 Peter 5:5; review 2 Peter 1:4-9

a. With what does Peter tell us to clothe (apron) ourselves?_____
_____
_____.

b. In light of the passage in 1 Peter 5:5, we in the body of Christ
are to take on the cloak of _____
_____.

We are to wear that cloak _____
_____
_____
_____.

c. What comes after kindness?_____.

12. Read 2 Corinthians 3:18

a. How does the change come that needs to take place in each of us? _____
_____
_____.

b. What is the only thing that changes the inner man? _____
_____
_____
_____.

c. What kind of people is the Lord looking for? _____
_____
_____
_____.

d. What will happen if we are willing to be changed? _____
_____
_____
_____
_____.

e. From what does fruit-bearing come? Explain. _____
_____
_____
_____
_____
_____
_____.

f. What should you do if you want to change, if you want to be like Jesus? _____

_____

_____.

Conclusion

1. In this study, what has the author tried to emphasize? _____
   _____
   _____
   _____.

2. What are *words*?_____.

3. Avoid all _____, _____,
   _____, and _____
   talk. Instead, learn to speak as _____ speaks.

4. What will the Word of God, spoken in truth and love from your
   lips, do?_____
   _____.

5. Why must your heart be right before the Lord in order to speak
   that Word in truth and love? _____
   _____
   _____
   _____
   _____.

6. You are bound by your _____, by your _____.
   You are also _____ by them.

7. Why is it so important to place a guard upon your lips? _____
   _____
   _____
   _____.

8. You can change your action and behavior, but to do so what must you first change? _____
   _____.

9. What do you need to do that?_____
   _____.

10. _____ determines action.

11. If you truly want your life to be totally different, what must you do?_____
    _____
    _____
    _____.

Prayer for a
Personal Relationship
with the Lord

God wants you to receive His free gift of salvation. Jesus wants to save you and fill you with the Holy Spirit more than anything. If you have never invited Jesus, the Prince of Peace, to be your Lord and Savior, I invite you to do so now. Pray the following prayer, and if you are really sincere about it, you will experience a new life in Christ.

Father,

You loved the world so much, You gave Your only begotten Son to die for our sins so that whoever believes in Him will not perish, but have eternal life.

Your Word says we are saved by grace through faith as a gift from You. There is nothing we can do to earn salvation.

I believe and confess with my mouth that Jesus Christ is Your Son, the Savior of the world. I believe He died on the cross for me and bore all of my sins, paying the price for them. I believe in my heart that You raised Jesus from the dead.

I ask You to forgive my sins. I confess Jesus as my Lord. According to Your Word, I am saved and will spend eternity with You! Thank You, Father. I am so grateful! In Jesus' name, amen.

See John 3:16; Ephesians 2:8,9; Romans 10:9,10; 1 Corinthians 15:3,4; 1 John 1:9; 4:14-16; 5:1,12,13.

Answers

Introduction

1. The mind or intellect, the will, and the emotions.

2. Because it is full of "self."

3a. To what we think, feel, and want.

3b. What we think, not necessarily what God thinks.

3c. What we want, not what God wants.

3d. What we feel, not what God feels.

4. It is trained to carry God's thoughts, desires, and feelings; then we become a mouthpiece for the Lord!

5. That we have been given the mind of Christ and that we hold the thoughts, feelings, and purposes of His heart.

6. The body and soul corporately.

7. Come under the leadership of the Spirit; requires time and diligence.

8. Either to the flesh or to the spirit. It can be used to verbalize God's Word or as a vehicle to express the enemy's work.

9. "Death"; "life"; "eat the fruit of it [for death or life]."

10. It can be used to bring blessings or destruction not only to our own lives, but also to the lives of many others.

Chapter 1

1a. Talk *to* them.

1b. Not our will, but the will of God. His will is His Word.

1c. With the Word of God. He repeatedly said, "It is written," and quoted Scriptures that met the lies and deceptions of the devil head on.

1d. We stop speaking the Word to our problems and begin once again speaking our feelings, which is probably what got us into trouble to begin with.

1e. Know what we believe and be determined to stick with it until we see results.

2a. He will be sadly disappointed.

2b. Unforgiveness.

2c. Trying to operate one of God's principles while completely ignoring another.

2d. Obedience.

2e. Repentance and a return to submission and obedience.

2b. His faith-filled words go forth to establish God's order in his life.

2c. Things begin to change!

3a. Has been established in the spiritual realm since before the foundation of the earth.

3b. ". . . thoughts and plans for welfare and peace and not for evil. . . ." To give us hope in our final outcome.

3c. It literally begins to become reality.

3d. Bring their mouths as well as their hearts into God's service.

3e. Talking like the devil.

3f. We will not see positive results in our daily lives.

3g. Calling for. We are reaching into the realm of the spirit and drawing out according to our words.

3h. Evil, negative things.

3i. Good, positive things.

4a. God's mighty words.

4b. We are created in God's image (Genesis 1:26,27), and we are supposed to act like Him.

5. By speaking of those things that He has promised in His Word to us as if they already existed.

6a. Win them to Christ.

6b. Spiritual knowledge and understanding.

6c. The fruit of love, the "more excellent way"; is not rude or unmannerly.

6d. By love.

6e. Fact.

6f. We can "declare the decree" in private; then when someone asks how we are doing or how we are feeling, we can find a way to remain positive and yet not leave the other person thinking that Christians (along with everything they believe) are weird.

6g. "Spiritually."

6h. Wisdom; common sense. The Holy Spirit.

Chapter 3

1a. That of reaching into the realm where God is and calling "those things which be not as if they were" (author's paraphrase).

1b. Speaking forth the words that will shape their future.

2a. "Declaring the decree!"

2b. Yes, as long as we are reasonably sure that what we are declaring is God's will for our life and not just what we want.

2c. Muttering,[1] conversing aloud with oneself, or declaring something.[2]

2d. It helps establish it in the heart.

3a. They needed a new self-image before their miracle could occur.

3b. The future was being prophesied: Abraham would be the father of a multitude, and Sarah would be the mother of nations.

3c. Reaching into the realm of the spirit, where their miracle was.

3d. Draw out the miracle God had promised. Coming into agreement with God's Word, as spoken earlier in Genesis 15.

4a. Abram believed God.

4b. We believe that God can do the impossible and that He will do it for us.

4c. To release their faith.

4d. It helps keep our faith strong until our manifestation arrives.

4e. We are willing to agree with Him — in our hearts and with our words.

5a. To mentally agree with God or believe what He tells us.

5b. Because what is in our hearts will come out of our mouths.

5c. To what is in our souls.

5d. Whatever our souls are full of.

5e. We will draw those things to ourselves.

5f. That is what we will draw to us.

5g. The choice is ours!

Chapter 4

1a. ". . . if anyone does not offend in speech [never says the wrong things]. . . ."

1b. Words are very important and powerful, and we will be held responsible for them: "For by your words you will be justified and acquitted, and by your words you will be condemned and sentenced."

2a. Not by himself.

2b. It is wild and uncontrollable, always wanting to do its own thing.

2c. The help of the Holy Spirit.

2d. Learn to discipline our own mouths and take responsibility for what comes out of them.

2e. Cooperating with God, taking His Word and starting to speak it over your life.

2f. Yes. By speaking evil of it. Yes. By speaking well of it.

2g. A lie.

2h. "Liar . . . and the father of lies and of all that is false."

2i. He strives to give us trouble and then use it to influence us to prophesy that same kind of trouble in our future.

3a. 1) No person's words have as much authority in our life as our own, and 2) our future cannot be blessed until we let go of the past.

3b. By no longer considering (thinking about) the things of old, believing that God has a good plan for our future.

3c. Begin to think in agreement with God. Begin to speak in agreement with Him. Actually prophesy our own future.

4a. Because words are containers for power; they carry creative or destructive power.

4b. That in the tongue is the power of life and death.

4c. Carry weight in the spiritual realm.

5a. To *yourself.*

5b. Faith-filled words, believing, as Jesus said, that the words you speak are spirit and life. Speak life into your life, not death.

6a. Watch for the attacks of the enemy and pray immediately.

6b. He will never get a stronghold!

7a. Positives; negatives.

7b. The Word of God.

7c. In the spiritual realm.

7d. Defeats a spiritual (unseen) enemy.

8a. We will win.

8b. Declaring in the beginning what will happen in the end.

9a. First, He declares things; then He does them.

9b. Spiritual laws; cannot ignore them.

9c. Words are seeds. We sow word seeds and reap according to what we have sown.

10a. Speak forth and declare the Word of the Lord — *before it comes to pass.*

10b. By prophesying (speaking forth God's Word) over your own life at any time.

11a. Stop speaking the old things and start speaking some new things.

11b. By finding out what God's Word promises you and beginning to declare the end from the beginning.

11c. By saying about your situation what you believe He would say, you will open the door for the miracle-working power of God.

Chapter 5

1a. Mouthpiece.

1b. Their mouth and what comes out of it.

2a. Speak only when spoken through.

2b. Our mouth must belong to Him.

3a. "The way" by their lives as well as by the Word of God.

3b. The mouth.

3c. Encouragement, comfort; edification.

4a. That he ". . . should know how to speak a word in season to him who is weary. . . ."

4b. The words of our mouth; speak life to them.

4c. "A word in season," a word that will heal and encourage them.

5a. ". . . encourage (admonish, exhort) one another and edify (strengthen and build up) one another. . . ."

5b. The "gift of exhortation." One of the ministry gifts that the Holy Spirit confers upon certain individuals.

5c. "Helper." Exhorts people in their growth in God, encouraging them to be all they can be, for God's glory. As a Helper and an Exhorter, He anoints others for that ministry.

5d. A ministry; a much needed ministry.

5e. Backsliding or giving up!

5f. Exhorters bring comfort; they just simply make people feel better — about themselves, about their circumstances, about the past, about the present, about the future, about anything else that concerns them.

5g. To continue in exhorting one another.

5h. People are hurting and need to be encouraged.

6a. ". . . only such [speech] as is good and beneficial to the spiritual progress of others, as is fitting to the need and the occasion, that it may be a blessing and give grace (God's favor) to those who hear it."

6b. By the grace gift that was upon him. (Romans 12:3.)

6c.   Out of balance.

6d.   Mouths; mouthpiece.

6e.   Without God's cleansing power we are all people of unclean lips. (Isaiah 6:5.)

Chapter 6

1a.   Complaining is a sin! It is a corrupt form of conversation that causes many people a great deal of problems in their lives.

1b.   It opens many doors for the enemy.

1c.   Power.

1d.   They destroy the joy of the one doing the complaining and can also affect other people who have to listen to them.

1e.   Murmuring and complaining probably sound like cursing to Him. It is verbal pollution.

1f.   When we complain about our current situation we remain in it, when we praise God in the midst of difficulty, He raises us out of it.

1g.   Gratitude; thanksgiving.

1h.   They are too busy being grateful for the good things they do have; they have no time to notice the things they could complain about.

1i.   Good; evil. Good; evil. (See Romans 12:21.)

1j.   Overcome it with good.

1k.   Good; evil.

2a.   They can bring healing or they can open the door for disease.

2b.   Healing power.

2c.   It can actually destroy it.

2d.   Physical energy; healing.

3a.   He takes it personally. He considers that we are exploiting His goodness. God is good, and He wants to hear us tell Him and others about His goodness.

3b.   Giving a critical appraisal of the God we serve.

3c.   For our instruction, so we can see their mistakes and not make the same ones. We should heed their example and not follow their pattern.

4a.   Guards his words can keep himself from ruin; does not guard his words can bring destruction into his own life.

4b.   The Israelites complained and after four decades they were still wandering in the wilderness of death and destruction. Jesus continued to praise God no matter what, refusing to complain, and as a result God raised Him from death to new life.

4c.   We should guard against the temptation to complain and grumble, and instead purposely *choose* to offer up the sacrifice of praise and thanksgiving. (Hebrews 13:15 KJV.)

4d.   Complain and remain; praise and be raised.

5a.   Thanksgiving.

5b.   Weakens; releases power — power to bring answers to our prayers.

5c.   Spiritually mature enough to handle any type of promotion or increase.

5d.   If we don't feel like it, or if our circumstances don't dictate it, thanksgiving can become a sacrificial offering, made by faith, in obedience, because we love the Lord and want to honor His Word.

6a.   Only after he had offered the sacrifice of thanksgiving.

6b.   Negative (evil) power.

7a.   Constantly and at all times.

7b.   Things to complain about; reasons to give God glory.

7c.   "At all times"; "in every circumstance"; "for everything."

7d.   *For; in.*

7e.   Powerful.

8a.   The mouth.

8b.   Negative talk, complaining, grumbling, and all the related types of speech.

9a.   "Voice your thankfulness to God."

9b.   Complaining; critical; faultfinding.

9c.   Excuses of any kind.

9d.   Excuses; choke fruit.

9e.   Addicted.

9f.   Whistling for the devil. The devil, who will quickly come in to give us more misery.

9g.   Pride.

9h.   By humbling ourselves and realizing how blessed we are to have anything at all.

9i.   Major on the positive attributes and minor on the negative ones.

10a.   Unthankful; ungrateful.

10b.   Express gratitude to God.

11a.   The spirit of the world today.

11b. Living epistles, read of all men.

11c. By a lifestyle that lifts up His principles.

11d. So that we may be able to show the world a different way of living.

12a. Complain; find fault. It simply means that we make it our goal in life to be as positive as possible.

12b. The fruit of the lips will change.

12c. Sweeten your relationship with the Lord.

13. Provide us with negative circumstances.

14a. Complain; in the beginning.

14b. Sow seeds now for our future.

14c. More of what we are grumbling about. A bountiful harvest later on.

15a. A pledge of what was to come.

15b. A beginning of a great downpour. A pledge or foretaste of good things to come.

16a. It is a sign of greater things to come.

16b. By complaining over it.

16c. By believing over it.

16d. We will never see the harvest.

16e. "Be content with what you have."

16f. By faith. We know that the Lord is the Author and the Finisher. (Hebrews 12:2.) What He begins, He completes. (Philippians 1:6.) He will do that for us — *if* we will hold our faith firm until the end. (Hebrews 3:6.)

Chapter 7

1a. During a storm.

1b. Behave in the storm!

1c. He "decided" that it would be wise not to open His mouth. In His humanity He would have been tempted to do the same thing you and I do: doubt, question God, complain, say something negative, etc.

1d. Be quieter than usual.

1e. Be quiet and allow the emotional storm to subside.

2. It is time for a change.

3a. The middle where we encounter the storms.

3b. Place of testing.

3c. "The midnight hour"; "the dark night of the soul."

3d. "Use" our faith.

3e. Just how much faith we really have.

3f. "Using" it; talking about it.

3g. Equips us to handle the next one better.

3h. Know that we will win before the battle ever starts.

3i. Manifestation. Middle.

4a. Calmed; rebuked.

4b. Grow in faith, which is confidence and trust in God.

4c. Grow in self-control and discipline of the mouth.

5a. Hold fast our confession of faith; God has His eye on everything, including us and the storm.

5b. He will not allow us to sink.

6a. Saying one thing in good times and another in hard times.

6b. Control. Maturity. Glorify.

7a. "Worthless (futile, barren)."

7b. "A harness consisting of a headstall, bit, and reins, which fits a horse's head and is used to restrain or guide."[1]

7c. We may never experience deliverance.

7d. The Holy Spirit, if we accept His leadership and guidance.

8a. Our tongue gives direction to all the rest of our life. Our words draw borders for us, and we must live inside those borders.

8b. As, "The metal mouthpiece of a bridle that controls and curbs an animal. . . . Something that controls. . . ."[2]

8c. When we begin to say the wrong thing, we will sense Him trying to pull us in the right direction.

9a. Bit and bridle. We will end up at the right place and stay out of all the wrong places.

9b. We will end up with a lot of pain.

10a. Our thoughts.

10b. We are to lead every wrong thought captive unto the obedience of Jesus Christ. Second Corinthians 10:5 KJV tells us to cast down wrong imaginations.

10c. It must be renewed completely. (Romans 12:1,2.)

10d. It is our choice.

10e. ". . . whatever is true, whatever is worthy of reverence and is honorable and seemly, whatever is just, whatever is pure, whatever is lovely and lovable, whatever is kind and winsome and gracious . . . ."

10f. Because they work together.

11a. God's will.

11b. Through the eye of faith.

11c. They have never learned how to talk.

11d. Times of personal difficulty.

11e. Turn around and go back to where you came from.

11f. ". . . they endure for a little while; then when trouble or persecution arises on account of the Word, they immediately are offended (become displeased, indignant, resentful) and they stumble and fall away."

11g. He has overcome the world.

12a. We become His mouthpiece and prophesy His Word.

12b. Our own idle words; our mouths to take the lead role.

13a. Dead circumstance.

13b. God will make a way.

14a. She kept *saying!*

14b. Through her words.

14c. Through our words.

14d. Keep saying — and don't give up hope!

15a. We must be filled with hope, we must think hope, and we must talk hope. Hope is the foundation on which faith stands.

15b. Restore to us double everything we have lost.

16a. Because anything that offends God in our conversation needs to be eliminated.

16b. Purpose to keep our mouth from transgressing.

16c. Because nothing gets God's attention any quicker. It is His Word that carries the power of the Holy Spirit.

16d. You will begin to notice that you are changing.

16e. God-ordained results.

Chapter 8

1a. Mouth.

1b. "Working out."

1c. Deposits a seed in us, and then we must cooperate with the work of the Holy Spirit to see that the seed He has placed in us grows into a plant that occupies our entire life.

2a. As "the seed."

2b. Harvest.

2c. Everything good that God desires for us to have.

2d. God. It must be cultivated, nurtured, watered, and cared for.

2e. It must be kept plowed up and weed free.

2f. Our hearts and lives.

2g. By submitting to the Holy Spirit our wills, which means submitting the flesh to the leadership of the spirit.

2h. We would be amazed at how different we are now from what we were when we began.

2i. A life-changing revelation on *the mouth!*

3. He had to do something about their words, about their mouths, before He could use them the way He had planned.

4a. Because he immediately began to say things that God had *not* told him to say.

4b. No.

4c. What God says about us!

4d. "I speak not My own words, but the words of the One Who sent Me. I say only what I have heard My Father say." (John 8:28; 12:50, author's paraphrase.)

4e. Soul; spirit.

5a. New opposition.

5b. Open doors for the enemy that we don't want to open.

5c. Walk in the flesh until it is time to exercise our ministry gift, and then quickly try to get in the Spirit.

5d. There are things that must be moved out of the way in order for it to be ushered in.

5e. Rejoice over what is coming!

6a. That he wasn't eloquent enough to do what God wanted done because he had a "mouth problem."

6b. He does.

6c. "Now therefore go, and I will be with your mouth and will teach you what you shall say."

6a.   He has told us to take away from our midst the yokes of oppression, to stop pointing the finger in scorn toward the oppressed or the godly, and to stop speaking falsely, harshly, unjustly, and wickedly.

6b.   We are not doing what God has plainly told us to do.

6c.   Stop judging one another.

6d.   Falsely, harshly, unjustly, wickedly.

6e.   It is useless speech, nonsense talk.

6f.   Talking too much.

6g.   Exercise careful control over our words.

7a.   When we stop judging each other and put away from ourselves every form of vain, false, harsh, unjust, and wicked speaking.

7b.   Pour out of our mouths curses on others.

8a.   "If you really want to enjoy My blessings in this life, then don't run around doing your own thing. Instead, find out what I want you to do — and then do it. Don't seek your own pleasure, but seek first My will. Don't speak your own idle words, but speak My powerful words, for they will not come back void, without producing any effect, useless."

8b.   To bless God, to bless others, and to bless ourselves.

8c.   Live godly lives before them.

8d.   Bring forth a sweet-smelling aroma, pleasing to others and pleasing to God.

8e.   By oozing with the fruit of the Spirit, with kindness, gentleness, goodness, love, joy, peace, and all the other fruit.

8f.   God.

8g.   "Let the words of my mouth and the meditation of my heart be acceptable in Your sight, O Lord, my [firm, impenetrable] Rock and my Redeemer."

Chapter 10

1a.   It means that you and I go through life with an awesome power — like fire or electricity or nuclear energy — right under our noses, one that can produce death or life, depending on how it is used.

1b.   Good; evil; benefit; harm.

1c.   We can use it to create death and destruction, or we can use it to create life and health.

1d.   We can speak forth sickness, disease, dissention, and disaster, or we can speak forth healing, harmony, exhortation, and edification.

1e.   The choice is ours.

2a.   Whatever we sow is what we will reap.

2b.   Right under your nose.

2c.   The choice of our words.

2d.   If we are a blabbermouth, we are going to get into trouble.

2e.   We get unsettled and lose our peace — not necessarily because we are saying something evil, but simply because we need to be quiet and listen.

3a.   To keep one ear tuned to God.

3b.   To be quick to hear and slow to speak.

3c.   We might not say some of the things we say.

3d.   So that he would know how to "speak a word in season" to the weary.

3e.   The joy of the Lord.

3f.   In Christ alone.

3g.   Speaking words in due season to one another.

4a.   It disturbs Him that with the same mouth we use to bless and praise Him, we curse and condemn our fellow man, made in His image just as we are.

4b.   Realize that we have a long way to go before we become perfect.

4c.   The Lord looks upon our heart and counts us as perfect while we are on the way to becoming so.

4d.   Those who are guilty of finding fault with others and spreading criticism.[1]

4e.   No. Something can be spread if it is told to only one other person.

4f.   It means that when you and I slander someone or accuse another person falsely, we are allowing the devil to use our mouths.

4g.   Because He wants to do something good in our lives, but our mouths are affecting our anointing.

4h.   Somebody wounded or even broke their spirit so that they ended up with a failure image.

5a.   Healer of the brokenhearted.

5b.   He will heal you so you can go forth and bring that healing to someone else. Those whom you have hurt will also forgive you and receive healing.

5c.   Don't break another person's spirit!

6a.   How wives and husbands are to regard and treat one another in the Lord.

6b.   To "adapt" themselves to their husbands.

6c.   Calling in Christ Jesus.

6d. To be affectionate and sympathetic to their wives. It means that they are to be considerate of them, not harsh or unkind or bitter toward them.

6e. Just be sweet, kind, nice, and encouraging!

7a. He has a strong spirit within him to sustain him in those times of trouble.

7b. The encourager or exhorter.

7c. Because every time we get around them, they make us feel better by the things they say and do. It just seems to come natural to them to uplift, encourage, and strengthen others by their very presence and personality.

7d. We can encourage. We can exhort. We can build up, edify, lift up, and speak life. We can refuse to be slanderers. We can refuse to do the work of the devil with the words of our mouth.

8a. Take our burden to the Lord; He will hear us and help us.

8b. Pray; sow.

8c. Start being an exhorter!

8d. The healing balm of Gilead begins to drip down into that person's wounded soul. Suddenly he begins to think, "Yes, I believe I can make it!"

8e. Comfort us; encourage us; urge us to press on; propel us forward.

8f. Slander, accuse, find fault, and spread innuendoes and criticism; encourage, strengthen, help, inspire, and comfort.

8g. The devil; the Holy Spirit.

Chapter 11

1a. Wrath, passion, rage, bad temper, resentment, anger, animosity, quarreling, brawling, clamor, contention, slander, evil-speaking, abusive or blasphemous language, malice, spite, ill will, or baseness of any kind.

1b. (Your answer.)

1c. No. We have the ability in the Holy Spirit to be adjustable and adaptable.

2a. Quick; slow; slow; slow.

2b. Being slow to speak.

2c. Acceptance with joy.

2d. It is not going to reverse your bad situation.

3a. Adaptable; adjustable. Pliable; moldable.

3b. Pride and self-concern or self-centeredness.

3c. We are entitled to have everything our way.

4a. Selfishness. Our flesh (that is, our carnal nature) just loves itself. It always wants its own way.

4b. First, to prove they are right, because we all want to be right. And second, to have their way, because we all want to have our way in everything.

4c. Calm down and exercise a bit more humility, realizing that the minor things we fuss and argue over don't make that much difference in life anyway.

4d. Our willingness to dwell together in peace and harmony.

5a. "Love endures long and is patient and kind; love never is envious nor boils over with jealousy, is not boastful or vainglorious, does not display itself haughtily. It is not conceited (arrogant and inflated with pride); it is not rude (unmannerly) and does not act unbecomingly. Love (God's love in us) does not insist on its own rights or its own way. . . ."

5b. Love.

5c. By dying to self on a daily basis.

5d. Two reasons: because we want to be right, and because we want our way, which is selfishness.

5e. Love, which is caring more for the opinions and desires of others than for our own.

5f. To come up higher, to give up trying to have everything our own way all the time, and to remember that whatever is in your heart eventually comes out of your mouth. (Matthew 12:34.)

6a. The vital necessity of walking in peace. According to Ephesians 6:15, peace is part of the armor of God with which we are to clothe ourselves.

6b. If they remained in a house or city that was in strife, they could not do any real work there.

6c. Because it grieves the Holy Spirit. When peace leaves, the Holy Spirit leaves, and He is the One Who does the real work.

6d. Learn to hunger and thirst after peace. Because it is in this area that Satan is stealing from God's people.

6e. Mouth.

7. They all convey a message, just as much as words do.

8a. It does not promote the righteousness of God.

8b. Yes, there are times when it is all right to get mad and display anger.

8c. Yes. He cleaned out the temple because the people were defiling the house of God by buying and selling in it and not genuinely caring for the people.

8d. By what is called in the Bible "the law of kindness."

9a. Our words and speech.

9b. Pride; anger; resentment; expressing those negative traits and emotions; the abundance of the heart or spirit that the mouth speaks.

10a. Right under our noses — in our mouths.

10b. No man.

10c. We can submit it to God, asking that His Spirit take command of our tongue and bring it into submission to His will and way.

11a. ". . . the wisdom from above is first of all pure (undefiled); then it is peace-loving, courteous (considerate, gentle). [It is willing to] yield to reason, full of compassion and good fruits; it is wholehearted and straight-forward, impartial and unfeigned (free from doubts, wavering, and insincerity)."

11b. Patient and forbearing; firm and decisive; "be not angry"; display righteous indignation.

12a. Because he does not want us to gather together in an attitude of peace. He knows that if we are in turmoil inside, the words we hear will bounce right off us. They will not take root.

12b. Get the strife out of our own life.

12c. In a ground of peace; walking in peace.

12d. Get the strife out of your life.

13a. No. Because we have chosen to do so. The choice is always ours.

13b. By learning the Word of God and choosing to act upon it rather than to *re*-act to circumstances.

13c. The same one He told the children of Israel in the days of Joshua: "Choose you this day." In other words, "Grow up!"

Chapter 12

1a. We use our mouths, to pay attention to our words.

1b. "Let no foul or polluting language, nor evil word nor unwholesome or worthless talk [ever] come out of your mouth, but only such [speech] as is good and beneficial to the spiritual progress of others, as is fitting to the need and the occasion, that it may be a blessing and give grace (God's favor) to those who hear it."

1c. It breaks down the spirit.

1d. Depression of the human spirit.

1e. Hurt; break down; depress; heal; restore; uplift.

2a. Life; others; ourselves.

2b. To make larger.

2c. Making God larger than all our problems.

2d. To make it larger than the bad.

3a. They are going to cause us trouble.

3b. It is built up one brick at a time by rotating certain kinds of thoughts in the mind.

4a. Evil reports God considers negative reports.

4b. Other people.

4c. Magnify the good.

4d. Turning our face toward the Lord and crying out to Him to help us.

4e. Because every time we do so we add another brick to the stronghold that is being built up in our lives.

4f. Speak with purpose.

4g. We are going to be held accountable for our vain, useless conversation, what the *King James Version* calls "every idle word."

5a. Favorable; evil or negative.

5b. Because of the way they look at it. The one chooses to magnify the good, while the others choose to magnify the bad.

5c. Bigger and bigger in the eyes of the one doing the magnifying.

5d. Whatever you and I talk about — whether negative or positive.

6a. By cleansing ourselves "from what is ignoble and unclean," separating ourselves "from contact with contaminating and corrupting influences."

6b. One is not to give them, and the second is not to receive them.

6c. To talk to the other negatively; to let the other talk to us that way.

6d. That we are not to be involved in polluting our own minds or the minds of those around us.

6e. By thinking and speaking the way that God wants us to think and speak.

6f. Because God hears them and records them in His book of remembrance.

7a. By magnifying Him in our conversation.

7b. How we handle ourselves in all the circumstances we encounter in this life.

8a. They picked up the same spirit that was within them, and they began to murmur and doubt and fear.

8b. The opportunity of giving the good report or the evil report, of magnifying the Lord or magnifying the enemy.

8c. So we will choose to use our mouths not to speak evil, but to speak good.

9a. When to speak and when not to. Exhort and encourage others.

9b. Find fault with others and magnify problems. Bless others and to magnify the good.

10a. The works of the Lord and not the works of the devil.

10b. Exhortation, encouragement, and edification.

10c. To urge others to keep being all they can be in Christ Jesus and to encourage them to keep straining forward toward the prize.

10d. By talking about it, by being positive in our thoughts, in our attitudes, in our outlook, in our words, and in our actions.

10e. Surrender your will to the Lord, Who is all positive. Say to Him, "O Lord, I want to be like You. Help me to be positive and not to be negative anymore." Ask God to change you! Do whatever God tells you to do. Cooperate with His Spirit and follow His leadership and guidance as you move from darkness to light, from negativism to positivism, from death to life.

11a. Kings; priests; "priests."

11b. To give us life and peace.

11c. To give Him reverence and worshipful fear, to revere Him, and to stand in awe of His name.

11d. Use our mouths to speak evil against His people for whom we serve as His priests.

12a. Judgment.

12b. Pride.

12c. Because we think we are better than they are.

12d. Because it is a violation of your divine calling.

13a. The law of truth.

13b. Not judging or criticizing or condemning, not being a gossip or a busybody.

14a. "One who concerns himself with other people's affairs."[1] "A nosy, meddlesome person."[2] One who digs up evil reports and makes it his business to spread them by gossip, slander, whispering, and so forth.

14b. As "*n.* . . . one who habitually repeats intimate or private rumors or facts," "*vi.* . . . To engage in or spread gossip."[3] One who magnifies and sensationalizes rumors and partial information.

14c. "Those who are given to finding fault with the demeanor and conduct of others, and spreading their innuendos and criticisms in the church."[4]

14d. "*n.* . . . Utterance of defamatory statements injurious to the reputation or well-being of a person. A malicious report or statement," "*vt.* . . . To utter damaging reports about."[5]

14e. "*n.* . . . A surreptitiously or secretly expressed belief, rumor, or hint <a *whisper* of impropriety>," "*vt.* . . . To speak quietly or privately, as when imparting gossip, slander, or intrigue."[6] A *whisperer* speaks quietly or privately to surreptitiously or secretly impart gossip, slander, or intrigue.

14f. As being sin in the eyes of God.

14g. To mind our own business.

14h. As much a sin as any of these others.

14i. Because the people seek, inquire, and require instruction at the mouth of the priest, who is the messenger of God.

14j. The law of truth; the law of kindness; speak no evil with our lips.

Chapter 13

1a. Reputation. Others say about us.

1b. Plain, straightforward, honest, truthful communication.

1c. The fruits of the Spirit, especially kindness, gentleness, meekness, and humility.

2a. "One's usual mood: TEMPERAMENT," "habitual tendency or inclination," or "usual manner of emotional response."[1]

2b. (Your answers.)

3a. "Everyone proud and arrogant in heart is disgusting, hateful, and exceedingly offensive to the Lord; be assured [I pledge it] they will not go unpunished."

3b. Because they are so arrogant.

3c. They can't be told anything because they already know everything. Since they are so opinionated, they are always on the defensive, which makes it hard for them to receive correction because to them that would be an admission they are wrong — and that is something they find almost impossible to do.

3d. Usually busy trying to convince others how they need to change or what they need to do. Proud people feel that they have to convince others that they are right and others are wrong. Proud people are also usually very rigid, which explains why they are often such strict disciplinarians. Finally, proud people are often complicated people.

3e. They do not make very many other people happy either.

4a. The same soothing disposition that His Son Jesus displayed.

4b. One that brings encouragement and edification and exhortation everywhere we go.

4c. Soothing and kind, simple and humble, pliable and adaptable.

4d. Put off our old nature and put on the new nature — which is the nature of His beloved Son Jesus Christ.

5a. Conversation; speech.

5b. Mouth.

5c. Lay aside our pride and allow the Holy Spirit to work through us as He wills in every situation.

6a. Easily; quickly.

6b. Overnight; instant.

6c. Endure some suffering. Cooperate with the Lord as step by step He brings us into conformity to His will and way, gradually transforming us into the image of His Son Jesus.

6d. He says that He is gentle, meek, humble, and lowly of heart.

6e. We will find rest.

6f. As wholesome and good, not harsh, hard, sharp, or pressing, but comfortable, gracious, and pleasant.

6g. Peace.

6h. The peace that is on the inside of us.

6i. Be like Jesus, to take His nature upon us, even as He took our nature upon Himself.

6j. Whether we are harsh and hard or sweet and soothing.

7. "The sweet fragrance of Christ."

8a. Meekness.[3] Goodness.[4] Gentleness.[5]

8b. A mixture of meekness, goodness, gentleness, and humility.

9a. So that we may claim the full inheritance set apart for the children of God.

9b. Only when we are mature enough to handle them.

9c. By demonstrating that we have control of our mouths.

9d. That He wants us to have the same kind of mature disposition that His Son Jesus had, one that is not selfish and self-centered, but one that cares for others.

10a. We start our relationship with God in the outer court. From there we move into the inner court, and then finally into the Holy of Holies.[6]

10b. In the flesh. Takes us where we are.

10c. God used to allow certain things, but not anymore.

10d. Placed upon the altar before the Lord. We cannot reserve the little things that we want for ourselves. We must give it all up to God, becoming true worshippers in spirit and in truth. That means that we must be ready to live our lives before Him as He desires, trusting Him to give us the grace to do so.

10e. That we must take the promises of God and add to them diligence.

10f. Faith, which in turn develops virtue or excellence.

10g. Knowledge.

10h. Self-control.

10i. Steadfastness.

10j. Patience or endurance.

10k. Not just the ability to wait, but the ability to wait with a good attitude.

10l. Our lives are still giving forth a sweet aroma before the Lord.

10m. Something called godliness.

10n. Brotherly affection or kindness. True Christian love.

11a. Humility of Christ.

11b. Humility, meekness, kindness, and gentleness. Out into the world where we are to act like Jesus, giving forth a sweet-smelling aroma and having a soothing personality.

11c. The Kingdom.

12a. Not by our effort or strain or good works, but from knowing God personally and intimately.

12b. Sitting in the Presence of God and allowing Him to do a work on the inside.

12c. People who are willing to be changed from what they are to what only He can make them to be.

12d. The Lord will do the transforming and transfiguring of us — in His own way and in His own time — as we simply fellowship with Him in the inner man.

12e. It comes from abiding in the Lord and allowing Him to abide in you. It is His divine Presence that dissolves the hardness of your soul so that sweet-smelling fragrances pour forth from you.

12f. Learn to fellowship with Him so He can develop in you a soothing tongue and spirit.

Conclusion

1. The importance of how much blessing — and how much damage — we do by the words of our mouth.

2. Containers of power.

3. Empty; idle; vain; useless. God.

4. Return to Him after accomplishing His will and purpose.

5. It is out of the abundance of the heart that the mouth speaks — for good or for evil.

6. Words; declarations; judged.

7. So that what issues forth from them is not only truthful, but also kind and positive and edifying and in line with the will of God.

8. Your thoughts and words.

9. The help of the indwelling Spirit of God.

10. Attitude.

11. Submit yourself to the Lord and in humility ask Him to transform you into the image and nature of His Son Jesus Christ.

Endnotes

Chapter 1

[1] *Webster's II New College Dictionary* (Boston: Houghton Mifflin Company, 1995), s.v. "wisdom."

[2] Webster's, s.v. "prudent."

Chapter 2

[1] W. E. Vine, Merrill F. Unger, William White Jr., "New Testament Section," in *Vine's Complete Expository Dictionary of Old and New Testament Words* (Nashville: Thomas Nelson, Inc., 1984), p. 121, s.v. "CONFIRM, CONFIRMATION," A. Verbs, No. 1, *BEBAIOO*.

[2] Vine, A. Verbs, No. 3, *KUROO*.

[3] Vine, B. Noun, *BEBAIOSIS*.

Chapter 3

[1] James E. Strong, "Hebrew and Chaldee Dictionary," in *Strong's Exhaustive Concordance of the Bible* (Nashville: Abingdon, 1890), p. 32, entry #1897, s.v. "meditate," Joshua 1:8.

[2] Strong, "Hebrew," p. 115, entry #7878, s.v., "meditate," Psalm 119:148.

Chapter 7

[1] Webster's II, s.v. "bridle."

[2] Webster's II, s.v. "bit."

Chapter 10

[1] Vine, "New Testament Section," p. 580, s.v. "slanderer."

[2] James Strong, "Greek Dictionary of the New Testament," in *The New Strong's Exhaustive Concordance of the Bible* (Nashville: Thomas Nelson, Inc., 1990).

Chapter 12

[1] *Webster's New World Dictionary of the American Language* (New World Publishing Company, 1969), s.v. "busybody."

[2] Webster's II, s.v. "busybody."

[3] Webster's II, s.v. "gossip."

[4] Vine, "New Testament Section," p. 580, s.v. "slanderer."

[5] Webster's II, s.v. "slander."

[6] Webster's II, s.v. "whisper."

Chapter 13

[1] Webster's II, s.v. "disposition."

[2] Hannah Hurnard, *Mountains of Spices* (Wheaton: Tyndale House, Inc., 1979).

[3] Hurnard, pp. 222-229.

[4] Hurnard, pp. 168-174.

[5] Hurnard, pp. 136-144.

[6] Refers to relationship with God — the way man related to Him before Jesus came. In the Old Testament the outer court, inner court, and Holy of Holies were separate areas in the tabernacle. Under the Old Covenant, the tabernacle was the house of God, His dwelling place, the place of prayer for His people. (See Exodus 29:42,43.) Under the New Covenant, we believers are now God's house, His dwelling place, His temple (1 Corinthians 3:16); we can personally come into His throne room, into the Holy of Holies, which is His Presence, and we can have a personal relationship with Him.

Do you have a real relationship with Jesus?

God loves you! He created you to be a special, unique, one-of-a-kind individual, and He has a specific purpose and plan for your life. And through a personal relationship with your Creator—God—you can discover a way of life that will truly satisfy your soul.

No matter who you are, what you've done, or where you are in your life right now, God's love and grace are greater than your sin—your mistakes. Jesus willingly gave His life so you can receive forgiveness from God and have new life in Him. He's just waiting for you to invite Him to be your Savior and Lord.

If you are ready to commit your life to Jesus and follow Him, all you have to do is ask Him to forgive your sins and give you a fresh start in the life you are meant to live. Begin by praying this prayer...

Lord Jesus, thank You for giving Your life for me and forgiving me of my sins so I can have a personal relationship with You. I am sincerely sorry for the mistakes I've made, and I know I need You to help me live right.

Your Word says in Romans 10:9, "If you declare with your mouth, 'Jesus is Lord,' and believe in your heart that God raised him from the dead, you will be saved" (NIV). I believe You are the Son of God and confess You as my Savior and Lord. Take me just as I am, and work in my heart, making me the person You want me to be. I want to live for You, Jesus, and I am so grateful that You are giving me a fresh start in my new life with You today.

I love You, Jesus!

It's so amazing to know that God loves us so much! He wants to have a deep, intimate relationship with us that grows every day as we spend time with Him in prayer and Bible study. And we want to encourage you in your new life in Christ.

Please visit joycemeyer.org/salvation to request Joyce's book *A New Way of Living*, which is our gift to you. We also have other free resources online to help you make progress in pursuing everything God has for you.

Congratulations on your fresh start in your life in Christ! We hope to hear from you soon.

ABOUT THE AUTHOR

JOYCE MEYER is one of the world's leading practical Bible teachers. Her daily broadcast, *Enjoying Everyday Life*, airs on hundreds of television networks and radio stations worldwide.

Joyce has written more than one hundred inspirational books. Her bestsellers include *Power Thoughts*; *The Confident Woman*; *Look Great, Feel Great*; *Starting Your Day Right*; *Ending Your Day Right*; *Approval Addiction*; *How to Hear from God*; *Beauty for Ashes*; and *Battlefield of the Mind*.

Joyce travels extensively, holding conferences throughout the year and speaking to thousands around the world.

JOYCE MEYER MINISTRIES

U.S. & FOREIGN OFFICE ADDRESSES

Joyce Meyer Ministries
P.O. Box 655
Fenton, MO 63026
USA
(636) 349-0303

Joyce Meyer Ministries—Canada
P.O. Box 7700
Vancouver, BC V6B 4E2
Canada
(800) 868-1002

Joyce Meyer Ministries—Australia
Locked Bag 77
Mansfield Delivery Centre
Queensland 4122
Australia
(07) 3349 1200

Joyce Meyer Ministries—England
P.O. Box 1549
Windsor SL4 1GT
United Kingdom
01753 831102

Joyce Meyer Ministries—South Africa
P.O. Box 5
Cape Town 8000
South Africa
(27) 21-701-1056

OTHER BOOKS BY JOYCE MEYER

100 Ways to Simplify Your Life

21 Ways to Finding Peace and Happiness

Any Minute

Approval Addiction

The Approval Fix

The Battle Belongs to the Lord

Battlefield of the Mind*

Battlefield of the Mind for Kids

Battlefield of the Mind for Teens

Battlefield of the Mind Devotional

Be Anxious for Nothing*

Being the Person God Made You to Be

Beauty for Ashes

Change Your Words, Change Your Life

The Confident Mom

The Confident Woman

The Confident Woman Devotional

Do Yourself a Favor…Forgive

Eat the Cookie…Buy the Shoes

Eight Ways to Keep the Devil Under Your Feet

Ending Your Day Right

Enjoying Where You Are on the Way to Where You Are Going

The Everyday Life Bible

Joyce Meyer Spanish Titles

Belleza en Lugar de Cenizas (Beauty for Ashes)

Buena Salud, Buena Vida (Good Health, Good Life)

*Cambia Tus Palabras, Cambia Tu Vida (Change Your Words,
Change Your Life)*

El Campo de Batalla de la Mente (Battlefield of the Mind)

*Como Formar Buenos Habitos y Romper Malos Habitos (Making Good
Habits, Breaking Bad Habits)*

La Conexión de la Mente (The Mind Connection)

Dios No Está Enojado Contigo (God Is Not Mad at You)

La Dosis de Aprobación (The Approval Fix)

Empezando Tu Día Bien (Starting Your Day Right)

Hazte Un Favor a Ti Mismo...Perdona (Do Yourself a Favor...Forgive)

Madre Segura de sí Misma (The Confident Mom)

Palabras de Poder (Power Words)

Pensamientos de Poder (Power Thoughts)

Sobrecarga (Overload)

Termina Bien tu Día (Ending Your Day Right)

Usted Puede Comenzar de Nuevo (You Can Begin Again)

¡Viva con Esperanza! (Get Your Hopes Up!)

Viva Valientemente (Living Courageously)

Books by Dave Meyer

Life Lines

* Study Guide available for this title